D1547031

WHAT THE
BIBLE SAYS
ABOUT
MONEY

WHAT THE BIBLE SAYS SERIES

WHAT THE
BIBLE SAYS
ABOUT
MONEY

Alger Fitch

College Press Publishing Company, Joplin, Missouri

Printed and bound in the
United States of America
All Rights Reserved

Library of Congress Catalog Card Number: 87-072773
International Standard Book Number: 0-89900-257-9

Table of Contents

PREFACE

"The love of money" may be "a root of all kinds of evil" (1 Tim. 6:10),[1] but the Christian use of money has been the root of tremendous good. Two thousand years of church history bears witness to that fact. Look calandar-wise across the centuries or geography-wise across the globe. Wherever the church has gone, she has left behind schools for the mind, hospitals for the sick, orphanages for the parentless and loving care for both the poor, the aging and the hurting.

Before we explore the mines of Scripture for what the Bible says about money, listen to what money says about the Bible for "money talks" indeed! It not only speaks, it expresses itself with clarity. Visit the mission stations across the world. Look into the happy eyes of the children in India or Africa finding hope and

---

1. All biblical quotations (unless otherwise noted) are taken from The New International Version (Grand Rapids: Zondervan, 1978).

purpose in life, because a caring believer thousands of miles away has reached out with hands of love. View in another part of the world a poor farmer being taught ways to make his small plot of land to be more productive for the future care of his family. Note the young girls on a far-away shore getting the education that gives them a future in nursing. See the young men challenged to believe in themselves as future leaders for their church and community. All of the above, and much more, is provided abundantly and freely by common folk who never saw in their flesh the recipients of their gifts. Rather they read in a book called the Bible about the stewardship responsibility of one who knows Christ to reach out as the Lord's hands touching the world for him.

The consecrated cash, that flows week by week through the coffers of the church, shouts testimony regarding the Bible and its array of teachings. The free-will giving of the church-man is an action that speaks louder than words. The believer's "tithes and offerings" talk about God as an all-wise planner, his church as a vitally important institution and his mission as of supreme value. The donor's contribution, "on the first day of every week" (1 Cor. 16:2), claims that daily work is sacred and not secular. But loudest of all, the money cast into the treasury of the church cries out that the Bible is one hundred percent reliable. Its promises can be counted upon. When the book says, "Give and it will be given to you" (Luke 6:38), you can rely on it. When the Scripture gives its word, that "he who supplies seed for the sower and bread for food will also supply and increase your store of seed" (2 Cor. 9:10), you will not endanger your future when you conclude that hoarding all you have for the rainy day is not necessary. The Christian, who in faith makes a life practice of supporting his church, hears his money shout the "amen" to the Bible's testimony, "you will be made rich in every way so that you can be generous on every occasion" (2 Cor. 9:11).

The Bible has not only motivated inspiring acts of generosity, it has spoken on the topic of money in all its aspects. This study, *What the Bible Says About Money,* is an effort to let the ageless book counsel us with the wisdom of God regarding how his creatures ought to make it, save it, spend it and give it. "Blessed is the one who reads . . . those who hear it and take to heart what is written" (Rev. 1:3).

INTRODUCTION

Be warned: the Christian view of wealth and that of the world are opposites. An appropriate posture for reading the Bible on the topic of money is standing on one's head. At least by the time your exploration is complete your values may be turned upside down. It is no surprise that the Christian Bible has a great deal to say about possessions. Christianity is not an other-worldly religion. In spite of the Marxian charge that the church deals with "pie in the sky bye and bye," at base the Christian faith is realistic and materialistic in a God-oriented way. Gnosticism could not overcome the Biblical reality of the doctrines of creation, incarnation and resurrection. Belief in a heaven to come does not erase practical life in our earthly abode. Since money and sex are powerful realities in human life, they both receive considerable space in the Scripture's teaching. Prayer and faith references are in the Bible about five hundred times each, but material possessions are there

11

over a thousand times. Of Jesus' parables, which are thirty-eight in number, sixteen have a stewardship concern. That is close to one out of two. Strong's Concordance has three columns of textual references to "silver" and three and a half columns of texts with the word "gold."

If God has joined together faith and finances, let no man put them asunder. If most humans have some money and desire more money, a religion that did not speak to the subject would be cast aside as impractical. While your hands can touch the precious metals and know them to be material substances, your heart finds them to be spiritual in character, function and significance. You recognize that birds, fish and animals have no interest in cash. It is only the beings who have souls that use, exchange and multiply money.

We are entering an investigation that in no sense can be considered a game of trivial pursuit. It demands on our part prime time and careful thought, because destinies are at stake. Since God has given priority space in his Revelation to the topic, let "he who has an ear . . . hear what the Spirit says to the churches" (Rev. 2:7). The New Testament begins with Matthew's account of the Magi bringing gifts of "gold" with incense and myrrh (Matt. 2:11). It closes with John's description of the heavenly "city of pure gold" with streets to match (Rev. 21:18,21). Today some library shelves carry *The Second Coming Bible,* in which prophetic passages are marked, aware that readers want to know the future. Would not a *Money Bible* be more helpful, since readers need to know how to both live and make livings in this present world.

THE NEED FOR THE STUDY

"We the people of the United States of America," as the preamble of our constitution begins, especially need to hear the word of the Lord who has made the whole world. I have no desire to stir guilt in our fortunate lives, but rather to raise understanding gratefulness and stewardship responsibility in our daily walk. We need to be aware that we are but a small percent (six?) of the world's population, yet it is estimated that we own fifty percent of the earth's wealth. We are an island of plenty in the sea of poverty. We are a rich man's suburb far removed from the slums where many humans daily live. Our men wrestle with the profound problem of finding a parking space, our women with the difficulty of finding a diet-plan that works, while brothers die of starvation, freezing and injustice. Is this a day for seeking more distracting and diversionary playthings to fill up our leisure time? Is this an hour to sip our drinks by some warm fireplace and let the rest of the world go by? Is this a time for eyes to be closed to human want, while our assets multiply through keen business acumen?

God's book has an answer to our oppulence by the name of Christian stewardship. We can be constructive with what is in our hands. Instead of seeking for our own pleasure more garments for our closets, more epicurean delights for our tastebuds or more recent model cars for our driveways, we can find the greater satisfaction of being an instrument for God. We must count on the church for the solution to the problems that come from financial success. We will look in vain through modern works on business ethics for a page or a reference on the theme of financial stewardship responsibility.

The Soviet "iron curtain" is no more fatal a curtain than the plush curtain that shuts the underdog out from enjoying some of our bounties. The Bible reveals a God who feels the pains of the needy. The Bible warns men who disregard their neighbor's wants and become calloused to their pleas. In sharp and explicit terms God's book speaks to its reader with warnings against the pursuit of sheer wealth for wealth's sake. Heaven's book alerts the affluent of the possibility of gaining the world to the loss of his soul.

Now is the time to count our blessings more often than our

calories. Today is the day to discover that stewardship of wealth is as vital a church doctrine as the virgin birth or the bodily resurrection. The present crisis in world history is the appropriate moment for a resurgence of total dedication of life and substance to the service of Christ. Here and now is the hour to move first century texts out of cobwebbed antiquity and hear them speak in staccato clarity to our twentieth century ears: "Command those who are rich in this present world not to be arrogant nor to put their hope in wealth, which is so uncertain, but to put their hope in God, who richly provides us with everything for our enjoyment" (1 Tim. 6:17).

"Those who are rich in this present world" is a phrase more apt to apply to us than either the famine sufferers in today's Ethiopia or the average church member in Timothy's Asian congregations. We must quit considering ourselves among the poorest of the poor, when we only have black and white TV or have to do without the things our forefathers never had. We need to measure our financial condition and opportunities in the light of the Book of books. That Bible covers history from creation to the end of time and knows the peoples of East and West from the perspective of eternity. Only a fool would hide his head in the sands of chosen ignorance when the All-knowing Maker has put his thoughts regarding wealth on paper for the eyes of all Bible readers to see. We need to study what the Bible says about money. Bills, taxes, monetary concerns, debts, loans, wages, etc. are elements of life in this world. God's book deals with life.

THE DEFINITIONS IN THE STUDY

A book called *What the Bible Says About Money* raises the question, why was the title not *What the Bible Says About Wealth* or about *Possessions,* or *Riches* or *Stewardship?* Are there different shades of meaning? What are these terms to mean to us in this study? This is a difficult question, for the Bible covers thousands of years of time and, in its various English translations, uses different words for identical Hebrew and Greek terms.

Begin finding the answer to the problem by recognizing that while King Solomon was the richest man of his day there were several experiences he never had. He not once reached into his pockets for a coin or opened a billfold for some paper money. It was long after Solomon that minted coins were introduced in Palestine. The Jews of the exile became acquainted with coined money in Babylon. For centuries prior to that unminted metal served as money. Before that, goods were bartered. When in Genesis we meet the word "money" (Gen. 47:15 and 16), think of metals possibly in the form of wire, rings, ingots, lumps or pins.

The Oxford Dictionary traces our English word "money" to a goddess by that name, in whose temple Roman money was coined. But in common parlance the word money refers to any storeable form of wealth that both sets a standard of value and serves as a medium of exchange. There is no way humans of our time can return to simple village life where barter met the community's needs. You can't carry forty hours of labor in a billfold, but you can carry its equivalent in the more concrete form of cash. That makes money one's life blood — time, energy, ability — minted into coin. Ideas to be exchanged require a common language. Goods and services to be exchanged require the acceptable entity we call money. Our word "wealth" comes from the Anglo-Saxon term "weal" that described a state of well-being such as that provided by health and contentment. The word "wealth" over the years has evolved from a reference to the inner causes of our condition to the outer means by which we buy goods and services which we think will purchase such a state. Abram in Genesis 13:2 is said to be "very wealthy."

The forms that wealth went through are traceable in the Biblical record. There was first the barter system, and later the coins. Since Bible days, we have moved to paper and in our time to credit. In the barter days of any society, there is the swapping of cattle, animal hides, cloth, salt, articles of precious metals, etc.

Sometimes wealth was in perfumes and ointments. Indians on American soil used a string of beads (wampum). In the Old Testament period, we find as objects of trade: gold, silver, copper, tin, iron, ivory, glass, wood, bitumen, flax, cotton and wool. Eight metals are named: "gold" (Gen. 2:11,12), "bronze" and "iron" (Gen. 4:22), "silver" (Gen. 13:2), "tin" and "lead" (Num. 31:21-23), "steel" (Gen. 22:35 KJV) and "copper" (Ezra 8:27 KJV). In Exodus 28:17-20 and Job 28:17,18 alone twenty-one different precious stones were listed: sardius, topaz, carbuncle, emerald, sapphire, diamond, ligure, agate, amethyst, beryl, onyx, jasper, crystal, coral, pearl, ruby, chalcedony, chrysolite, chrysoprasus, jacinth and sardonya. Barter sometimes swapped a carpenter's labor on building construction for food (1 Kgs. 5:1-12) or grain for the purchase of a wife (Hosea 3:2).

Trading one item for another was a difficult system crying for improvement. Some goods were bulky and inconvenient to divide. Others were perishable and required immediate exchange. Something that was more durable, portable and divisible was needed. Trading is time consuming. It takes effort to find some individual who has what is needed to make the exchange. Out of the inevitable frustration of this system the weighing of metals was born. Gold, for instance, was a widely accepted commodity in and of itself. It was scarce, storeable and attractive even before minting coins was devised.

Both gold and silver came to be weighed out before they became a coined value (Gen. 23:16). The *gerah*, smallest of the Hebrew weights, signifies "a grain," because the Rabbis estimated weights by the grains of barley that had been taken from the middle of the grain's ear. The weighing of the precious metals was done normally at a city gate in the presence of witnesses. The Bible reader's confusion regarding coins is excusable in the light of the fact that words like *talent* or *shekel*, which later will denote minted currency, are used earlier for units of weight (Exod. 30:13; Num. 7:13,14; 1 Sam. 2:36; 1 Chron. 21:25; 2 Chron. 3:9). To further our confounding, the word "money" in the KJV of the Old Testament is used one hundred twelve times to translate a word that literally only means "silver."

Before Old Testament times were over, the move had gone beyond barter and weighed-out metals to coinage by governments. The very first coins, to our knowledge, arose in the Asia Minor area at the small kingdom of Lydia at about 700 BC. Coins, being regularly shaped and of known weight, became very convenient. They were immediately recognizable by the impressed image placed upon them. In Western Asia every planet of the heavens had its metal (silver for the moon, gold for the sun, etc.). The coins carried government propaganda, generally glorifying a king or emperor by reciting his deeds. The only actual coin mentioned in all of the Old Testament was the gold *drachma* in Ezra 2:69. It was a Persian coin. Since the pagan coins carried the images of gods and emperors, they could never be acceptable to Jews whose covenant forbade graven images. This fact explains the need for the temple "money changers," who for about a 12 percent charge would give Passover worshippers the correct Hebrew two drachmas in trade for the Roman currency.

During New Testament days in Palestine we find a basically rural setting. Yet we read of fishermen, craftsmen and carpenters. We learn of farmers owning small tracts of land they till and of shepherds renting pasture land for their flocks. All kinds of coins from various kinds of metals meet us in the Gospels and Epistles to our general confusion. Gold is likely thirteen to fifteen times more valuable than silver by weight, but we are in the dark as to the grade of the metals. Is the *talent*, or *mna*, or *shekel* in a verse made of gold or silver? When different English translations use different words for the same Greek word does the mind correctly equate?

In bronze (copper), the coins were *lepton* or *mite*, *quadrans*, equivalent to two *lepts* and *asserion* or *farthing* or penny worth four *quadrans* or eight *lepta*. The silver coins were *drachma*, valued at sixteen *assaria* (approximately the equivalent of the Roman *denarius* of Matthew 22:19), *didrachma* which had the

worth of two *drachma* and *shekel,* listed at four *drachma.*
As hard as one tries to get the correct Roman, Greek or
Hebrew coinage values straight by studying Bible dictionaries and
contrasting the varied English translations, we still flounder by
seeing words giving values in pound sterling rather than purchasing power. To speak of a "penny" (KJV) or a *denarius* being
worth eighteen cents takes on more flesh and blood when we
learn it was in apostolic times a day's wages. In purchasing power
Judas complained that Mary's annointing oil was a waste of about
a year's pay (three hundred days) and the betrayal price of his
Christ brought Judas a month's salary.

THE GOALS FOR THE STUDY

Since 1864 the words "In God We Trust" began appearing on
United States coins. Our present aim is that the truth of these
words become inscribed in our hearts and emblazoned in our actions. Reading Bible passages will convince us that money is more
than a quantity of hard and cold pieces of metal. Money is life in
coined form. Talents and energy applied over time have produced the wealth that is in our hands. It is either a potential blessing or a danger. Which it is to us will be determined by attitude, as
attitude will be molded by what we read and hear.

The Bible calls on its audience not only to "speak where the
Scriptures speak," but to act as they teach. The Sacred Writings
call man a steward that has been given a trust. That trust implies
opportunity, responsibility and accountability. As the book says,
"It is required that those who have been given a trust must prove
faithful" (1 Cor. 4:2).

The teaching of the Old Testament was delivered to a covenant people, the Jews. The teaching of the New Testament was
addressed to the new covenant people, the Church. Only as
covenant documents do the terms and promises of these writings
make sense to the parties in contract. The Bible is specifically ad-

dressed to chosen people — people in a special relationship with God. They recognize him as the owner and maker of all. They see themselves as persons in partnership with him. They know that a message for the world is theirs to deliver. They realize that while their entrusted truth is more valuable than gold, it will take gold and grit, silver and striving, talents and tithes to fulfill their part of the partnership.

Our aim, as parties in covenant, is to learn from God how to manage what he has placed in our hands. We hope to let the Bible clarify our goal, organize our steps and motivate us to act according to his purposes. Charles F. Banning once said, "If all the gold in the world were melted down into a solid cube, it would be about the size of an eight-room house." He added, "If a man got possession of all that gold — billions of dollars worth — he could not buy a friend, character, peace of mind, a clear conscience or a sense of eternity." True as this is, the Bible calls on us "to be rich in good deeds, and to be generous and willing to share," promising in return "treasure . . . for the coming age" (1 Tim. 6:18,19).

THE PLAN OF ATTACK

If these are our goals, by what steps will we meet them? Having spotted our pole star, how shall we plan our course? I suggest four intermediate steps toward our final destination.

First, it is foundational that we look at our topic *Question by Question*. Nothing could be more profitable than to interrogate the Bible with specific inquiries that seek practical answers to the questions men are asking. What does the Scripture have to say about the gaining, saving and spending of money? Does it inform us regarding giving to the poor, to the mission or to the church? Is there advice to guide us as to "how much" or "for what" or "by whom" such giving is to be done?

Part Two will give us a chance to see the theological connection of stewardship to the rest of the Bible's teaching. Here we will consider our topic *Doctrine by Doctrine*. As surely as love and marriage go together, so do heaven's commission and man's wealth. Christian economics is applied theology in its highest form.

Having viewed money in relationship to the questions of the people and to the doctrines of the church, we will in Part Three and Four simply listen to the Scripture speak in all its parts about wealth *Book by Book*, first New Testament, then Old Testament. In these sections it is proposed that we start not with Genesis but with Jesus. We will begin with the Master Teacher himself, then move to what his followers (apostles and disciples) have written on the subject (Part Three) and only finally search Christ's Bible — the Old Testament (Part Four) — to find the roots of his concepts regarding riches. At the end of our search we will know that the Holy Bible is not aiming to separate us from our money but to bind us to our Master. Let us pray that it succeeds.

Part One

Question by Question

1

ASKING THE BIBLE ABOUT THE
ACCUMULATION OF MONEY

The Bible is the right anvil on which to hammer out monetary question-marks until they become exclamation points. Every reader of Scripture hopes that his very human questions can receive divine answers that will help him live in confidence. Often the pulpit quotes verse after verse that deal with the giving away of wealth but leave in silence the prophetic voices that teach God's will regarding the gaining, saving and spending of that wealth. Stewardship is a more inclusive subject than our pulpit practice suggests. Let's begin asking about possessions from the angle of gaining riches.

TO A CHRISTIAN, IS MONEY OF VALUE?

The Christ whom Christians follow was not an ascetic. He did not become a mendicant. When he laid down his carpenter tools as he began his ministry, he did not replace them with a begging bowl. He associated with people of every class, including the poorest (Matt. 3:4; 11:8) and the richest (Mark 10:17-31; Luke 8:1-3). As certainly as Peter was the spokesman of the twelve and Matthew the secretary, Judas was appointed treasurer (John 13:29). The Rabbi from Galilee saw no inconsistency in receiving and expending money in his mission. His famous parables, like that of the ten minas, speak of heaven's expectations of good stewardship on the part of earth's trustees. Jesus' words were, "Put this money to work . . . until I come back." At the king's return "he sent for the servants to whom he had given the money, in order to find out what they had gained with it" (Luke 19:13,15).

The followers of Jesus are not to consider material things evil or non-existent. Neither are they to hold them as the all-important item in life. Rather they are to consider them tools to be used for the spiritual end of advancing the kingdom of God.

How does one act the part of the Good Samaritan, if he has nothing to share (Luke 10:25-37)? How do I follow my Lord's command to feed the hungry, give drink to the thirsty, or invite into my home the stranger, if I have taken the vow of poverty (Matt. 25:36-46)? Should a rigorist give everything he has away, is he not the one who will become a burden to the community down the road? By what miracle, after total impoverishment, can such a one exercise the gift of "contributing to the needs of others . . . generously" (Rom. 12:8)?

Are we not forced to conclude that Biblical ethics does not reach detachment from money but a stewardly use of money? Having modest means becomes the channel of showing love to our neighbors. There is nothing innately evil in either science or money. We need to recognize that both at one time have served destructive ends and at other times have blessed the world. It is all a matter of use. The inanimate check-book in your pocket can exploit, dominate and harm. It can in godly service bless, lift and help. The lost "silver coin" in Jesus' story was considered a valuable, worth searching for with care (Luke 15:8-10).

TO A CHRISTIAN, IS MONEY THE HIGHEST VALUE?

The Bible is quick to answer this question. Many elements in the realm of heaven are beyond purchase with the coins of earth. By God's grace, every believer enjoys the indwelling of his Spirit. The Christian knows the forgiveness of all his sins. He possesses eternal life because he is possessed by him who is "the way and the truth and the life" (John 14:6).

Money can buy many things but among them is neither exemption from death (Psa. 49:8) nor genuine love (Song of Sol. 8:7; Prov. 15:17). Of more value than money is "wisdom" (Prov. 3:15; 8:10,11; 16:16; 17:16; 20:15; 25:11,12; Job 28:15-19) and "peace" (Prov. 15:16; 17:1). Synonymous to peace is the "quiet spirit, which is of great worth in God's sight" (1 Pet. 3:4) and the "godliness with contentment [that] is great gain" (1 Tim. 6:6). The wise Solomon found reputation and "a good name . . . more desirable than great riches" (Prov. 22:1; 11:16; 28:6). The Psalmist counted God's law "more precious than gold" (Psa. 19:10; 119:72,127). Moses "regarded disgrace for the sake of Christ as of greater value than the treasures of Egypt (Heb. 11:26). Peter held out the "precious promises" to his readers (2 Pet. 1:4). John reminded the materially poor how "rich" they were in Christ (Rev. 2:9; 3:18). Paul gave a hearty amen to that truth, when he related his experience as "poor, yet making many rich; having nothing, and yet possessing everything" (2 Cor. 6:10 cp. James 1:9; Hebrews 10:34).

"The fear of the Lord" is not only the beginning of wisdom, it is of higher value than "great wealth" (Prov. 15:16) and offers a more certain security (Job 31:24). Jesus knew how gold without God would be no comfort at the judgment bar. He taught, "woe to you who are rich, for you have already received your comfort" (Luke 6:24). Years later his half-brother James echoed, "Now listen, you rich people, weep and wail because of the misery that is coming upon you" (James 5:1-5). Their Old Testament was right, "Wealth is worthless in the day of wrath" (Prov. 11:4).

Men can have cash and not Christ, gaining "the whole world," yet forfeiting their souls (Matt. 17:26). Their bank accounts need to show investments producing "treasures in heaven" (Matthew 6:19-21). That heavenly kingdom is worth selling "all" for it (Matt. 13:44,45). To make the accumulation of earthly goods one's primary and single aim is to miss the "joy" God intended to accompany abounding wine and grain (Psa. 4:7). The Master offers a better way than materialism, where earthly values are divorced from their source and their proper use. The blind secularist and humanist offer to lead the blind who follow them into the pit of self-deception. Men cannot lift themselves by their own bootstraps nor in their own strength overcome the problems of their world. Pleasure, ease and physical satisfaction form a poor trinity to substitute for the heavenly Father, the incarnate Son and the eternal Spirit. William C. Sanford's paraphrase of a materialist's 2 Peter 1:5-7 would read, "make every effort to suppliment your stove with a refrigerator, your refrigerator with a washing machine, your washing machine with a dryer, your dryer with a vacuum cleaner, your vacuum cleaner with a deep freeze, your deep freeze with a dish washer, your dish washer with a garbage disposal" (Methodist Church, Paradise, California).

The cure for greed is God. Economics that includes God makes life have meaning. Finances plus faith equals purpose. Stewardship causes our dollars to make sense, for in the church "whatever you do" is "all for the glory of God" (1 Cor. 10:31). As the coins go into the till, the voice of Jesus is heard, "a man's life does not consist in the abundance of his possessions" (Luke 12:15).

DOES THE BIBLE REVEAL AN AWARENESS OF EVERYDAY LIFE WITH JOBS TO BE DONE, WAGES TO BE EARNED, RENT TO BE PAID, ETC.?

The Sacred Scriptures have been penned by flesh and blood

people, who write concerning bread and butter issues. The Carpenter of Nazareth drew from everyday experiences to illustrate eternal truths. He told of vineyards to be rented (Matt. 21:41) and the collecting of such rent (Mark 12:1,2). He spoke of dishing out silver coins to innkeepers for a night's lodging (Luke 10:35). The words "hired . . . out" (Luke 15:15; Matthew 10:10), "settle accounts" (Matt. 18:23) or "agreed . . . pay" (Matt. 20:2) were not terms foreign to him. What "eight months' wages would . . . buy" (John 6:7) or what the differences in attitude might be between a "hired hand" and an owner (John 10:12) was understood by him.

The Book of books knows of money earned in a great variety of ways. An incomplete listing in alphabetical order reveals wages received by adventurers (Jdgs. 9:4), builders (Ezek. 27:4; 2 Chron. 34:10), beggars (Luke 18:35; John 9:8; Acts 3:2), carpenters (2 Chron. 34:10), craftsmen (Ezek. 27:9), dancers (Mark 6:22,23), dealers in purple cloth (Acts 16:14), designers (Exod. 35:35), farmers (2 Tim. 2:6; Jer. 31:5; Zech. 13:5), fishermen (Mark 1:16; Ezek. 47:10), flax workers (Isa. 19:9), fortune tellers (Acts 16:16), hired workers (Lev. 25:6; Job 7:1), masons (Ezra 3:7), managers (Luke 16:8), merchants (Psa. 107:23; Isa. 23:2; Ezek. 27:22; Rev. 18:3,11-15), mercenaries (Jer. 46:21), money changers (Matt. 21:12; John 2:14), money lenders (Luke 7:41), musicians (Rev. 18:22), nurses (Exod. 2:9), oil sellers (Matt. 25:9); oarsmen (Ezek. 27:26), partners (Luke 5:10), plowmen (1 Cor. 9:10), priests (Jdgs. 17:10), robbers (Matt. 27:38), sea captains (Rev. 18:17), sailors (Ezek. 27:9; Isa. 23:2), shepherds (1 Cor. 9:7), soldiers (Luke 3:11; 1 Cor. 9:7; Num. 31:27; 2 Sam. 10:6), silversmiths (Acts 19:24), sellers (John 2:14), shipwrights (Ezek. 27:9), tax collectors (Matt. 5:46; Luke 3:11; 5:27; 7:34; 19:1), tentmakers (Acts 15:3), traders (Isa. 2:16), treasurers (Acts 8:27), vinedressers (Jer. 31:5, 1 Cor. 9:7), and "weavers" (Exod. 35:35).

Whatever the labor done for another, the wage was to be paid on time (James 5:4) and in full (Jer. 22:13). Surely he, who had worked as a carpenter in Nazareth would count producing food, clothing and shelter for self and others as a sacred calling. Hands were not considered contaminated by labor but sanctified by it. God is served in the midst of toil as much as in the monastery or the temple.

To work at one's trade with "design and skill" is expected (Acts 17:29). To use "great skill" increases "wealth" (Ezek. 28:5). Proverbs predicts that a man "skilled in his work . . . will serve before kings . . . not obscure men" (Prov. 22:29; 24:3,4). The world is ever looking for "capable" persons (Exod. 18:21) of "special ability" (Gen. 47:6), who work "faithfully" (2 Kgs. 22:7; 1 Pet. 4:11). Caring for one's equipment — the tools of his trade — is twin brother to learning that trade (1 Sam. 13:20,21). We who pray for the money needed to pay the bills, often find the answer in the stewardly use of God-given abilities. Should modest means multiply into abundant supplies, God will get a partner or a man will lose his soul.

AT WHAT POINT DOES LIVING MODESTLY END AND LIVING SUMPTUOUSLY BEGIN?

We are led by some early church fathers to believe that two roads that never intersect are Easy Street and the Straight and Narrow Way. In the ancient church and that of the Middle Ages, there arose monastic orders which demanded the vow of poverty as a prerequisite of membership. Had these opened their ears to the apostolic records which were rooted in Jewish and Christian tradition, and had they closed out the Greek and Oriental influence, they might have arrived at a different conclusion. The slogans, "Do not handle! Do not taste! Do not touch!" (Col. 2:21) are the words of apostates and not apostles. Paul, an apostle of Christ, knew God as the one "who richly provides us with everything for our enjoyment" (I Tim. 6:17). Jesus himself had been criticized as one who put feasting ahead of fasting (Luke

5:33).

Paul's Christ had not chosen the option of joining ranks with the Essenes. His Bible knew of ancient heroes God had used that were men of wealth. There had been Abraham (Gen. 13:2), Isaac (Gen. 26:12), Jacob (Gen. 30:43), and the twelve patriarchs (Deut. 8:7-10; 28:1-12). There were righteous kings including David, Solomon, Jehoshaphat and Hezekiah (2 Chron. 32:27,28).

Piety and poverty were not synonyms in Scriptural terminology. The church fathers, who taught only the road of poverty as agreeable to their Maker, ought to have remembered the Old Testament's glowing reports of the patriarchs' riches. They should have pondered Jesus' practice of attending banquets with men of means (Luke 5:29; 7:36) and borrowing the home of a modestly well-to-do for his final supper (Mark 14:14). They should have thought out their Master's teaching about supporting parents (Mark 7:11), helping the needy (Matt. 6:2) and lending to the poor (Matt. 5:42; Luke 6:30,34). They ought to have restudied Paul's congregations that had in their membership at least a few from the upper classes. There was Erastus "the city's director of public works" (Rom. 16:24), Philemon whose home was adequate in size to hold the Colossian congregation (Phile. 2), and the list goes on (Acts 18:8; 1 Cor. 1:16; Rom. 16:5).

The Christianity of the first century held to a holy materialism. It asked not self-divestment but self-investment. The rich young ruler, who had been ensnared by his wealth, was ordered to "sell all" in order to cut the chain that bound him. The simple hermeneutical principle that advises the reader to ask "who is speaking?" and "to whom is he speaking?" should save readers from turning a specific command to one individual into a general rule for all.

The Bible recognizes wealth as a gift from God. It points to men who gained and used it in full harmony with heaven-taught values. Yet, it just as clearly warns how it can distract us from our mission and draw us away from our reliance on God. Since increased wealth means increased power and influence, it can blind us to what is happening in our own souls as the means of service slips into the slot of master. Even church elders and evangelists need the flashing yellow light, "be not greedy for money, but eager to serve" (1 Pet. 5:2). Proverbial wisdom sees in greed "trouble" (Prov. 15:27), harsh "answers" (Prov. 18:23) and egotism (Prov. 28:11).

Someone has quipped, "to be green with envy is to be ripe for trouble." Each person in his or her own heart must answer the question as to what point modest living gets out of bounds. Too many have fallen into the trap baited with glitter and gold. Too few have kept their eye on the ambition to do well rather than make the swap for the ambition to be well-to-do. Only the individual that follows the golden rule in his business can be saved from the rule of gold.

Each young family must wrestle with the real problem of deciding if the extra income the new or additional job offers is of higher value than the more modest life-style its absence would require. Would spending the first half of life expending health for wealth, justify the latter half of life using up the wealth in regaining some of that health? "The worries of this life and the deceitfulness of wealth" do choke out Jesus' teaching. The anxieties that go with gaining, losing, investing and using riches are sapped of their harming power when "moderation in all things" becomes the guiding star. The prayer of Agur is appropriate for all, "O Lord . . . give me neither poverty nor riches . . . otherwise, I may have too much and disown you . . . or I may become poor and steal, and so dishonor the name of my God" (Prov. 30:7-9).

WHAT MONEY PROBLEMS ARE EXPRESSLY ADDRESSED IN SCRIPTURE?

In addition to the basic error of having the wrong priority of wanting to get rich quick (1 Tim. 6:9,10; Prov. 28:22) and the partner evil of holding to an upside down value scale (Luke 12:15), the Bible speaks to many other issues on the financial scene.

It speaks highly of putting in an honest day's work for an honest day's pay. "Wicked, lazy servant" are words no one on judgment day wants to hear (Matt. 25:26). The apostolic example is that of hands supplying one's "own needs" (Acts 20:34) and working "night and day in order not to burden" others (1 Thess. 1:9). The apostolic admonition is "to work with your own hands, just as we told you to do" (1 Thess. 4:11). The apostolic judgment rings out, "If a man will not work, he shall not eat" (2 Thess. 3:10). The apostolic illustration is "the hardworking farmer" (2 Tim. 2:6). The apostolic hope is that God's people "provide for daily necessities and not live unproductive lives" (Titus 3:14). From one end of Proverbs to the other idleness is condemned (Prov. 6:10,11; 10:4; 13:4; 18:9; 19:15; 20:4,13; 21:25; 22:13; 24:30; 26:13-16) and diligent labor praised (Prov. 12:11,14,24; 14:23; 16:26; 21:5; 27:18; 28:19; 31:14,17,20,24). To live and not work productively is to be draining the pond another has filled. To deliberately set out to get more than one gives is not to play life's game in fairness.

The book of God also gives high priority to total honesty. It matters to God how wealth comes into our possession. A wag once said, "No matter how low in value the dollar may eventually fall, it will never fall as low as some people will stoop to get it." John the Baptist was God's prophetic voice, when he informed the tax collector to not "collect any more than you are required to" and instructed the soldier to not "extort money" (Luke 3:13,14). We need modern prophetic voices to protest a greedy raping of today's environment, disdaining the next generation's need for what the inherited environment will provide for them. We must have a twentieth century voice like John's to point out the unethical practice of voting in benefits for us, who could make our way, while passing on to our grandchildren a burden of debt that will be unbearable to them. Not only Ananias and Sapphira with Judas misappropriate funds. Honesty is not only the best policy, it is the only policy for a Christian.

Ever since the stones from Sinai called for the covenant people of God not to "steal," honesty has been the cry of the Law (Gen. 14:11; 20:14ff; 30:31-34,43; 31:1,7,30,32,39,31; 34:29; 37:23-36; 39:1; 43:20; 44:8ff; Exod. 1:11; 2:23; 3:7; 6:5; 15:9; 18:21; 20:15; 21:2ff; 22:1ff; 23:3ff; Lev. 6:2ff; 19:13,35-36; 25:13; 27:2ff; Num. 5:5ff; 16:15; 31:9ff; Deut. 3:7; 5:19; 13:16; 14:21; 16:19; 22:19,29; 24:14; 25:13-16; 27:17,25; 28:4-68; 29:9; 30:2,3), the Prophets (Jdgs. 14:12,13,15,19; 16:5,18; 1 Sam. 8:1,14ff; 12:3,4; 14:32,36; 15:19,21; 30:18ff; 2 Sam. 8:7ff; 18:12; 2 Kgs. 12:15; 21:14; 22:4ff; Isa. 1:23; 2:7; 8:4; 10:1-6; 11:14; 33:4ff.; 49:24; 61:8; Jer. 2:14; 6:13; 7:9; 8:10; 17:11; 21:12; 22:3,11,17; 34:8ff; 49:9; 51:34; 52:15ff. Ezek. 13:19; 18:6,7,18; 22:13,25,27-29; 25:7; 26:12; 28:18; 29:19; 34:8; 36:5ff; 38:12,13; 45:10ff; Amos 1:6; 5:12; 8:5; Obad. 13; Micah 2:1,2,8-11; 3:5,11; 4:13; 6:10; 7:3; Nahum 3:16; Hab. 2:6,12; Zech. 11:5,12ff; 14:14), the Writings (Psa. 12:5; 15:5; 26:10; 37:21; 44:10,12; 50:18; 62:10; 68:12,13; 89:41; 94:6; 105:16,17; Prov. 1:13ff; 6:30,31; 10:2,3,16; 11:1,18; 12:12; 13:11,23; 14:11,31; 15:6,27; 16:8,11; 17:8; 19:22,26; 20:10,17,23; 21:6; 22:16,22; 23:10; 24:15,16; 28:3,8,16,21,24; 29:2,7,13,14, 24,27; 30:9,14; 31:9; Job 1:15ff; 6:27; 24:2-20; 31:6; 36:18; Neh. 6:12, Esther 3:9; 8:11; 9:10,16; Dan. 5:17; 12:7), the Gospels (Matt. 4:9; 5:40; 12:29; 19:18; 26:15; 27:3-38; 28:12-15; Mark 3:27; 5:25ff; 10:19; 12:40; 14:10ff; Luke 3:13ff; 10:30; 11:21ff; 16:10ff; 18:11,20; 19:1,45; 20:14,47; 22:3ff; John 10:7; 19:23ff), the Acts (Acts 1:8; 16:16; 19:19,37, 24.26) and the Epistles (Rom. 2:21; 1 Cor. 5:10-11; 2 Cor. 7:2; 8:19ff; 12:17; 1 Tim. 3:8; 2 Tim. 2:6; Titus 1:7,11; 2:9; 3:14; Hebrews 10:34; James 2:5ff; 5:1ff; 2 Peter 2:18; 4:15; Jude 11).

This impressive list of texts on honesty should convince anyone cutting corners in a business deal or using false scales at a sale that the Bible promises swift justice at the bar of God.

Another business issue worthy of note in the Bible is its counsel to avoid debt when at all possible. Solomon noted that "The rich rule over the poor, and the borrower is servant to the lender" (Prov. 22:7). Financial advisors today encourage the newly marrieds to cut up their credit cards to give more hope to their marriages. Past debts need to be paid off and future obligations entered with exceptional care.

"Let no debt remain outstanding, except the continuing debt to love one another," wrote Paul (Rom. 13:8). It would be stealing not to pay just debts. It would be lying not to pay an obligation agreed to. Either situation would muffle the believer's testimony to his world. It is "the wicked [who] borrow and . . . not repay" (Psa. 37:21).

Closely related to debt is the question of interest charges. When does charging interest on money loaned become usury? In our modern day, citizens of North America would be hard put to own a home or operate a business were it not considered moral to take out a loan at the bank. Is there a legitimate distinction between a small loan a neighbor makes to a friend that meets an immediate need and a business arrangement that adds to the borrower's resources to accomplish a self-set goal? The first case is a matter of charity. The latter a banking activity in which charity has little or no place.

We get the impression that not all interest charges are condemned, for Jesus' Parable of the Talents commends putting "money to work" to gain "more." The "well done" is heard by the investors. The "wicked, lazy" charge is hurled at those who did not at the bankers receive the capital back "with interest" (Matt. 25:14-27; Luke 19:23; Deut. 23:19,20). What the Scripture attacks is the practice of "usury" (Psa. 15:5) or "exorbitant" (Prov. 28:8) and "excessive interest" (Ezek. 22:12). Jesus rankled at the fees the temple money changers charged, lowering the holy place to "a den of robbers" (Luke 19:46). "Let the exacting of usury stop!" is the prophetic command (Neh. 5:10). The poor are to be helped on a love level rather than a business level by God's covenant people. From those in need "do not take interest of any kind" (Lev. 25:36). From those in need do not "require a pledge for a loan" (Ezek. 18:16). From Mosaic days the rule was, "do not take a pair of millstones — not even the upper one — as security for a debt, because that would be taking a man's livelihood as security" (Deut. 24:6). From those in need the follower of Christ is not to "expect repayment," for love should lead us to do more for hurting humanity than sinners who expect "to be repaid in full" (Luke 6:34).

2

ASKING THE BIBLE ABOUT THE MANAGEMENT OF MONEY

New Testament stewardship does not find its fulness in the giving of one tenth of one's possessions to the work of God. True Biblical theology asks for all a person is and has to be ministered for the Lord's purposes. The genuine tither under both the Old and New Covenants counts his first tenth as the recognition of the fuller obligation to use the remaining nine tenths as his Lord directs.

Our Savior has committed unto his church the gospel message. Every member of that body is entrusted with the great commission (Ephesians 3:10). Since, "it is required that those who have been given a trust must prove faithful" (1 Cor. 4:2), it is prerequisite that we sharpen our management skills in relation to our talents, time and money. Success never comes to a person that lets everything drift along, while he simply hopes for the best. Planning responsibility is a must. Thinking out how to provide for old age, sickness, unemployment and unexpected emergencies can not be avoided. Biblical principles are an unfailing road map. If the Scriptures have spoken on the theme of making money, what do they say to the questions regarding its distribution? Some persons, even with large incomes by two family members, seem to have problems meeting their bills. Others with modest means appear to have it all together. Is there a key to unlock the jail called financial problems? Is there a decalogue from some Mount Sinai that has "thou shalts" and "thou shalt nots" regarding Christian management principles? I propose ten questions that lead to ten such affirmations. The first three from God's book will be of the "thou shalt not" variety.

AT WHAT PACE SHOULD A PERSON SEEK TO AMASS HIS FORTUNE? (THOU SHALT NOT BE GREEDY)

"He who gathers money little by little makes it grow," said Solomon (Prov. 13:2). Get rich quick schemes appeal to man's lowest of low desires named greed. Of that danger we hear the alarm ring throughout the Bible. Jesus called "greed" an evil "from inside . . . a man" making him "unclean" (Mark 7:22-23). Jeremiah saw this affliction affecting Israel from top to bottom as he preached, "From the least to the greatest, all are greedy for gain; prophets and priests alike" (Jer. 6:13; 8:10). He asked, "Does it make you a king to have more and more cedar?" (Jer. 22:15). Isaiah echoed the same woe to those who would "add house to house and join field to field" (Isaiah 5:8). Habakkuk announced woe to "him who piles stolen goods" (Hab. 2:6). Amos scathed those "who hoard plunder and loot" (Amos 3.10). And Zechariah saw some had "heaped up silver like dust and gold like the dirt of the streets" (Zech. 9:3).

The "love of money" had tainted the Pharisees of Jesus' time (Luke 16:14) and was prophesied to affect the people "in the last days" (2 Tim. 3:1,2). The church was admonished to

36

"keep . . . free from the love of money" (Heb. 13:5). Greed has a way of ensnaring us (Deut. 7:25), making us "proud" (Deut. 8:14; Ezek. 28:5), "weighing [us] down" (Luke 21:34), engrossing us (1 Cor. 7:31), stirring us to dissension (Prov. 28:25) and enticing us (Job 36:18).

To make the making of money primary in life is to become like "the pagan world" (Luke 12:30). The fault by any other name would smell as unsweet. By alias it has been termed covetousness (Rom. 7:7; James 4:2), envy (Job 5:2) or being "eager to get rich" (Prov. 28:20). "Greed" is what it is (Eph. 5:3; Col. 3:5) even when the party involved speaks of it as carrying on "business" and making "money" (James 4:13). Paul was not a preacher to "put on a mask to cover up greed" (1 Thess. 1:5; 1 Tim. 6:8). Peter knew false teachers who had become "experts in greed" (2 Pet. 2:14).

A man married to his money has looked at his wealth and said "I do" to the pledge "to have and to hold until death do us part." That death does part a man from his material assets was well illustrated by Alexander the Great. He is reported to have ordered from his deathbed that his hands unwrapped on his funeral bier should be seen by all viewers to be totally empty as he went into eternity. The divine arithmetic Jesus taught called on his followers to subtract when others said "add" and to divide one's wealth when materialists admonished "multiply." As John Wesley taught: "Make all the money you can. Save all the money you can. Give all the money you can."

Have you "learned the secret of being content whatever the circumstances . . . to be in need" or "to have plenty" (Phil. 4:12)? Many who are not content with what they have would not be contented when they did receive what they wanted to possess. Moderate wealth is a good. Trying to get something for nothing is a danger. "Life's worries, riches and pleasure" can choke out the supreme values as do "thorns" (Luke 8:14). Enjoy making money. Enjoy saving money. Get the biggest joy in giving money. Prove that it is your possession and not something that possesses you. Money exists for you. You do not exist for money.

IS PERSONAL DEBT PUBLIC ENEMY NUMBER ONE? (THOU SHALT NOT BE BURDENED WITH DEBT)

When out go exceeds income, upkeep is downfall. How often we pray "forgive us our debts" (Matt. 6:12) and on the same day sign another promissory note. One of life's thrills is paying the last installment on some purchase. One of life's traumas is to seem forced to enter another stint with the loan company at interest rates that will double the price of your purchase. You have reasoned with yourself that it is illogical to assume that, when you can't pay cash today, you will be able to pay the principal plus the high percentage of interest tomorrow. But the TV advertising has created the desire to buy what you don't need with money you don't have. The finance schemes sound so plausible. Yet in thirty days depression begins to set in. You are distressed. Your family is discouraged. You and your spouse begin to feel divided.

Because God cares about people and families, his Bible calls for realism. Advertisers are motivated by their financial returns. If the customer is benefited, that is to the good. If the appetite is stirred to desire the higher life-style and the purchaser drowns in debt, that is simply too bad. There is a limit to what any family can afford.

Once obligated, "you will not get out until you have paid the last penny" (Matt. 5:26). Some men have "owed money to a certain moneylender," as in Jesus' parable (Luke 7:41,42), but have not experienced the gracious cancellation of that obligation, as the fortunate debtors in Christ's story. Their experience has been more like that of the servant whose lender "ordered that he and his wife and his children and all that he had be sold to repay the debt" (Matt. 18:25). As soon as possible move to the Pauline ideal, "let no debt remain outstanding" (Rom. 13:8). In Old Testament language, "Do not say . . . 'Come back later; I'll give it tomorrow' — when you now have it with you" (Prov. 8:28). The wisdom of Solomon that warns of being indebted to others, especially warns against getting indebted for others. "Free yourself" is his cry (Prov. 6:1-3). You "will surely suffer" (Prov. 11:15). "Your very bed will be snatched from under you" (Prov. 22:27). It proves a man to be "lacking in judgment" (Prov. 17:18; 27:13).

One debt we never will be able to repay is the obligation we have to those who brought us the gospel (Rom. 15:27). Another debt no man can escape is that of paying taxes. Citizens of heaven's kingdom are also citizens of some earthly realm. They "pay taxes, for the authorities are God's servants, who give their full time to governing" (Rom. 13:6,7). Jesus, the "friend of tax collectors" (Matt. 11:19; Luke 15:1), was accused falsely of opposing "payment of taxes to Caesar" (Luke 23:2). He rather instructed his audience to "give to Caesar what is Caesar's" (Luke 20:25). For one of his twelve apostles, he selected "Levi sitting at his tax booth" (Luke 5:27).

DO WINE, WOMEN AND WEALTH MIX?
(THOU SHALT NOT INVEST IN SELFISH PLEASURES)

Write it down as a truism, "he who loves pleasure will become poor [and] whoever loves wine and oil will never be rich" (Prov. 21:17; 23:21). The apex of all foolish investments is one made in sensuality. "Sexually immoral people" (1 Cor. 5:9) have, like the prodigal of Jesus' parable, "squandered [their] wealth in wild living" (Luke 15:13) "with prostitutes" (Luke 15:30). Prophets warned against them (Jer. 8:2; Hosea 2:5; 9:1; Micah 1:7). Wise men called them "deep pits" and "bandits" (Prov. 23:27,28), announcing to the unlearned that strangers would feast on their wealth reducing them "to a loaf of bread" (Prov. 6:26).

After the three negatives follow seven positives. Following the "thou shalt nots" regarding greed, debt and waste, are the "thou shalts" that point us in upward mobile directions.

WHAT IS ALWAYS WORTH THE MONEY PAID OUT? (THOU SHALT INVEST IN LIFE'S NECESSITIES)

"Why spend money on what is not bread, and your labor on what does not satsify?" (Isa. 55:2). That is a serious mistake.

If we are to chart our course in a way that we neither crash our boat on the rocks of asceticism on the one side nor become grounded in the quicksands of personal gratification on the other, we must follow the polar star of prudence in spending. The exemplary characters of the Bible used funds for life's necessities. Israelites paid for "water" for themselves and their livestock (Num. 20:19; Deut. 1:6,28). Christian leaders did not "eat anyone's food without paying for it" (2 Thess. 3:8). "Daily bread" was worthy of their best prayers (Matt. 6:11) and their highest concerns (John 6:5; Luke 9:12; Matt. 14:5). It was regarding "the daily distribution of food" (Acts 6:1) that the first local church functionaries arose. It was partly for the purchase of food that Jesus' funds were expended (John 4:8; 13:29; Luke 22:8). Does money go out today for food? It did way back when (Gen. 42:3,7,19). Do we need money for clothing? That is no new thing (Gen. 37:3). Is housing an expensive item of the budget? Bible characters paid for housing (Acts 28:30; Rom. 16:19; Ezek. 28:26) for land (Matt. 27:5-10; Luke 14:18; Acts 7:16) and for burial plots (Gen. 23:3; 33:19; 49:30; 50:12,13). "There is nothing new under the sun" (Eccl. 1:9) when it comes to life's necessities and their cost.

In the Gospels we read of money being paid out for "oil" to keep the lights burning (Matt. 25:9,10), for the services of a "doctor" to keep the body going (Mark 5:26) and for "myrrh and aloes" to make the funeral arrangements up to expectations (John 19:39). "Expensive perfume" purchased by a woman out of love for Christ, was an elaborate but approved expenditure that will be told "wherever this gospel is preached throughout the world" (Matt. 26:7,13).

In contrast to the Scriptures' verbal moving pictures of practical men and women, are the snap shots of wastrels. Such a one "stores up things for himself but is not rich toward God" (Luke 12:21). An Esau will sell a birthright of agelong significance for a momentary meal (Gen. 25:31-33; Heb. 12:16). A weak nation will melt their earrings and jewelry, shaping a golden calf that will be a blight and not a blessing (Exod. 32:2-4,24; Isa. 46:6). Jeremiah saw in idolatry the economic calamity mingled with the theological heresy, saying, "From our youth shameful gods have consumed the fruits of our father's labor" (Jer. 3:24). Satan argued, "A man will give all he has for his own life" (Job 2:4). Job, Jesus and a gallery of faith's heroes have refuted that slander with lives lived out in stewardship.

IS EDUCATION A GOOD INVESTMENT IN ONE'S FUTURE? (THOU SHALT MAKE EXPENDITURES ON YOUR MIND)

Books and schools are costly. One thing more costly is to be uneducated. Or, so Solomon believed. He could not imagine a price tag so high that he would not find a way to pay it. He pled, "Listen, my sons, to a father's instruction . . . though it cost all you have, get understanding" (Prov. 4:7).

Jewish history recorded God's pleasure at Solomon's opting for wisdom above "long life or wealth" for himself (1 Kgs. 3:10; 2 Chron. 1:11,12). The All-Knowing One puts priority on the mind. If such advice was valid in ancient days, how much more in the modern hour of mechanical devices and computer chips. Sharpen your ax and you can hew more wood. Surround yourself with counselors. Be a disciple of the wise-ones, for "whoever loves discipline loves knowledge" (Prov. 12:1). When you "listen to advice and accept instruction . . . in the end you will be wise" (Prov. 19:20). Many of our "plans fail for lack of counsel." With "many advisers they succeed" (Prov. 15:22). "Zeal without knowledge" was as taboo with Solomon (Prov. 19:2) as with Paul (Rom. 10:2).

WHEN IT COMES TO PUTTING MONEY OUT, SHOULD IT GO FIRST TO PEOPLE, PLACES OR THINGS? (THOU SHALT PUT MONEY INTO PEOPLE)

"The God who made the world and everything in it is the Lord of heaven and earth and does not live in temples built by hands" (Acts 17:24). That was true in Athens in the first century and is true in America in this century. If it is fitting to put church money into mortar, it is above all fitting to invest Christian money in mortals. Buildings may last for centuries, but human lives extend beyond funerals and grave sites. The body of man is mortal. The soul of man is immortal. That fact alone makes signficant the Master's exclamation, "How much more valuable is a man than a sheep" (Matt. 12:12).

Whatever it cost Matthew to put on the banquet, so that his friends and associates in business could meet Jesus, it was a profitable investment in human lives (Luke 5:29). Whatever it cost John over the years to care for Jesus' mother after the Lord's crucifixion, it was money well spent (John 19:26,27). However much Barnabas and the other Jerusalem disciples gave up in "lands or houses" to feed the church's hungry, it was money in the bank of heaven which pays dividends higher than any bank on earth (Acts 4:32-37).

Little drops of water make the ocean. Little investments in little ones, from Galilee or the orphanages of the world, make the returns on a certificate of deposit or an IRA seem unimpressive. We have the word of a gentleman, "if anyone gives a cup of cold water to one of these little ones because he is my disciple, I tell you the truth, he will certainly not lose his reward" (Matt. 10:42). Paul saw wisdom in parents saving up "for their children" and spending "very gladly . . . everything [they] have" including themselves "as well" (2 Cor. 12:14,15). Paul's payment of the expenses for the four men . . . who [had] made a vow" (Acts 21:24) or your support of some young seminary student's education, equally invest in the church's future.

When it comes to investing in parents during their sunset years, that placement of currency in people is likewise a transaction of transforming proportions. The apostle to the Gentiles calls it putting one's "religion into practice by caring for their own family and so repaying their parents and grandparents" (1 Tim. 5:4). Such a practice is "pleasing to God." The refusal of the responsibility is a denial of "the faith and is worse than unbelief" (1 Tim. 5:8). After all, the word "steward" makes the money at our disposal God's money and the distribution of the Heavenly Father's wealth to His family our privileged ministry. What a trust God has placed in our hands! What an opportunity lies before us! The compassionate use of wealth is our divine instruction.

One person worth the investment of many dollars is your marriage mate. For a man of earth to ask "What is a wife of noble character worth?" is to hear the answer of heaven, "She is worth far more than rubies" (Prov. 31:10). Rebekah was worth her weight in gold (Gen. 24:22,28,35,47,53). Leah and Rachel came at the high price of many year's labor by Jacob (Gen. 29:18,27; Hosea 12:12), Boaz bought Ruth (Ruth 4:9,10), Hosea paid for Gomer (Hosea 3:2) and Saul offered his daughter Michal at a price to David (1 Sam. 18:20,25). We do not have that custom today, but we have Biblical precedent that wives are so precious they deserve not to be neglected. To lose the wife of one's youth in the mad pursuit of the wealth of the world is to receive low grades in the Golden Street Journal of that big city where people count more than pesos.

SHOULD A BUDGET FOR HOUSE OR
BUSINESS HAVE AN AMOUNT FOR UPKEEP?
(THOU SHALT KEEP EQUIPMENT IN GOOD REPAIR)

The sons of Zebedee did not spend all their time casting their nets into the sea. There were hours spent in mending their nets. Without that kind of care for their fishing gear, they would soon have been out of the fishing business. Stewardship of equipment saves the means of production for future years. This principle extended requires mankind as a whole to leave the land, the water and the air in better condition for later generations than when inherited.

The Holy Writ looks in unbelief at a thoughtless steward of the earth: "I went past the field of the sluggard, past the vineyard of the man who lacks judgment; thorns had come up everywhere, the ground was covered with weeds, and the stone wall was in ruins" (Prov. 24:30,31). The message from heaven admonishes, "Be sure to know the condition of your flocks, give careful attention to your herds; for riches do not endure forever" (Prov. 27:23,24).

There have been times when congregations have overbuilt, making the adequate funding of local program and world mission next to impossible. In such cases we could paraphrase Paul saying, "The love of property is a root of all kinds of evil to a church" (1 Tim. 6:10). Sound planning in faith looks to future growth. Wise planning in wisdom considers upkeep costs in its deliberations. A building erected as a tool in carrying out the Nazareth Carpenter's commission (Matt. 28:19,20) should reflect the worshippers' love for God and their awareness of his wisdom. Inside and out there should be attractiveness to the gospel. There is nothing to hamper evangelism's progress when the rooms are neither too poorly furnished for the wealthy, nor too elaborately equipped for the poor.

The Old Testament temple was a magnificent edifice. The Bible tells not only of its erection, it tells of its repair. Joash devised a chest to receive "a great amount of money." This was used to hire "masons and carpenters to restore the LORD'S temple" (2 Chron. 24:11,12). Later, under Josiah, Hilkiah the high priest "paid the workers who repaired and restored the temple" (2 Chron. 34:10), as did others (Neh. 3:31).

WHAT ABOUT SPENDING MONEY ON
THE BUILDING OF HARMONIOUS RELATIONSHIPS?
(THOU SHALT INVEST IN PEACE)

If the Biblical records of how its characters spent some of their wealth models for us how we ought to dispense our funds, then investing in peace has a place. Abraham, the father of those who walk by faith, made a treaty at Beersheba with Abimelech by bringing "seven ewe lambs from the flock" (Gen. 21:27-32). Jacob, suing for peace with Esau, "selected a gift for his brother Esau: two hundred female goats and twenty male goats, two hundred ewes and twenty rams, thirty female camels with their young, forty cows and ten bulls, and twenty female donkeys and ten male donkeys." The purpose of Jacob toward Esau was "to pacify him with these gifts I am sending on ahead" (Gen. 32:13-15,18,20 and 21; 33:10,11).

Many kings considered peace with potential enemies a priority item (Jdgs. 3:15-18; Isa. 36:16). Saul looked at the death of Goliath as a guns over butter issue, offering "great wealth to the man who kills him" (1 Sam. 17:25). Nabal's wife Abigail hoped for peace with David by a generous gift (1 Sam. 25:1,2,18,27). Ahab thought money might make things better between him and Ben-Hadad, but to no avail in this case (1 Kgs. 20:1-12,34). Ben-Hadad in turn offers "as a gift forty camel-loads of all the finest wares of Damascus" to Elisha (2 Kgs. 8:8-9). Asa, with "silver and gold out of the treasuries of the LORD'S temple and of his own palace," sought to get the king of Aram to break treaty with Israel and make treaty with Judah (2 Chron. 16:2,3).

The Jewish exiles in Babylon were given a message from Jeremiah that said "the LORD Almighty" wanted the Israelites to "seek the peace and prosperity" of the city of their captivity, "because if it prospers, you too will prosper" (Jer. 29:4-7). "War is hell" are not the words of Jesus. But these words on the high value of reconciliation are: "As you are going with your adversary to the magistrate, try hard to be reconciled to him on the way"

(Luke 12:58). Peace, amity and harmony, *et al* may come at a high price, but discord, battle and strife no one can afford.

SHOULD THOUGHT BE GIVEN
TO SAVING FOR THE FUTURE?
(THOU SHALT GET PREPARED FOR THE RAINY DAY)

The eyes of every Christian are focused on the future. The believer is banking on the bank of heaven, where he is heavily invested in the heavenly "treasure . . . that will not be exhausted" (Luke 12:33). Yet the awareness that eternity is to have the prime rate in importance, does not mean we should not have a growing rate of interest in our life in this world.

Bees save honey for the winter. Farmers save seed for next year's harvest. Governments save grain for possible lean years ahead. Ants teach economics courses by the storing of "provisions in summer" and gathering of "food at harvest" (Prov. 6:6,8; 30:25). Bibles instruct with this wisdom: "In the house of the wise are stores of choice food and oil, but a foolish man devours all he has" (Prov. 21:20). It goes on, "The wisdom of the prudent is to give thought to their ways" (Proverbs 14:8).

If you would "laugh at the days to come" (Prov. 31:25) and have no fear for your household "when it snows" (Prov. 31:21), it will be because the future was provided for in the past. Solomon considered money in the bank a "fortified city" (Prov. 10:15) and a potential "ransom" for his life (Prov. 13:8). He declared "money is a shelter" (Ecclesiastes 7:12). In and of itself the accumulation of money cannot be evil for the Holy God of Abraham, Isaac, Jacob and Israel smiled on these people as they "accumulated" possessions (Gen. 12:5; 31:18; 36:6; 46:6). The Son of God, source of abundant supply, upon feeding the multitudes spoke out, "Let nothing be wasted" (John 6:12). The Apostle Paul knew it to be fitting for "parents" to save up "for their children" (2 Cor. 12:14). The wise Solomon realized it was "good and proper . . . to find satisfaction . . . during the few days of life God has given." He knew "possessions" could enable a happiness (Ecclesiasties 5:18,19). What Solomon could never imagine was a day like our day, when the innovation of retirement at sixty-five with social security, medicare and annuities could set before many senior citizens in their golden years so many golden opportunities for helping their families, their friends and their churches.

At that time your earthly holdings can prove to be effective instruments by which you continue your ministry of love. If you would find your later years enjoying the highest gift of giving, start now by investing one-tenth each pay check into your church and another one-tenth into your savings. And along the road from your first job to the retirement banquet, carry adequate insurance to better your chances of having something left come time to go to glory.

IN THE MANAGEMENT OF MY MONEY, WHAT PART DOES MY LOCAL CHURCH PLAY? (THOU SHALT BE GENEROUS)

This final financial commandment should well have been the first. It is of such high importance in Scripture that the Bible's teaching will fill the next chapter where the question of giving falls under the spot light. The Bible speaks on the accumulation of money in firm but quiet tones. It speaks on the management of money with moderate voice and crescendo in concern. And, when it speaks on the giving of money, there is little *pianissimo* (ppp) and much *triple forte* (fff). Please do not reach for your spiritual ear plugs. We both need to hear the grand *finale* of stewardship as the organ of divine revelation, with all the stops out, peals forth the vibrant truth about giving.

3

ASKING THE BIBLE ABOUT THE GIVING OF MONEY (WHO? TO WHOM?)

Who should give? To whom? Why? How much? When and where? Does it matter to God? Are his instructions clear? The questions that surround the Christian's giving to the work of God are many and the Bible answers are mighty. The trail is long but the journey is worth every step.

A good beginning point is the recognition that God has a will in the matter and has revealed his will. The prophet Isaiah labeled some gifts "meaningless offerings" (Isa. 1:13) and God's Son charged some worshippers with the guilt of turning his "Father's house into a market" (John 2:16) and a "den of robbers" (Matthew 21:13). Apostles spoke of giving "in keeping with God's will" (2 Cor. 8:5 cp. Ezra 7:18). Moses wrote of one offering receiving God's "favor," while another his disfavor (Gen. 4:4,5). The author of Hebrews explained that the "better sacrifice" of Abel over Cain had to do with "faith" (Heb. 11:4). As Paul based his instruction regarding giving on what "the Scripture says" (1

Tim. 5:18), let us determine to do the same.

WHO SHOULD GIVE?

Asking the Bible about Christian giving commences with the question "Who should give?" Should it be all people, or just the believers? Should it come from all ages present, or just the business men? Ought it be given week by week, or only when in attendance? Are there some Sundays when the gift should not be given until one's attitudes have changed?

The first of this present list of questions raised the issue of church funds and their source. Ought they to be monies from members? Do communists support the advancement of free enterprise? Ought the tamborine be passed in the beer hall or the gamblers buy an organ for the church? Before you answer, remember that chief priests argued that "it is against the law to put [Judas' money] into the treasury, since it is blood money" (Matt. 27:6). Recall John's praise of the workers, who "for the sake of the Name . . . went out, receiving no help from the pagans" (3 John 7). Ask yourself "what do righteousness and wickedness have in common? Or what fellowship can light have with darkness?" (2 Cor. 6:14).

The support of the Lord's church is the high privilege of the Lord's people. However, since some are in debt, should they be excused? Would the government forgive us of our tax responsibility, since we owe for a car? Was our debt to God incurred before our debts to Visa, Mastercard and United Air Lines? Might our accepting financial responsibility for God's work teach us better accountability in the rest of our monetary dealings? In the light of the following promises, the poor man can not afford to withhold his gift. Read afresh Prov. 3:9,10; Eccl. 11:1; Matt. 6:33; Luke 6:38 and Phil. 4:19.

When a child passes by the Lord's Treasury or the offering plate passes by him or her, should that child share in the giving?

Does the father do all the worshipping for his family? Does he do the breathing for his wife and children? Are Paul's words to be taken literally when he says "each one of you should set aside a sum of money" (1 Cor. 16:2)? Babies at birth are basically selfish and need to be taught early to share. If you train up a child to give nothing or bring but a penny to worship, when he is old he will not depart from it. If you teach your child what God asks, he will hear the Lord say, "No one is to appear before me empty-handed" (Exod. 23:15; 34:20).

Another practical question deserving of a Biblical answer is that regarding whether "on the first day of every week" (1 Cor. 16:2) only means those Sundays when you are in attendance at the assembly. We only pay in restaurants and ball parks when we attend, so why should we not give only to the church when we are there? Irregular heart beats may signal a danger to the doctor and irregular giving to the Great Physician. We are the part of a congregation and its expenses go on both when we are present and when we are absent. All of us know that our own regular bills go on month after month. Each one requires money, a certain amount of money and at weekly, monthly or annual times. Nehemiah "made provision for contributions . . . at designated times" (Neh. 13:31). Solomon advised, "Do not say . . . 'I'll give it tomorrow' — when you now have it" (Prov. 3:28). Paul rejoiced in the Philippian example of partnership in the gospel from the first day" (Philippians 1:5). Once a part of the body, each member should be a functioning part, contributing to the health of that body.

One would be tempted in the face of financial need in the congregation to cover over the topic of giving only when one's attitudes are right. Fairness to the declared theme of what the Bible says expects full disclosure. Jesus is Lord of his Church and he said that, at the point of remembering that a brother has something against you, the settlement of that problem must precede the offering to God of your gift (Matt. 5:23,24). To give all one possesses without love is to gain nothing (1 Cor. 13:3).

TO WHOM SHOULD WE GIVE?

Akin to the questions, regarding who the givers are to be, are those dealing with the recipients of our gifts. To whom is the worshipper to give his gifts? People in love love to give gifts to the object of their affections. In the love song of the Old Testament the beloved sings to the king, "my own . . . is mine to give; the thousand shekels are for you, O Solomon" (Song of Sol. 8:12). Put the name of your beloved, King Jesus, in the place of Solomon's name. Then, like the Magi, you will present "him with gifts of gold" (Matt. 2:11).

The Bible's instruction is to "bring gifts to the One to be feared" (Psa. 76:11). The Psalmist sings, "Ascribe to the Lord the glory due his name; bring an offering and come unto his courts" (Psa. 96:8). If Caesar is to get what is Caesar's, then surely God is to get what is God's (Matt. 22:21). The Lord said to Moses, "Tell the Israelites to bring me an offering" (Exod. 25:1). He seeks the same from his New Israel, the church.

Since we pray, "Our Father in heaven," how do we get our money gifts to him? If you answer we give to Christ by giving to his body the church, you are not far from the truth. In the words of Jesus, "whatever you did for one of the least of these brothers of mine, you did for me" (Matt. 25:40). Before we emphasize the validity of the "storehouse" giving concept (Mal. 3:10), let us note other ideas equally clear in the Book.

The Book knows of giving "food" and "water" to one's enemies and promises God's blessing to accompany the action (Prov. 25:21,22). The same Book suggests that the recipients of one's *largesse* be persons of discernment. A "gold ring in a pig's snout" (Prov. 11:22) is a misplaced valuable. Would a sane man "throw . . . pearls to pigs" (Matt. 7:6)? Good stewardship looks for a return for God in one's investment in people. As we "do good to all people, especially to those who belong to the family of believers" (Gal. 6:10), it is not sinful to be selective. The Bible asks, "Of what use is money in the hand of a fool?" (Prov. 17:16).

Most preachers know where to find the modest but meaningful texts on tithing. As one preacher, I am overwhelmed at the quantitative abundance of passages showing heaven's concern for the poor of earth. If I speak where the Bible stresses, I need to say more and do more about hurting humans. Over twenty Hebrew Psalms sing of God's care for the poor (Psa. 9:9,17; 10:12,14; 12:5; 14:6; 34:6; 35:10; 40:17; 68:10; 69:32,33; 70:5; 72:4,12-14; 73:12; 74:21; 82:3,4; 86:1; 102:17; 107:9,41; 109:16,22; 113:7; 132:15; 146:7,9). The Prophets are not silent regarding the injustices that have caused the poverty of God's people (Isa. 1:17,22; 3:14,15; 5:22,23; 10:1-3; 14:30; 25:4; 26:5,6; 29:19; 58:6,7,10,11; Jer. 2:34; 5:28; 7:6; 20:13; 21:12; 22:16; 39:10; 40:7; 49:9,11; Lam. 1:11; 2:19; 4:3; Ezek. 16:49; 18:7,16; 22:7,29; Amos 2:6,7; 4:1; 5:11,12; 8:4-6; Zech. 7:9,10; Malachi 3:5). The rest of the Old Testament contains laws to aid the poor and kind words to assure them of God's love (Lev. 19:9,10,15; 22:11; 23:22; 25:35; Deut. 10:18; 15:7-15,18; 24:6-22; 27:19; I Sam. 2:5,8; 2 Sam. 12:1-6; 2 Kgs. 5:26,27; 2 Chron. 28:14,15; Neh. 5:3,4,10-12; Esther 9:22; Prov. 14:21,31; 21:13; 22:9,16; 25:20; 27:7; 28:22,27; 29:7,13; 31:6-9,20). The Creator sees "the tears of the oppressed" (Eccl. 4:1).

The new and better convenant introduced by Jesus calls for "compassion" for the poor (Matt. 19:21; Mark 8:2; 10:21; 14:5-7; Luke 3:11; 4:18; 6:20,36; 12:33; 14:13,21; 15:32; 16:20; 18:35; 19:8; John 13:29; Acts 20:35; 24:17; Rom. 12:13; Gal. 2:10; Eph. 4:28) and for the feeding of the hungry (Matt. 25:35-46; Acts 2:45; 4:32-37; 6:1; 10:2; 11:27-30; James 1:15,16). It calls on a follower of Christ to "give to the one who asks [him]" (Matt. 5:42; Luke 6:30), because to see a "brother in need" and show "no pity" is evidence of the absence of "the love of God" (1 John 3:17).

It is helpful to note that the word "alms" is in the plural in every instance, as if to suggest that a single act of charity is scarcely worthy of mention. The Greek word ἐλεημοσυνη means compassion and implies that the giver has a "fellow-feeling" toward the one he helps. The Latin word benevolence means "good feeling" and points to the warm glow that comes into the heart of the giver.

The church is not to be silent on the compassionate use of one's wealth. One Christ-like objective for acquiring material means, is to enable the Christian to minister to the needy. That love de-institutionalized is love in its most effective form. One caring person using his hands, his smile and his dollars to meet a need, brings more strength and satisfaction to the recipient than standing in a slow line that finally yields some food stamps to be redeemed at still longer lines.

Falling under the "to whom" category of questions are those that ask about wills. Does leaving wealth to others in a will get high or low points in the Scripture?

Seven out of eight Americans die without a will. Is that good or bad? It can be logically argued that money left to persons living outside of God's will can hurt them more than it helps them. A big spender will have more to waste. A drug addict and sot will spend it on the momentary highs that are followed by the ever deeper lows. An undisciplined spender will put what he inherits down on further and bigger debts, rather than getting above water for the first time.

Prodigal sons are famous for proving that wealth can be "squandered" (Luke 15:12,13). Solomon knew of that possibility when he wrote, "An inheritance quickly gained at the beginning will not be blessed at the end" (Prov. 20:21). That sad observation did not keep him from the glad recommendation that "a good man leaves an inheritance for his children's children" (Prov. 13:22).

David saw the blessing of God on men who "store up wealth for their children" (Psa. 17:14) and leave to their descendants the inheritance of "land" (Psa. 25:13). Paul reasoned, "After all, children should not have to save up for their parents, but parents for their children" (2 Cor. 12:14). Since Christians speak convenantal language, they think in terms of the last will and testament of Jesus Christ. They distinguish the gospel of Christ from the law of Moses and explain the dividing line between them as the time of Jesus' death. The case is illustrated thus: "In the case of a will, it is necessary to prove the death of the one who made it, because a will is in force only when somebody has died; it never takes effect while the one who made it is living" (Heb. 9:16,17).

This Hebrews passage makes clear the New Testament Jesus initiated went into effect after his death. We are glad to know that this last will and testament included us. That is evidence beyond refutation that we are loved by him. It also contains the clear suggestion that we also should consider those we love in wills that we make.

"Abraham left everything he owned to Isaac" (Gen. 25:5). God saw to it that Moses would give guidelines to Israel in will making (Lev. 25:46; Num. 27:5-11; 36:7). Prophets spoke of Israel's sons as "heirs" (Jer. 49:1) and called for the land to be divided "equally among them" (Ezek. 47:13,14,22,23). Anyone intending to render accountable stewardship of his assets beyond death, not leaving to others to decide where those assets should go, should get at it. Jesus called the man "fool" (Luke 12:20) who was overconfident about having many future days to "take life easy" (cp. Prov. 27:1; James 4:13-15). You can't take it with you but you can have something to say about whom you can someday help.

Asking the Bible about the "to whom" of stewardship has brought the reply that our giving is to be to God. That answer has been honed down to reveal that we give to God when we help the needy and care for our families both before and after death. But there is a very important further response. We are to give to and through the church, as surely as Jews gave to and through their temple and synagogues. The temple had a "treasury"

(Josh. 6:19,24) and Jesus with interest "watched the crowd putting their money into the temple treasury" (Mark 12:31-43). The last prophet, prior to John the Baptist, called for the entire tithe to be brought to "the storehouse." Malachi gives the Lord's reason: "that there may be food in my house" (Mal. 3:10). On top of all the good to be done in one-to-one situations day by day, there was the collective good to be done through the center of worship.

In our day the temple is gone and Jerusalem is not the center of the Christian work. But, across the globe, local congregations gather to carry out their Lord's commission. There still needs to be "food" in each house ready to meet the needs of each community. Paul's instruction regarding "the collection for God's people" was to be the same in Corinth to whom he was writing as it was in Ephesus from which city he was writing. As in Galatia, the believers on their day of weekly assembly were to "lay by in store" (ASV). *Thesauros*, the Greek word Paul uses, carries the idea of treasury. Into whatever receptical the congregation provides, from a collection plate to a box by the door, the Christian puts a part of himself to be used in the service of God and the salvation of men (1 Cor. 16:1,2).

4

ASKING THE BIBLE ABOUT THE
GIVING OF MONEY (WHY?)

WHY SHOULD WE GIVE

Ask a child to do something and you are apt to get the question "Why?" The children of God find themselves having the same word come to their minds when giving is under discussion. The God of these children is ready, willing and able to answer. Christian giving has tremendous consequences in heaven, in the world, in the church and in the giver. Why we give is important. Motives rank higher than outward religious acts.

Are there really results in heaven when I give? There were when the Roman centurion Cornelius gave. An angelic visitor told him, "Your . . . gifts to the poor have come up as a remembrance before God" (Acts 10:4,31). God sees givers as persons who love him. There is such a thing as "the proof of . . . love" (2 Cor. 8:24). John says "love for God" is known when we "obey his commands" (1 John 5:3). Ask yourself what convinces you that God loves the world. The John 3:16 answer is "he gave." In the same way God knows of our love.

When we back heaven's cause, God sees us as people who trust him. If we put our "hope in wealth," we cling to each dollar. Those who release their funds through Christ's church show that their "hope [is] in God" (1 Tim. 6:17). They "say with confidence, 'The Lord is my helper; I will not be afraid' " (Heb. 13:6).

In the eyes of God, the giver is seen as one who obeys his heavenly Father. Giving is commanded of the church members, you know. "The Lord has commanded that those who preach the gospel should receive their living from the gospel" (1 Cor. 9:13,14). The imperative is clear to "each one" (1 Cor. 16:2). Do you want your Master to know you appreciate him? Then, as you have "freely . . . received, freely give" (Matt. 10:8). Do you want him to count you a worshipper? Then be "devoted . . . to the fellowship" (Acts 2:42). Do you want the Almighty to see you a faithful steward? Then act like "the earth is the LORD'S, and everything in it" (Psa. 24:1; 50:10), including all "the silver . . . and the gold" (Haggai 2:8) plus you (1 Cor. 6:19).

The Bible does tell us of results in heaven when we give, but are there consequences we can see here on earth? There were dire results in Old Testament times among the Levites. They did not receive "the portions assigned" and "the house of God [was] neglected," when the people of Judah fell short in their tithing (Neh. 13:10-12). A similar black situation, or an opposite bright situation, will be ours in New Testament days regarding support for preaching, when the church gives or withholds its giving. Paul's chain of logic has many links. He reasons that believing is dependent upon hearing, hearing upon preaching and preaching upon sending (Rom. 10:14,15). No money to send the worker means no proclamation with the bottom line of a lost world. How blessed is planet earth when week after week faithful givers place their gifts into the church's coffers with the prayer "go into . . . the world and the preach the good news" (Mark 16:15).

It is worth our asking ourselves if the world would be evangelized in two decades, if every Christian gave at the minimal level of every Old Testament Jew. It is a helpful query to investigate if missionaries have ever been called back from their field due to lack of support. Do you know of preachers who found it necessary to work at secular employment so their families could eat? Is the problem that God's Word is not clear, or is it that God's people are not willing? And while we are tossing out questions to ponder, is my example in giving important (Matt. 17:21) and might your living conditions improve if you gave more faithfully (Mal. 3:11,12; Prov. 3:9,10)? Was the temporal aid promised to tithers just for Old Testament times? Are the tithing Christians you know any more faithful in their church attendance than the rest?

If there are results in both heaven and earth because of our giving, are there some in the church? The Bible answer is that there are many. The church's spiritual life is increased. Paul said so. He wrote, "This service that you perform is not only supplying the needs of God's people but is also overflowing in many expressions of thanks to God" (2 Cor. 9:12,14). He apologized for not taking money from Corinth for his services. He considered that to have resulted in making them "inferior to the other churches" by taking that "burden" from them (2 Cor. 12:13).

A giving church has an enlarging ministry (Acts 4:32-37). It carries on its work "in a fitting and orderly way" (I Cor. 14:40). It can send out more missionaries, enlarge its facilities and add to its staff. It does not have to be embarrassed by old debts nor forced into questionable money-raising schemes. It knows that no congregation is a spiritual success while it is a financial failure.

Let's get personal. We are asking the Bible why we should give. Answers about heaven, earth and church are not personal enough. If I give, will there be tangible results in me? Will material blessings be included, or only spiritual ones?

Read Proverbs 11:25 that argues, "A generous man will prosper; he who refreshes others will himself be refreshed." Read

Matthew 6:33 that promises those who "seek first [God's] kingdom and his righteousness" will find life's necessities added "as well." Read Luke 6:38 where Jesus teaches, "Give, and it will be given to you. A good measure, pressed down, shaken together and running over, will be poured into your lap. For with the measure you use, it will be measured to you." You reap what you sow (Gal. 6:6,7). Some tithers see an indirect relationship between their giving practice and their health. They reason that many of the numerous and obvious tensions that originate in the gaining and protecting of wealth are eliminated in their lives. They sense a growing confidence that God does bless his consistent stewards. By their acknowledgment of God's ownership in sharing the first of all increase, they find God to be their business partner. That lifts a tremendous load off the shoulders of all junior partners in that trust relationship.

Joining other givers, in meeting needs in God's world, brings inner satisfaction. The mind is relieved to know that brothers in trouble were not meant to face their trials unaided. God prescribed for that need in ancient Israel and in the modern church. A side effect, when taking the Bible's prescription of giving either tithes or offerings, is unavoidable. A wonderful law of the universe is that the happiness and peace of mind we seek become our own as we give them to others.

A Reader's Digest footnote told of a maid who told her employer that she had been "buying things on the lay-awake plan." She referred to the all-too-common experience of purchasing beyond one's means and then laying awake many a night wondering how to pay the bill.

Let us again distinguish between Old Testament promises to Israel and New Testament promises to Christians. Admittedly material blessing were covenanted to the obedient Jew. Since Christ has come, have we moved from type to antitype, from lower to higher, from physical to spiritual? Before we draw our conclusions or confusions, hear how it was under the Old Covenant.

Thumb through Proverbs and the equation is: human giving plus God's blessing equals material rewards. "Honor the LORD with your wealth, with the firstfruits of all your crops; then your barns will be filled to overflowing, and your vats will brim over with new wine" (Prov. 3:9,10). "He who sows righteousness reaps a sure reward" (Prov. 11:18). "One man gives freely, yet gains even more; another withholds unduly, but comes to poverty" (Prov. 11:24). "A generous man will himself be blessed, for he shares his food with the poor" (Prov. 22:9). "He who gives to the poor will lack nothing" (Prov. 28:27). The Preacher in Ecclesiastes preaches the same message: "Cast your bread upon the waters, for after many days you will find it again" (Ecclesiastes 11:1). The last prophetic voice before John the Baptist gave "amen!" to the truth: " 'Test me in this,' says the LORD Almighty, 'and see if I will not throw open the floodgates of heaven and pour out so much blessing that you will not have room for it' " (Mal. 3:10).

When Jesus came incarnate into history, what did he say on the subject to the disciples that followed him? Hear the word of a gentleman upon whose pledge you can rely. Christ said to his disciples, "Your Father, who sees what is done in secret, will reward you" (Matt. 6:4). "If anyone gives a cup of cold water to one of these little ones because he is my disciple, I tell you the truth, he will certainly not lose his reward" (Matt. 10:42; Mark 9:41). "Give to the poor, and you will have treasure in heaven" (Matt. 19:21; Mark 10:21). "Lend to them without expecting to get anything back. Then your reward will be great, and you will be sons of the Most High" (Luke 6:35).

These promises of "reward" and "treasure in heaven" may be limited to spiritual blessings or those in the age to come. To be "rich toward God" (Luke 12:21) will make a difference in heaven. That Abraham pointed out to the rich man who had neglected the beggar Lazarus at his gate, "Son remember that in your lifetime you received your good things, but now he is comforted here and you are in agony" (Luke 16:25). Did the Lord ever hint that an earthly reward might come to a disciple in this world? Here is Jesus' answer: "I tell you the truth . . . no one who has left home or brothers or sisters or mother or father or children or fields for me and the gospel will fail to receive a hundred times as much in this present age (homes, brothers, sisters, mothers, children and fields — and with them, persecutions) and in the age to come, eternal life" (Mark 10:29,30; Luke 18:29). "Seek first his kingdom and his righteousness, and all these things will be given to you as well" (Matt. 6:33; Luke 12:31). "Give, and it will be given to you. A good measure, pressed down, shaken together and running over, will be poured into your lap. For with the measure you use, it will be measured to you" (Luke 6:38).

The apostles, in the years following Jesus' earthly ministry, touched on the topic of reward tied to the giving of a saint: "Anyone who receives instruction in the word must share all good things with his instructor. Do not be deceived . . . a man reaps what he sows" (Gal. 6:6,7). "My God will meet all your needs according to his glorious riches in Christ Jesus" (Phil. 4:19). Of course the Christian, like Moses, is "looking ahead to his reward" and knows that this coming reward is "of greater value than the treasures of Egypt" (Heb. 11:26). Yet, that which "may be credited to your account" for future enjoyment (Phil. 4:17), does not cancel out the apostolic prayer for the present: "Dear friend, I pray that you may enjoy good health and that all may go well with you [you may prosper ASV], even as your soul is getting along well" (3 John 2). So twentieth century Christian, "Cast all your anxiety on him for he cares for you" (1 Pet. 5:7).

Even more valuable than material blessings that accrue to the giver are the spiritual ones. Isaiah exhorted, "If you spend yourselves on behalf of the hungry and satisfy the needs of the oppressed, then your light will rise in the darkness, and your night will become like the noonday. The LORD will guide you always" (Isa. 58:10,11; Psa. 112:9). Jesus promised "reward from your Father in heaven" (Matt. 6:1-4). He guaranteed results in the "heart" (Matt. 6:21). Paul saw beyond the gift what was "credited" to the giver's heavenly "account" (Phil. 4:17).

Among the spiritual blessings are many to be received in the future world. These "treasures in heaven" (Matt. 6:19,20; Luke 12:33) include the salvation of one's "soul" (Matt. 16:26) and entrance into "the kingdom of heaven" (Matt. 19:23,24). Are you "rich toward God" (Luke 12:21)? Do you list among your future assets the "true riches" (Luke 16:11)? Every investment in your church is an investment in your future. Social security stops at death. Eternal security is a much sounder program.

5

ASKING THE BIBLE ABOUT THE GIVING
OF MONEY (HOW?)

HOW SHOULD WE GIVE?

"It's not what you do, it's the way that you do it," went an old song. Why we give, to whom we give, how much we give are important issues. Yet none of these upstage the vital Biblical concern of how we give. In what manner should every one of our gifts be given? For example, where does free will fit into the Christian concept of stewardship?

If God-likeness or Christ-likeness is the Biblical norm for the believer's life style, then it is basic to remember how Jesus died. He was no martyr whose life was snatched away. "The Son of Man did not come to be served, but to serve, and to give his life as a ransom for many" (Mark 10:45). His death was voluntary. He did not have to die. He could have called legions of angels to his defense (Matt. 26:53). But he chose to die, so men could be redeemed. In other words, his death, while not necessary *per se*, was necessary if humans were to be saved. The option of not giving himself "a ransom for many" and saving his own life was rejected. The option freely chosen was to give his life in death. In a way the Christian has options regarding giving to support the telling of this saving gospel. There is no law demanding his contributions to the gospel cause. But there is love. No, he does not have to give. But yes he must give, if the world is to know of God's way of salvation. He responds willingly to the magnificent obsession to help get the story out.

What a different kind of institution the church is from those of the world. It is the only institution supported solely by the voluntary giving of its people. Love cannot be commanded, but neither can it be kept silent. When famine spread across the Roman world, Luke reports that "the disciples, each according to his ability, decided to provide help for the brothers living in Judea" (Acts 11:29). Note the word "decided." Paul carried contributions "for the poor among the saints in Jerusalem." He says the monies came from "Macedonia and Achaia" and he happily observes, "they were pleased to do it" (Rom. 15:26,27). That same willingness shines off the sacred page in Paul's response to the request by James, Peter and John that he help the needy. The apostle states, "All they asked was that we should continue to remember the poor, the very thing I was eager to do" (Gal 2:10).

The Mosaic Torah makes constant reference to offerings being "freewill offerings" (Num. 15:3; Deut. 12:6; 16:10). When the tabernacle was built, "the LORD said to Moses, 'Tell the Israelites to bring me an offering. You are to receive the offering for me from each man whose heart prompts him to give' " (Exodus 25:1,2). In this place it is heart-prompted gifts. In a later chapter the call is for "everyone who is willing to bring to the LORD an offering" (Exod. 35:5). The response was, "everyone who was willing and whose heart moved him . . . brought an offering (Exod. 35:20). The voluntary spirit did not quickly fade. "The people continued to bring freewill offerings morning after morning" (Exod. 36:3).

At Jesus' call fishermen "at once left their nets" (Matt. 4:20) and tax collectors their booths (Matt. 9:9). All who became Christ's apostles heard the order, "Freely you have received, freely give" (Matt. 10:8). No disciple is expected to bear only burdens thrust upon him by circumstances beyond his control. Rather, in choices completely within a man's control, each one voluntarily "take[s] up his cross and follow[s]" (Matt. 16:24). In amazement at how walking with Jesus transforms the selfish into the selfless, Paul points to the evidence of conversion in his missionary churches: "I testify that they gave as much as they were able, and even beyond their ability. Entirely on their own, they urgently pleaded with us for the privilege of sharing" (2 Cor. 8:3). To the Corinthian Church members, the apostle made the matter of giving clear: "I am not commanding you," he said. Then he added, "For if the willingness is there, the gift is acceptable" (2 Cor. 8:12). In all giving there is first the being "willing to share" (1 Tim. 6:18).

What does compassion have to do with the manner of giving? Behind voluntarism and willingness is the good-will feeling called love. Many of Jesus' miracles of healing were prompted by his being moved with compassion for those blind or lame. The thousands were fed because Christ said, "I have compassion for these people" (Mark 8:2). The imprisoned apostle to the Gentiles received helpful gifts initiated by brotherly "concern" (Phil. 4:10). The launching pad of stewardship is love. Therefore Paul, in the midst of two chapters dedicated to offerings for the poor (2 Cor. 8,9) says, "I thank God, who put into the heart of Titus the same concern I have" (2 Cor. 8:16). If the Bible declares "a righteous man cares for the needs of his animal" (Prov. 12:10), it certainly teaches concern for the human species. The same Bible that calls for our giving to be voluntary and compassionate, warns that giving without love is barren. Take a hypothetical case. "If I give all I possess to the poor . . . but have not love, I gain nothing" (1 Cor. 13:3). Love is more than a nice accompaniment for our giving. Compassion is essential. How we give is as basic as what we give.

We have begun to answer the interrogative, "How much more valuable to God is unselfish giving compared to simply giving in itself?" The Book speaks, "An unfriendly man pursues selfish ends; he defies all sound judgment" (Prov. 18:1). We have wondered, "Is boasting about a gift all that bad?" Again the Bible gives answer, "Everything in the world — the cravings of sinful man, the lust of his eyes and the boasting of what he has and does — comes not from the Father but from the world" (1 John 2:16). "False apostles, deceitful workmen" like to "boast about" everything (2 Cor. 11:12). True Christians are "not to be arrogant" (1 Tim. 6:17. They are to remember an important point Jesus made in his Sermon on the Mount, warning, "Be careful not to do your 'acts of righteousness' before men, to be seen by them. If you do, you will have no reward from your Father in heaven . . . when you give to the needy, do not let your left hand know what your right hand is doing, so that your giving may be in secret" (Matt. 6:1-4). How far from the Christian ideal were the Israelites who were regular in "sacrifices," "tithes" and "freewill offerings," but accompanied them with a "brag" and a "boast" (Hosea 4:4,5). One rung farther down the ladder of acceptable givers were the objects of Solomon's ridicule: "Like clouds and wind without rain is a man who boasts of gifts he does not give" (Prov. 25:14).

The how of giving is not answered completely until the Bible adverb "generously" comes into view. Dozens upon dozens of Scripture verses call for generosity. In a religion that has as a symbol the cross, "sacrificial" is a descriptive that rightly belongs to the noun "gifts." Hands open to receive the blessings of God remain open to share what has been received.

David describes "the righteous" as "always generous" (Psa. 37:26). Solomon believes "the righteous give without sparing" (Prov. 21:26). The Psalmist sees good coming to him "who is generous and lends freely" (Psa. 112:5,9). The general Old Testament assumption is that "a generous man will himself be blessed" (Prov. 22:9). The Book has no good to say about a "stingy" person (Prov. 23:6; 28:22). It encourages the reader to "not hold back offerings" (Exod. 22:29), but to "bring the best . . . to the house of the LORD" (Exod. 23:19; 34:26).

In the days of tabernacle construction the plea for generosity brought such a willing response that workmen told Moses, "The people are bringing more than enough for doing the work the LORD commanded to be done" (Exod. 36:5,7). Imagine such a happy state that the donors needed to be "restrained from bringing more" (Exod. 36:6).

Listen to the laws of giving; "Give generously . . . without a grudging heart . . . be openhanded toward your brothers and toward the poor and needy in your land" (Deut. 15:10,11). Give ear to the spirit of giving: "I insist on paying the full price. I will not take for the LORD what is yours, or sacrifice a burnt offering that costs me nothing" (1 Chron. 21:24). Hear the prayer about giving: "But who am I, and who are my people, that we should be able to give as generously as this? Everything comes from you, and we have given you only what comes from your hand . . . O LORD our God, as for all this abundance that we have provided for building you a temple for your Holy Name, it comes from your hand, and all of it belongs to you" (1 Chron. 29:14,16). Read the historical record of Israelite giving: "As soon as the order went out, the Israelites generously gave . . . they brought a great amount, a tithe of everything" (2 Chron. 31:5). "Plenty to spare," "great amount . . . left over," "faithfully brought . . . contributions . . . dedicated gifts" are phrases descriptive of a people that "worked wholeheartedly" (2 Chron. 31:10,11,21).

The church, growing out of such rich Old Testament soil and fertilized by Jesus' example of self-giving, found the word "generous" an applicable description of Christian giving. Church leadership called for the congregation's membership "to be rich in good deeds, and to be generous and willing to share" (1 Tim. 6:18). Those "contributing to the needs of others" were to "give generously" (Rom. 12:8). And that they did? Even "out of the most severe trial, their overflowing joy and their extreme poverty welled up in rich generosity" (2 Cor. 8:2; 9:14). What a delight to read of that time when "all the believers were one in heart and mind" and "shared everything they had" so that "there were no needy persons among them" (Acts 4:32,34).

In the light of Christ's cross, a follower of Jesus is ready to "deny himself" and forsake the way of seeking to gain "the whole world" (Matt. 16:24,26; Mark 8:34,36; Luke 14:27). Peter "left everything to follow" (Matt. 19:27; Mark 10:28) as did the other fishermen (Mark 1:18-20; Luke 5:11a) and Levi (Luke 5:28). Paul volunteered to the church "I will very gladly spend for you everything I have and expend myself as well" (2 Cor. 12:15). There were exceptions in the early church, like Ananias and Sapphira (Acts 5:1-7), and there will be "in the last days," when "people will be lovers of themselves, lovers of money" (2 Tim. 3:1,2). Even in the Lord's earthly ministry, the rich young ruler's "face fell" at the command to "sell everything" (Mark 10:21,22). But no exceptional part here or there changes the remarkable miracle of generosity so beautifully evident in the church of all times and places. The opening line of one of Jesus' parables began, "The kingdom of heaven is like a landowner" (i.e. God). The closing thought of the story has the landowner referring to his "own money" and saying "I am generous" (Matt. 20:1,15).

It can be safely said that the adverbs which blend well Biblically with the questions on how to give, are "voluntarily," "compassionately" and "generously." An additional word describing the manner of Godly giving is "exemplary." Apostolic stimulus for Corinthian giving was the example of God's grace among the Macedonian churches to the north (2 Cor. 8:1-5). The most inspiring case of the desired kind of giving was that of Jesus himself, who "though he was rich, yet for your sakes he became poor, so that you through his poverty might become rich" (2 Cor. 8:9). As surely as the good example of others stirred the church of God at Corinth to generosity, so will noble sharing on their part quicken others to higher and nobler acts of giving. At least, that is what the epistle's author believed as he wrote, "show these men [the representatives of the churches] the proof of your love and the reason for our pride in you, so that the churches can see it" (2 Cor. 8:24).

"No man is an island," wrote John Donne. Every man is an influence, believed Paul and his companions. "Make it your ambition . . . to work with your hands, just as we told you, so that your daily life may win the respect of outsiders" (1 Thess. 4:11,12). He commanded, "follow our example" and he expressed his desire to be "a model . . . to follow" (2 Thess. 3:7,9). Jesus thought it vital to set the right example in temple tax paying so as not to mislead or "offend" observers (Matt. 17:27). In the same vein Paul told the Ephesian elders of his open life for all eyes to read: "In everything I did, I showed you that by this kind of hard work we must help the weak remembering . . . it is more blessed to give than to receive" (Acts 20:35). Like it or not we are examples, either good, bad or indifferent. Children learn from our actions more than our words. So do believers and unbelievers alike in our church and community learn. It is time to shape up.

6

ASKING THE BIBLE ABOUT THE GIVING OF MONEY (HOW MUCH?)

HOW MUCH SHOULD WE GIVE?

How much? Now we are down to a question that cannot be avoided and ought not be delayed. How much is a Christian to give to God's work? Our attitudes in the giving and our methods count, but so does the amount. How much? How a believer discharges his stewardship obligations to God is a larger question than how much of income and increase ought to find its way into the church's coffers. Admitting that, the money-amount question is still there. How much?

Should that vital issue be resolved by the amount of money in my pocket or purse as the collection plate goes by, or should a more serious and basic life decision make the determination? Is that amount to be established by considering one's own needs first or by finding the Bible's teaching? Do I make up my mind by noting what I budget for pleasure and then setting a percentage of that for my church? Should the average man spend time to find what expenses his congregation might have to carry out modestly the Lord's program in his neighborhood and then decide?

In Matthew 21:12 and 13 you read of Jesus as an angry custodian of God's temple, unhappy at the scheme of money-making devised by the religious leaders. Since houses of worship and programs of service do take money, would the Lord be pleased with some more modern fund-raising ideas churches have dreamed up? The Bible has called for spontaneous, free-will and generous giving. But how does each individual decide what amount of money in his case would be "generous" in the eyes of God (Matt. 6:1)? One wag said he was a cheerful giver because he enjoyed getting away with giving as little as possible.

To help each church member make his personal decision, the Scripture suggests that giving should be proportionate to one's assets. The Corinthian Christian was taught to bring "a sum of money in keeping with his income" (1 Cor. 16:2). Macedonian believers "gave as much as they were able, and even beyond their ability" (2 Cor. 8:3). "According to your means" (2 Cor. 8:11) was the apostolic standard. "Each according to his ability" (Acts 11:29) was the example of the early church. In Old Testament days proportionate giving was normative as well. God asked the Jew to give "a freewill offering in proportion to the blessings the LORD your God has given you" (Deut. 16:10,17). After all, how can you offer the required "lamb," if you "cannot afford a lamb?" Will not "two doves or two pigeons" have to suffice (Lev. 5:7)? And in cases where the birds are too costly for a person's budget, will not "a tenth of an ephah of fine flour" serve as well (Lev. 5:11)? There will be times when the finest of God's men will have to say to the needy, "Silver or gold I do not have, but what I have I give you" (Acts 3:6).

To say "proportionate giving" is still a hazy answer. For the question "what proportion?" cries out for specifics. Is the Pharisee who gave "a tenth" the model (Luke 8:12)? Or, is Zacchaeus our example in the giving of fifty percent to the poor (Luke 19:8)?

Would you believe that the widow who gave one hundred percent (Luke 21:4) is the standard? Are there further details in Scripture to help us clarify what is expected in proportionate giving? One miser is reported to have been considered by his neighbors as a proportionate giver. The community was certain that he gave in proportion to the amount of religion he had.

We do need outside help to determine amount. The human heart must be weaned from its natural selfishness. Without the Holy Spirit's light of revelation, each believer might yield to the tug of self-protection. Cornelius prior to his conversion to Christ "gave generously" (Acts 10:2). KJV and ASV word it: "gave much." Leave the topic of money and turn for a moment to time. How much time do you give to prayer? Of the one thousand four hundred forty minutes in a day, is ten minutes "much" time in communion with God? How much time to Bible Study? Of the one hundred sixty-eight hours in each week do you spend six hours at the assembly? Would that pass for "much?" Now back to money. How much is "much?" Any proportion is a proportion, but what is a respectable proportion for the Christian?

Let us move from a prior inquiry regarding the proportion for Israel to the asking about the Church — from Moses to Christ, from Old Testament to New Testament, from Law to Gospel. How much should the people of God give? The Old Testament answer was two fold. Tithes were to be paid and offerings given.

The first Bible mention of tithing is that by Abram (Gen. 14:20) and the second is that by Jacob (Gen. 28:22). Historical records of heathen nations indicate that idol worshippers and pagan priests considered the tenth a proper portion to be given to Hercules, Apollo or any of their gods. We are not exploring the writings of Herodotus, Diodorus Siculus, Xenophon, Hesiod and Pliny. Our interest is the Bible. However it is of interest to note how worldwide was the awareness of the tithe portion. If Arabians, Babylonians, Carthagenians, Phoenicians, Egyptians, Greeks and Romans knew of tithing, could its practice have been remembered from prehistoric times? The answer is not finally in on that question.

Some early Christian writers, such as Tertullian in the third century, used the Cain and Abel offerings as a basis for teaching the tithe. Using the Septuagint (LXX) of Genesis 4:7, they considered the sin of Cain to be bringing the wrong percentage of his field increase. That Greek Old Testament translation said, in effect, "Hast thou not sinned if thou hast brought it rightly, but not divided it?" To others the problem with Cain's offering was that "you can't squeeze blood out of a turnip." If God asked a blood sacrifice, a generous amount of grain given would not be fulfilling what was asked. Add Romans 10:17 to Hebrews 11:4 and find tithing in Genesis 4:7, if you desire. At least the word "tithe" is not there, however the passage is translated.

What we do know is that tithing as a law was the practice of the Jewish nation. But, what a unique law it was. All other laws carried penalties to be inflicted upon violation. All Mosaic law, including violating the Sabbath, had proscribed penalties. The exception was the law of the tithe. Prophets and priests could denounce and persuade — they could announce that God would bless or withdraw his blessing — but they personally and their nation collectively could apply no penalty. Moral persuasion that the tithe belonged to God could be applied to the conscience, but pain or punishment could not be brought against the body. But let the Bible speak for itself.

"A tithe of everything from the land, whether grain from the soil or fruit from the trees, belongs to the Lord; it is holy to the Lord. If a man redeems any of his tithe, he must add a fifth of the value to it. The entire tithe of the herd and flock — every tenth animal that passes under the shepherd's rod — will be holy to the Lord" (Lev. 27:30-32). "Be sure to set aside a tenth of all that your fields produce each year . . . if that place is too distant and you have been blessed by the Lord your God and cannot carry your tithe . . . then exchange your tithe for silver, and take the silver with you" (Deut. 14:22-29). "I give to the Levites all the tithes in Israel as their inheritance in return for the work they do

while serving at the tent of meeting" (Num. 18:21,23,24).
"Speak to the Levites and say unto them: 'When you receive
from the Israelites the tithe I give you as your inheritance, you
must present a tenth of that tithe as the Lord's offering' " (Num.
18:25,26,28).

In the light of such laws, Israelites vowed, "We will bring a
tithe of our crops to the Levites, for it is the Levites who collect
the tithes in all the towns" (Neh. 10:37; 12:44). Keeping their
vows, "all Judah brought the tithes of grain, new wine and oil into
the storerooms" (Neh. 13:12). In the days of Hezekiah it was said
that the people "brought a great amount, a tithe of
everything . . . a tithe of their herds and flocks and a tithe of the
holy things dedicated to the Lord" (2 Chron. 31:5,6). But, by the
time of Malachi the people were indicted with the charge of robbing God "in tithes and offerings" with the result of
"pests . . . devouring . . . crops, and the vines" losing their fruit
(Malachi 3:8-11).

The advocate of tithing in the Christian era does need to be
solid in his facts. The Levites were the recipients of the entire first
tithe (Num. 18:21). To understand Paul's words in 1 Corinthians
9:13 and 14 as some do, will bring a tremendous raise in pay to
all preachers I know. Paul's statement was, "Don't you know that
those who work in the temple get their food from the temple, and
those who serve at the altar share in what is offered at the altar? In
the same way, the Lord has commanded that those who preach
the gospel should receive their living from the gospel." If "in the
same way," οὕτως, is pressed to refer specifically to the tithe rather
than to the more general awareness that workers are to be supported, then the ancient way of Levites getting it all poses problems for the church in finding other funds for the other expenses. In context, is Paul's point the discovery of how money
was raised, or was it the fact that workers are eligible for support
from those for whom they labor?

Before dogmatically deciding the tithing issue for the church
age, be aware that there seems to have been more than one tithe

expected of the Jewish people. It was more like two and one third tithes. One tithe, the primary one, was for the support of the Levitical priesthood (Lev. 27:30-32). Another was required in the support of the national feasts of Passover, Pentecost and Tabernacles (Deut. 14:22-27). Last, but not least, was a third tithe for the sustenance of the fatherless, the widow and the alien (Deut. 14:28,29). This portion was paid every three years.

Beyond the paying of the tithes was the giving of offerings in the Old Covenant era. "Tithes and offerings" (Mal. 3:8) were joined in Jewish thought. The offerings were often called "freewill offerings." The tithes were in a sense neither voluntary nor always spontaneous. They were like taxes. They were a matter of law. They were, however, different from taxes, for men were not assigned to apply penalty where failure to comply occurred. The tenth was a decimal of duty — a taught obligation.

Jesus, the Lord of the church, was "born under law" (Gal. 4:4) and kept every jot and tittle of Mosaic teaching. Since his critics tried to find flaws in his obedience, you can be sure, if he had failed to keep the titihing regulations, the world would have heard about it. The opponents tried to label him anti-government or anti-temple, but no voice broke the silence labelling him an enemy of the tithe. During our Lord's three-and-a-half-year ministry, his enemies would have discovered in short order the flaw of failing to tithe had there been such a flaw. In his parables and sermons the Messiah spoke often of money, yet on only two recorded occasions referred to tithing by name. In a woe pronounced against the hypocrisy of the law teachers, he revealed his awareness that they gave "a tenth of [their] spices — mint, dill and cummin," while neglecting what he termed "more important matters." However he spoke a good word for tithing by suggesting they begin the practice of "justice, mercy and faithfulness . . . without neglecting" their bringing the tithe (Matt. 23:23; Luke 11:42). At another time, in one of Christ's stories, he described a Pharisee who bragged to God "about himself," proud to say, "I . . . give a tenth of all I get" (Luke 18:12). We must neither draw too much nor too little from Jesus' criticisms of the warped religion of the Pharisee. The pride in tithing on their part is no more an argument against the tithe, than the warped prayer, "God I thank you that I am not like other men" (Luke 18:11) is a case against genuine praying.

As Jesus said much about money but little regarding the tithe, so Paul teaches a great deal on giving yet makes no use of the word "tithe" in his writings. Which direction shall we go with that fact? Shall we reason that his silence on the subject establishes his opposition to tithing for the Christian age? Or, might we argue that, when believers were already far beyond the giving of the tenth in their life in grace, to fill his epistles with calls for the tithe would be a waste of paper? As much as we wish we had in some epistle all that was in Paul's mind on our subject, we are left with a blank page. He did not mention tithing by name.

The records of the first century are silent. When tithing appears in church writings of the second century, the emphasis is upon the believer going beyond the tithe as he lives under grace. In the following years ten councils in "Christendom" bind the law of tithing on those willing to submit to their authority. At the present hour the Fundamentalist and Pentecostalist agree on one thing with the Ecumenical Denominations that they consider liberals. With one voice, they preach tithing as the God-given plan for financing the work of the Church.

Here we have it. From the law of Moses to the prophecy of Malachi, we have tithing as a topic of historical record, legal regulation and prophetic exhortation. From the ancient councils of the church to the modern promotional-bulletins from denominational headquarters, we read admonitions to tithe. Yet, from the lips of Jesus and the pens of apostles, there is all too little. Paul does not use the word. Jesus mentioned it twice. The author of Hebrews draws a lesson on Christ's superiority by showing a typology (which includes the tithe) between Melchizedek and Christ, Abraham and Christians (Heb. 7:4-10).

Let us draw a worst case and a best case scenario for tithing.

There could be the danger that a modern tither might become proud in his practice. The Pharisee did (Luke 18:11,12). The Christian could, but I have yet to meet one who has. Self-righteousness is an admitted danger, but I am glad to report that the humble tithers I know are abstainers, when it comes to parading their virtues. Another precipice over which a church-man could fall is the steep cliff of legalism. It is conceivable that a follower of Jesus might measure himself by the ten-percent yard-stick, while shutting his eyes to the spirit of mercy. But my eyes have yet to see brothers and sisters frolic even close to that dangerous potential fall.

Perhaps a hazard more perilous to the soul could be to turn the joy of tithing into a heated debate over the practice, leaving divisive scars in the body. Quiet example, overflowing gratitude and the confident assurance of God's partnership will be a stronger magnet to attract others to try tithing than the banging of Bibles on heads well-insulated against the idea.

To search for a case against tithing is to find one. Tithing as a fund-raising gimmick to meet the church budget is not the highest of motives for any practice. But again, while this may be a possi-ble reason for beginning the practice, it was not the way it was with my friends who tithe. They point to their Bible study as the stimulus to their giving the practice of tithing a go. It must also be said that to none in my acquaintance was their tithing counted a substitute for total stewardship.

Yes, imagination allows the mind to visualize a redeemed man becoming self-righteous, legalistic and argumentative, led down the road not by the Bible but by the critical condition of the Church's budget. But, let us be fair and consider a best case scenario.

The tither knows the practice to come from God's Old Testa-ment revelation and not from a frustrated church treasurer's im-agination, while seeking an answer to the lagging support of the congregation. It was not originally a human scheme, but a divine plan. Granted, the Christian is under the grace of Christ and not the law of Moses. However, did Jesus raise or lower standards for those who followed him? A glance at the sermon on the mount answers that question. In the contrasts, "You have heard that it was said to the people long ago . . . But I tell you" (Matt. 5:2,27,31-34,38,39,43,44), the Messiah always called for his own to have a "righteousness [that] surpasses that of the Pharisees and the teachers of the law" (Matt. 5:20).

Consider a situation where your beloved child is in anguish with the pangs of disease. One doctor, able to relieve some pain but not able to cure the critical disorder, charges a high fee. A new physician brings total cure, but requires no set fee. He only asks that you give him what you consider appropriate. Can it seem right to any reasoning person that the prior physician receive his stated amount and the one bringing the cure receive but a pittance? Under the law the fatal disease of sin found no abiding cure. Under Christ all sins are removed. To decide in our total freedom to start our giving-norm below the ancient tenth may only be an excuse for self-centeredness.

For a Christian under the Gospel to give less than a Jew under the Law, is not an evidence of grace but of disgrace. Can we not agree that in the Bible to tithe is the lowest standard of giving recognized? In the glorious gospel age the tithe is an appropriate starting line for those in the race, but an inadequate goal at which to stop running forward. He who refuses to run the first mile will never go the second. "The law was our schoolmaster to bring us unto Christ" (Gal. 3:24 KJV). That "schoolmaster" ("tutor" ASV) taught tithing as a lesson to be learned. The Master Teacher now takes the pupil on to the next lesson based on what was learned from the pedagogue before. No moral bankruptcy law ought to be claimed allowing each disciple to pay as he chooses. Standing on New Testament ground and viewing one's monetary responsibility for the support of the gospel, the tithe makes a fine floor but a terribly low ceiling.

Shall we sing an old hymn with just one word altered? "Blest be the tithe that binds our hearts in Christian love." The tithe can be a love-tie to the church, the ministry and the mission. Under grace it is never to be reduced to law but always lifted to love. It, in no way, is to be seen as a test of fellowship. Yet it may prove in the eyes of God to be a test of our love, our faith and our sincerity.

Each person in the closet of his heart must ask himself before his God, "Is the gospel of less value than the law? Is the maintenance of world proclamation of our Savior of lower priority than the maintenance of yesterday's Jewish worship on Jerusalem's holy mount Zion? Are we under grace honoring God with "left-overs," when ancients honored him with the first-fruit of their increase (Prov. 3:9)? However a believer answers these questions, let his giving reflect concern for the world and its people for whom Christ died. Let his giving confess the depth of his conviction that Jesus is Lord. Let his answer to the "how much" question reflect his awareness that God is the maker and owner of all creation. Let his eagerness to follow his Master be evident in his choice of a system of giving that is Biblical at root.

Does that word "system" and its relative "systematic" seem incongruent to one living under the gospel? Do not words like "creative" or "spontaneous" seem less legalistic or less calculating? Will our doctor be pleased, if we turn from the systematic intake of regular meals to spasmodic dining as we feel like it? How about the landlord's appreciation of our rent-paying habits, if we turn from the regular first of the month practice to sending in the sum on occasions when we are emotionally moved? Unless a Christian follows some systematic plan, other obligations will push into secondary place his debt to God. The tither sees himself as an investor, putting God's money into His program according to His plan. The tither doubts that Jesus went to heaven at the ascension leaving his bride the church a victim of non-support.

If you have found a system that is an improvement on the tither's plan of proportionate, systematic giving, go for it. But, before you make a clean break from the tithing taught in the Old

Covenant Scriptures, be sure to temper utopian thinking with the Biblical awareness of man's tendencies to selfishness. A man who keeps no account of his giving may be saving himself from the realization of how little he gives. A joking budget-committee person remarked that from the amount some people give to the Lord, they must be positive that it is the little things in life that count. The weekly *Lookout* of Standard Publishing Company, in a regular column titled "Deacon Jones Says," once ran the line, "The only danger I can see in tithing is that some church folks'll use it as an excuse to limit their gifts to a tenth."

To the charge that tithing enslaves, the answer is given that many have found it to be liberating, freeing from their dubious human schemes and personal doubts about their minimal share. Once again I must confess that chapter and verse cannot be found in the New Testament to establish beyond question the tithe as law for the church. But once again I must express my appreciation for the Christian parents and teachers who recommended to children to consider the first dime of every dollar as belonging to God. To paraphrase Solomon: "Remember to tithe in the days of your youth, before the stingy days come and the years approach when you will say, 'I find not pleasure in it' " (Eccl. 12:1). A child reared in bringing "tithes and offerings" to Jesus has a protective wall about him holding back the flood of materialism reaching out to engulf him. All the world cares about is money. All the liquor industry cares about is money. All the tobacco industry cares about is money. All the movie and TV industries care about is money. From infancy, let the child learn there is one organization that cares about people. The high point of worship in the church assembly is the sacrificial gifts of the saints to the support of its ministry to the world.

Should my study of the Bible lead me to want to give tithing a try, would pledging or promising to do so be an acceptable thing to do?

Making vows regarding giving is neither foreign to the Old Testament (Num. 29:39; Deut. 12:26) nor the Gospels (Matt.

23:16-19; Mark 7:11-13). The Psalmist sang, "Make vows to the Lord your God and fulfill them; let all the neighboring lands bring gifts to the One to be feared" (Psa. 76:11). He promised, "I am under vows to you, O God; I will present my thank offerings to you" (Psa. 56:12) and "I will come to your temple with burnt offerings and fulfill my vows to you — vows my lips promised and my mouth spoke" (Psa. 66:13,14). He declared that it would be "in the presence of all [God's] people" that his vows would be fulfilled (Psa. 116:18). In Apostolic times the inspired apostle considered it fitting to "finish the arrangements for the generous gift . . . promised" by the Corinthians (2 Cor. 9:5). The only caution is, "If you make a vow to the Lord your God, do not be slow to pay it" (Deut. 23:21).

7

ASKING THE BIBLE ABOUT THE GIVING
OF MONEY (WHAT?)

WHAT SHOULD BE DONE WITH THE GIFTS?

The question of how much believers should regularly bring into the coffers of their churches dare not be the final question. "What should be done with these gifts?" is next in line for the one who cares about responsible stewardship. Should the church or the individual disperse the funds? Is the judgment of a dozen Christian minds better than one? Is there safety in a multitude of counselors? Who would get the credit and the glory, if I gave directly to a missionary's support? Who, if it was sent by a congregation? Does it matter?

It is easier to come up with hard questions than with easy answers. But, lay this text as a foundation stone: "Everything should be done in a fitting and orderly way" (1 Cor. 14:40). Following his own advice for good procedure, Paul named the time ("the first day of every week"), the people ("each one of you"), the amount ("a sum of money in keeping with his income") and the seemly procedure ("when I arrive, I will give letters of introduction to the men you approve and send them with your gift to Jerusalem" 1 Cor. 16:2,3). The gifts were delivered "to the elders" (Acts 11:30), who were responsible for the oversight of its distribution. So there could be no criticism of mismanagement, Paul took care in the receiving, transporting and distribution of all monies. Note the caution of Paul's instruction. He uses men "chosen by the churches" to accompany himself and his workers as they administer the fund in a way that will "honor the Lord himself." Why the care? He responds, "We want to avoid any criticism of the way we administer this liberal gift. For we are taking pains to do what is right, not only in the eyes of the Lord but also right in the eyes of men" (2 Cor. 8:19-21). Apostles (Acts 4:35,37) and Prophets (Mal. 3:10; Ezra 7:18; Neh. 13:12) sought to follow "a manner worthy of God . . . for the sake of the Name" (3 John 6-7).

The church has a divine mission and funds are well spent that foster that mission. Gospel preaching is to be financed (Gal. 6:6) for "the worker is worth his keep" (Matt. 10:10) and "deserves his wages" (Luke 10:7). He has a "right to food and drink" (1 Cor. 9:4,7-14). God so ordained in Old Covenant days and again in the Church age. It is not left to doubt, "the Lord has commanded that those who preach the gospel should receive their living from the gospel" (1 Cor. 9:14). The whole church shares "partnership in the gospel" (Phil. 1:4), when it shares with the gospel heralds "in the matter of giving and receiving" (Phil. 4:15).

Besides investing in the lost by gospel preaching, the wise church makes investment in hurting humanity by meeting benevolent needs. "To look after orphans and widows in their distress" is a part of pure religion (James 1:27) and a manifestation of "the love of God" in a Christian (1 John 3:17). Acts of sharing with the needy should happen "as we have opportunity" (Gal. 6:10). Care should be given that none be "overlooked" (Acts 6:1). What the earthly familiy cannot provide, the extended church family should try to furnish (1 Tim. 5:8,9,16).

There will always be poor that need help (Matt. 26:11). That being so evidently true, should any money be invested by a congregation in buildings for the saints to gather? If the Old Testament is the measuring rod, a temple of worship is to be adorned as a "glorious temple" (Isa. 60:7). To read Kings (1 Kgs. 6:14-22; 8:13,62ff) and Chronicles (1 Chron. 22,28,29; 2 Chron. 3-7,24), or to examine Ezra (1,2,5-8) and Nehemiah (7), is to find the same exalting of the temple as in the Law (Lev. 24:4; Num. 4:11; 7:1-88; 10:2) and the Prophets (Zech. 4:2,12; 5:10,11). Jesus' disciples were proud to view their Jerusalem temple. They often talked "about how the temple was adorned with beautiful stones and with gifts dedicated to God" (Luke 21:5).

The buildings a congregation may erect for service and worship ought to be built in the awareness that God dwells in his people and in no facility of mortar and brick. If they construct a "house" or a "room" for the Lord and his disciples to break bread together (Luke 22:11,12), wisdom and purpose should have first say. Money, given in loving adoration for Christ, is not to be "rebuked" or called a "waste" (Mark 14:4,5). Yet neither is any follower of the Carpenter of Nazareth to start "to build" without an estimate of the cost to see if he has "enough money to complete it." To do otherwise is to ask for "ridicule" (Luke 14:28,29). Faith and foolishness are not twin sisters. To build elaborately and call it walking by faith may be rather rejecting Christ's words, "Do not put the Lord your God to the test" (Matt. 4:7).

"Of making many books there is no end" (Eccl. 12:12). It is the same with honest questions worthy of group discussion. Should a congregation ever go into debt? Is it an honor not to owe one red cent to anyone and always have money in the treasury? Should a Christian, like a business man, as a matter of good business practice, keep investing in a project without making inquiry as to the results coming forth? Would designating my gifts dropped in the church treasury be a way to be sure I only supported what I totally favored? If everybody followed that practice, how would the phone bills get paid? Does stewardship require keeping oneself informed on the congregation's expenditure of its funds? One could wish for easier roads for the accountable Christian to travel, but who said following the way of the cross was to be easy?

Part Two

Doctrine by Doctrine

8

MONEY AND THE NATURE OF GOD

The members of the first Christian church in all the world "devoted themselves to the apostles' teaching" (Acts 2:42 "the apostles' doctrine" ASV). Where would a study of that doctrine or theology place money? Would it be listed as a sub-topic under worship? It belongs under every category from Theology and Christology, through Anthropology and Soteriology to Ecclesiology and Eschatology. With the Bible as our guide, we will be led to see that Christian theology and church stewardship were not meant to be placed in different compartments. Put on your Biblical glasses and take a good look at the apostles' teaching on money from the A of Ananias to the Z of Zachaeus. A wholeness view has a holiness result.

GOD IS ONE

The Christian serves a God that is not satisfied with second place. Christianity is a thoroughly monotheistic religion. It cannot accept the competition of an "Almighty Dollar." As Jesus put it, "No one can serve two masters . . . You cannot serve both God and Money" (Matt. 6:24; Luke 16:13). "Mammon" (KJV) was a Syrian god whom the populace worshipped when they desired riches. Etymologically the word "mammon," in its Aramaic root, carries the meaning "to trust in." Since God is "a jealous God" (Exod. 20:5), he does not allow for rivals in the hearts of his people. If even one's family is not to take first place in the disciple's affections (Luke 14:26), how much more is money forbidden first place in the human heart.

Paul saw clearly that "greed . . . is idolatry" (Col. 3:5). Anyone with Jewish descent knew that. At the formation of their nation at Mount Sinai, Israel received the uncompromising order, "Do not make for yourselves gods of silver or gods of gold" (Exod. 20:23). In very short time the people succumbed to the appeal of a visible and radiant god in the form of a "golden calf" (Exod. 32:2-4,24,31). The Jewish people needed the constant reminder that to their God it was the pagan that had "detestable images and idols of wood and stone: of silver and gold" (Deut. 29:17). The nation needed to recall their susceptibility — their proneness, their weakness — toward the enamourment with gold. The book of Judges relates how even the hero Gideon made some "gold into an ephod." The record tells the black incident, when "all Israel prostituted themselves by worshipping it there, and it became a snare to Gideon and his family" (Jdgs. 8:27). That kind of sad tale repeats itself when Micah's mother consecrated "two hundred shekels of silver and gave them to a silversmith, who made them into the image and the idol" (Jdgs. 17.1-4).

The prophets God raised up continued to warn the covenant people of the dangers of turning from monotheism to polytheism even in a nation pledged to the one God. Isaiah saw that the "land full of silver and gold" was also "full of idols" (Isa. 2:7; 40:19,20; 46:6). He foresaw the happy day coming when Jews would "reject the idols of silver and gold [their] sinful hands [had] made" (Isa. 31:7) and return to the sure foundation" of "the fear of the Lord" (Isa. 33:6). Then they would recognize that "all who made idols are nothing, and the things they treasure are worthless," plus they would then realize their "craftsmen are nothing but men" (Isa. 44:9,11).

Jeremiah speaks in ridicule of an idol maker who would "cut a tree . . . adorn it with silver and gold," only to be "shamed by his idols" (Jer. 10:3,9,14). How much wiser to boast, not " 'of riches, but . . . that he understands and knows me, that I am the Lord, who exercises kindness, justice and righteousnes on the earth, for in these I delight,' declares the Lord" (Jer. 9:23,24). Hosea's voice decried Israel making "idols for themselves to their own destruction" (Hosea 8:4), but Daniel's pen celebrated heroes like Shadrach, Meshack and Abednego who refused to serve or worship the image of gold (Dan. 2:31; 3:1,5,7,10-12,14,18).

The song-book of Israel sang the truth into Jewish minds that "the idols of the nations are silver and gold, made by the hands of men," unable to speak, see or hear (Psa. 135:15). They also chanted the proud truth, "Our God is in heaven; he does whatever pleases him. But their idols are silver and gold, made by the hands of men" (Psa. 115:3,4). The music of the Old Covenant church made it evident that gold, even when not crafted into an idol, can be a substitute god in the heart; "Deceivers . . . trust in their wealth and boast of their great riches" (Psa. 49:6,16; 52:6,7). Their songs admonished, "Though your riches increase, do not set your heart on them" (Psa. 62:10). They also recognized the frailty of each worshipper, confessing, "As for me, my feet had almost slipped; I had nearly lost my foothold. For I envied the arrogant when I saw the prosperity of the wicked" (Psa. 73:2,3).

The wisdom literature warned that "whoever trusts in his riches will fall" (Prov. 11:28). It revealed that the wealth of the rich was falsely considered by them a "fortified city . . . an unscalable wall" (Prov. 18:11). When needed, that tightly held money would "surely sprout wings and fly off to the sky like an eagle" (Prov. 23:5). He who transfers total allegiance and trust to his bank account, saying, "Who is the Lord?" (Prov. 30:9), may find out too late that "riches do not endure forever" (Prov. 27:24).

When the curtain is pulled back to reveal end times, the Revelator finds unrepentant mankind still "worshipping demons, and the idols of gold, silver, bronze, stone and wood — idols that cannot see or hear or walk" (Rev. 9:20). The real God — the only true God — the One worthy of man's highest adoration, is not to be thought of as "like gold or silver or stone — an image made by man's design and skill" (Acts 17:29). Paul preached that "man-made gods are no gods at all" (Acts 19:26).

In the face of Jesus' insistence that those who follow him, "Worship the Lord . . . God, and serve him only" (Matt. 4:10; Luke 4:8; Deut. 6:13), many like the rich young man go away from the Christ sadly, because they refuse to dethrone their "great wealth" (Matt. 19:22; Mark 10:22). Money is not worthy of our total surrender. To love money is to "wander from the faith" (1 Tim. 6:10). To put "hope in wealth" is to settle for a demi-god that will disappoint. They who put "hope in God" (1 Tim. 6:17) are properly placing their adoration in their Maker, rather than being "lovers of themselves, lovers of money" (2 Tim. 3:2).

Money is not a dependable ally. It can be lost or stolen. You will find it devalued or taxed away. Swindlers can take it by fraud. Inflation can sap its strength. Through the ages money has been a god universally enthroned in all ages and lands. In man's preoccupation with money, he has allowed pure gold to come into his life and the true God be crowded out. "God is spirit" (John 4:24) and is too easily rejected for the visible and tangible cash in the bank. But, if money's lack of qualification for the status of God is not evident before, at the point of death the truth will come out.

Values are frightfully mixed when an athlete can become an overnight millionaire and a genuine life-long servant of humanity go unrecognized into oblivion. Our world needs to sit at the feet of the Master Teacher and learn about the true values and the genuine priorities in God's sight. Eternal well-being is of more lasting consequence than temporal well-being. "First" before "things" is God's "kingdom and righteousness" (Matt. 6:33). Money has a rightful place. It is not to claim our unswerving allegiance as an entity to be fully trusted and endlessly served. Money is to be put in its place. That place is the place of servant by our side and not the place of God over all. Let the rich refuse to submit to avarice and the poor to envy. Let neither allow the pursuit of wealth to become a tyrant stripping them of dignity. Let all master the acrostic on "Joy," where Jesus is first, others come second and yourself is placed last. Gold-fever cannot drive mad a disciple of Christ who has been taught that the greatest command is "love" (Matt. 22:36,37) and the highest position is that of servant (Matt. 23:11). Money on a heart's pedestal is guilty of insubordination.

The nature of money is to be seen in relationship to the nature of God. "Hear, O Israel; The Lord our God, the Lord is one" (Deut. 6:4). That oneness of monotheism refuses a place on a person's "god shelf" for some other than the Maker and Sustainer himself. Our "God and Father of all . . . is over all and through all and in all" (Eph. 4:6).

GOD IS CREATOR

He is the Creator of all. Telescopes and microscopes join in disclosing the wonders of that creation. Stewardship practices remember and stand in awe of that fact. The Christian looks up to the one who "created all things" (Eph. 3:9). "Heavens declare the glory of God; . . . skies proclaim the work of his hands" (Psa. 19:1). Once God is recognized as the Maker, the stewardship question is settled. There is no other song to sing than, "The earth is the Lord's, and everything in it, the world, and all who live in it"

(Psa. 24:1).

The opening line of the Bible sets that straight: "God created the heavens and the earth" (Gen. 1:1). Farmers are to see their crops as bounties from the Creator's hand (Gen. 1:11). Fishermen are to see their "catch" (Gen. 1:20-23) and breeders their livestock (Gen. 1:24,25) as gifts from the One who made the laborers as well (Gen. 1:26,28-30).

God owns all by the right of creation. He speaks, "Everything under heaven belongs to me" (Job 41:11). That includes "the silver . . . and the gold" (Hag. 2:8). That includes "every animal of the forest . . . and the cattle on a thousand hills" (Psa. 50:10). That includes us for "we are his . . . his people, the sheep of his pasture" (Psa. 100:3). Humanism starts on assumptions that are totally foreign to a Bible reader. The Bible believer cannot leave God out of the equation. In the light of Scripture God is over all and created men are exceedingly small. Each human being is a creature of the Almighty and will one day stand before his Maker to be judged. While on the earth, nothing ultimately belongs to the man. He is entrusted to use what comes his way in responsible stewardship. What he considers his, is God's. The Christian's creed speaks of Christ as "the firstborn of all creation. For by him all things were created . . . and for him" (Col. 1:16). Each believer owns nothing but is a steward of everything. He handles much, but holds ultimate title to less than little. As the sheep of God's pasture, believers hold no right to the wool. Rather they are grateful for the Shepherd's care. The Psalmist would be the last to bleat that the wool was not rightly the Shepherd's.

GOD IS PROVIDER

Joined to the concept of God as Creator is that of God as Provider. It is a fair conclusion that, if God has created the world and everything in it, then wealth falls under the approbation: "God saw all that he had made, and it was very good" (Gen. 1:31). It is likewise a logical deduction that the Originator of life is the Sustainer of life. Both Old and New Testament writings presuppose a God who cares for his creation as a father would provide for his offspring. Mary sings, "He has filled the hungry with good things" (Luke 1:53). David joined in the same hymn of praise, "The Lord is with me; he is my helper" (Psa. 118:7). Apostles told the church, "Cast all your anxiety on him because he cares for you" (1 Pet. 5:7). The sweet singer of Israel taught his nation, "Cast your cares on the Lord and he will sustain you" (Psa. 55:22). Insurance companies advertise, "You are in good hands with Allstate." The best offer ever to reach man's attention is the Biblical offer, "You are in good hands with God." Refuse the choking effect of "the worries of this life and the deceitfulness of wealth" (Matt. 13:22; Mark 4:19). Steer a wide course from "the anxieties of life" that weigh down your heart and "close on you . . . like a trap" (Luke 21:34). As you make your living day by day, remember that the God you follow is a Provider who "supplies seed to the sower and bread for food." You can count on him to "also supply and increase your store of seed" (2 Cor. 9:10). Concern is what every wage earner has for the family dependent upon him. But the person in Christ is buoyed up with the assurance that he is not left alone to deal with his economic problems. He has a divine partner.

GOD IS LOVE

The most basic of all Christian doctrines is that "God is love" (1 John 4:8). The highest of all Christian hopes is to become more and more God-like. The most rational of all conclusions then is that stewardship is the warp and woof of Christian theology. It is the nature of love to give (John 3:16).

Never in the ancient mystery religions of old, nor in the modern animistic religions of the present, was love a factor between the diety and the devotee. No kinship existed between the god or goddess and the worshipper at the shrine. The seeker was looking for protection or seeking some favor. How different is the revelation of God in Scripture. George Dewey claims to find 1520 references to giving in the Bible. Only the word "love" is found in Scripture to outnumber the instances of "give." You can't have one without the other. Love always finds a way to give. Philippians 2:5-11 is a stark contrast to Philippians 3:17-19. False religionists serve "their god [which] is their stomach" for "their mind is on earthly things." True servants of Christ follow his willing example of self-emptying for the sake of others. God's abundant generosity grows out of his love as will ours. You may give without loving, but it is impossible to love without giving. The nature of God is basic to the reality of money. It is as clear as ABC unless one chooses to be DEF.

9

MONEY AND THE NATURE OF CHRIST AND THE HOLY SPIRIT

THE INCARNATE JESUS

Doctrine matters. "False doctrines" are defined by apostles of Christ as those theologies that do "not agree to the sound instruction of our Lord Jesus Christ and to godly teaching" (1 Tim. 6:3). At Christmas the world is pointed to the vital Biblical teaching that Jesus is God incarnate. Heaven has come to earth in flesh and blood. The One over history has entered history. God has put his stamp of approval on the material world. He, who made it in the beginning, has shown in the first advent that he deems the earth worth rescuing.

All dualism, with its eternal distinctions between "spirituality" and "materialism," is discredited forever. With doctrines like creation, incarnation and resurrection can the church look with disdain on material assets or label morally suspect every tangible thing? See Jesus born of Mary laboring in Joseph's carpenter shop in Nazareth and you view human toil as dignified. Listen to this Rabbi and nothing can be brushed aside as secular and unfit for the kingdom. Daily toil and tangible goods are ordained into the ministry. Work days and Sabbath days are both holy to the Lord. Jesus the carpenter will build his church with leaders expert at fishing, taxing, doctoring *ad infinitum.*

THE ANOINTED ONE

This God-Man was proven to be the long-awaited Messiah. As the Christ, he is the priest more worthy of our gifts than Melchizedek to receive the tithe of Abraham (Heb. 7:4-10). As the Anointed King, he is not the subject of his people but rather they are his possessions. As the Anointed One, his prophetic teaching on money became the norm for his disciples. As the Perfect One, his life became the model or example to be followed. By his words and his works the Christian walks each day. Christ's many parables on riches opened their eyes. His generous self-giving challenged their hearts. It never can satisfy the person, who has made Christ-likeness his goal, to only talk about loving the poor and needy while leaving them unfed, unhoused or unhappy.

The Christian life is the application of Jesus' ways and words in all aspects of daily living. It is the twenty-four hour day — the three hundred sixty-five day year — of Jesus' church, as his body, continuing his ministry across the world (Acts 1:1). It is Galatians 2:20 reenacted in every disciple. It is the unison voice of each baptized believer saying, "I have been crucified with Christ and I no longer live, but Christ lives in me" (Gal. 2:20).

THE PERFECT MAN

The topic of money, or coined life, is addressed at every turn when we consider Jesus. He is God-incarnate. He is the anointed servant. He is the ideal man, the Adam more to be model for us than the sinner in the opening chapters of Genesis. He is above all the crucified savior, whose giving defines what giving really means.

THE CRUCIFIED SAVIOR

The cross of Christ becomes the symbol of the church and the definition of what a sacrificial gift is. Jesus gave up heaven for earth, a royal palace for a stable, a King's court (where being served is the way) for a basin and towel (where humble acts lead to the hard agony of Calvary). "It was not with perishable things such as silver or gold that you were redeemed . . . but with the precious blood of Christ" (1 Pet. 1:18,19). The name "disciple of Christ" fits the follower who chooses the discipline of giving, where a daily dying to one's own desires becomes the stepping stone to being like the Master.

THE SANCTIFYING SPIRIT

Any person who has taken self off the throne of his life and has crowned Jesus Lord of all has presented irrefutable evidence that the Spirit of Christ has been operative within him. A miracle has occurred. The sanctifying Spirit of God alone can be the sufficient cause for such a transformation. The once "greedy" are now "washed . . . sanctified . . . justified in the name of the Lord Jesus Christ and by the Spirit of our God" (1 Cor. 6:11).

Sanctified means to be set apart for a holy use. In the ancient temple former common utensils were sanctified, or set aside, for exclusive use in the service of God. The people once seen as vessels for Satan's service are purchased by Christ's precious blood. From the day of their redemption, their Master being changed they henceforth are to be tools for their newly crowned King. The practice of stewardship over time produces the *de facto*

101

reality which was *de jure* thinking from day one of conversion. Complete surrender is the final goal. Starting to take on steward-ship responsibilities gets the runner started in the race toward Christ-likeness (Heb. 12:1-3). Stewardship is not a human gim-mick, the goal of which is raising funds. It is a divine prescription that has as its drive the raising up of people in God's image. The former "aints" become present "saints" by the power of the Holy Spirit. His holiness is catching. His presence is transforming.

THE FRUIT-PRODUCING SPIRIT

"No one can say, 'Jesus is Lord,' except by the Holy Spirit" (1 Cor. 12:3). "We were all baptized by one Spirit into one body" (1 Cor. 12:13). "The Spirit and the bride" were the voice that called you to faith, confession and baptism (Rev. 22:17). The Spirit is the *paraclete* — the helper called to your side — to produce the lovely fruit described in Galatians 5:22 and 23. "Love, joy, peace" are traits of Christ. "Kindness, goodness, faithfulness" are traits of Christ. Whoever has these qualities reveals the family-traits of God's people. Who is a Christian? "By their fruit you will recognize them" (Matt. 7:20). Only the Spirit of Christ can pro-duce in men the nature of Christ. Apple trees do not bring forth olives. "Christ in you, [is] the hope of glory" (Col. 1:27) and the only hope of bearing the fruit of a redeemed life. Put inanimate rocks in the ground and they will never reproduce. Put the living Spirit of Jesus into the soil of a penitent heart and heavenly life will spring up everywhere. Make way for the sanctifying, fruit-producing, life-changing Spirit.

10

MONEY AND THE NATURE OF MAN AND SIN

IMAGE OF GOD

The Bible, like a family album, is filled with snapshots of man. In one photo the human is seen as a created being (Gen. 1:26-28; 2:7; Acts 17:26; Job 33:4; Psa. 100:3; Mal. 2:10), loved by his Maker (Psa. 8:5; Matt. 6:26; 12:12). In another picture the descendants of Adam and Eve show the family traits of rationality (Job 35:10,11), emotion (1 Chron. 29:3), sexuality (Gen. 1:27) and mortality (1 Cor. 15:22; Heb. 9:27; 1 Pet. 1:24). Especially related to our money theme are the Bible pictures of man as a moral, volitional and spiritual being with social responsibilities.

Yes, man is a physical being (1 Cor. 15:47) that must have resources to buy food and clothing for the body (Gen. 1:28-30; Matt. 6:25). But he is also a social person that will live with, and be responsible for, others (Gen. 2:18). From the time of man's creation, he has been divinely given the stewardship of the world and its resources. Adam was placed "in the garden of Eden to work it and take care of it" (Gen. 2:15). With everything placed "under his feet" (Psa. 8:6), man assumed the entrusted responsibility for earth. He will one day account for his success or failure with that stewardship (Rom. 2:6).

SERVANT OF ALL

Being a volitional creature and not a programmed automaton, each man is responsible for his choices. Every human elects whom to serve (Josh. 24:15) and by that willful act selects blessings or curses (Deut. 30:19,20). The choice to give or refrain from giving to the needy or to missions, etc. is ever a free-will choice (2 Cor. 9:7). To bear the "image of God" (Gen. 1:27; James 3:19) is to be a moral and willing being, having responsibilities toward others.

To recognize man as spiritual in nature (Zech. 12:1; Job 32:8; 1 Cor. 2:11), is to know his worth. A man in the ghetto or a woman with child sleeping in the street must be seen as of more value than gold. To be Biblically conscious is to opt for being servant of all, rather than a runner in the rat-race, where every man looks out only for himself. It is to vote for rendering humane service, rather than grasping for dominating power. It is to choose the way of servant-leadership that asks not how much will be made but how many will be helped. Looking through the eyes of Jesus, you see a small child or an aged woman of far more worth than sheep, or oxen, or birds (Matt. 6:26; 12:12).

STEWARDS OF EARTH

The miracle of miracles, resulting from the touch of Jesus on a life, is that the person begins to give and do for others with the undreamed consequence of having and becoming more himself or herself. It is a law of God that clipping roses to give them away produces more roses. Milking cows assures more milk for tomorrow, where refusing to take the milk dries up the source. Generosity is the nature of God. Woe to that human, who follows the animal instinct of self-preservation in the creatures below him. Fortunate the human, who adopts the divine instinct of self-giving in the Creator above him. Let your motivation be the service of others rather than personal profit. God came to earth in the person of Jesus to demonstrate what man was intended to be. He declared, "even the Son of Man did not come to be served, but to serve, and to give his life as a ransom for many" (Mark 10:45).

In the light of that revelation as to what man ought to be, you can estimate how much you personally are worth. If the banks defaulted or your possessions were all stolen, then how much would you be worth? "A man's life does not consist in the abundance of his possessions" (Luke 12:15). Once a person is possessed by Christ rather than his possessions, his scale of values is inverted. He remembers who he is. His insomnia is cured. He is a son of God. His investments in this life store up "treasures in heaven" (Matt. 6:20).

REBEL AGAINST GOD

The Chinese have the proverb that, while gold is tested by fire, man is tested by gold. The Hebrew and Christian Scriptures tell the same truth but use different words. Adam and Eve were guilty of the original sin, but their descendants dare not point the finger "for all have sinned" (Rom. 3:23).

What was Adam's sin? Do words like "covetousness" or "greed" come close? God had given the first man the world and all in it, withholding but one thing — the tree in the middle of the garden" (Gen. 3:3). As a reminder of divine ownership "the tree of the knowledge of good and evil" was to go untouched, but the abundant supply from the rest of the garden was for man's use and enjoyment. Not satisfied with the *largesse* of God toward him, Adam wanted it all.

EXPERT IN GREED

Sin is, at base, selfishness. It is a hand upraised in the face of God. It is a seeking one's own satisfaction rather than God's will. The love of God produces beneficent results, the "love of money . . . all kinds of evil" (1 Tim. 6:10). Covetousness is an assertion of the ego against God and the rest of humanity. Greed or avarice dethrones God. Nowhere in Scripture are wealth and success condemned. But everywhere in Scripture the warning sounds forth that loving money is man's greatest danger.

Covetousness climaxes the spiritual threats engraved in the ten commandments (Exod. 20:17). It is the evil viewed with alarm in the Gospels and Epistles. The Greek word for greed, πλεονεξία, describes the person who ever desires to have more (Mark 7:22; Rom. 1:29; 1 Cor. 5:11; Eph. 5:3; Col. 3:5). It is not only a sin committed by people of wealth, but by the poor who either resent the well-to-do or suffer total preoccupation with money.

Greed is the most prevalent sin in the Bible records (Achan, Gehazi, Ananias, Judas, etc.). Its harmful spread is difficult to stem in that those afflicted with the disease are unaware that they have its cancerous cells. Preachers often remind us of Francis Xavier's experience. After years of listening to confessions of heinous sins of every kind, he could not recall one person ever confessing to the sin of covetousness. Jesus knew that the Pharisees "loved money" (Luke 16:14), but they did not realize it. Jesus was aware that the "certain rich man" of his parable was a "fool" (Luke 12:20), but Christ's hearers who fit the category were numb in conscience to the barb. The Lord could see the symptoms of greed in priests and Levites headed for the temple

(Luke 10:31,32) and for unconcerned Jews who thought their riches were a sign of God's approval while they were unmoved by beggars at their gates (Luke 16:19-21).

If your favorite pronouns are "I" and "me," or your pet adjectives are "my" and "mine," you need a grammar lesson from the Master Teacher. Baptism in water is taught in God's book but total immersion in self is condemned in every section of the Scripture.

"Man's envy of his neighbor" (Eccl. 4:4) is sin. But who would recognize it as such had "the law not said, — 'Do not covet' " (Rom. 7:7)? The modern Christian needs to see the guilt by association implied by Paul when he places greed in the very center of sensual evils that destroy the soul. He wrote, "Do not be deceived: Neither the sexually immoral nor idolaters nor adulterers nor male prostitutes nor homosexual offenders nor thieves nor the greedy nor drunkards nor slanderers nor swindlers will inherit the kingdom of God" (1 Cor. 6:10). "Ruin and destruction" plus "many griefs" can be avoided by shunning the sin of greed that dethrones God and corrupts man.

REDEEMABLE BY CHRIST

The nature of man and the nature of sin throws light on the nature of money. In itself this thing called money can be neither moral nor immoral. It is amoral. It takes on the trait of virtue or vice by the human hand that touches it. It can be a tool to corrupt and destroy. It can be a constructive force to serve God's purposes. Whatever economic theory and management education can do for the mind, if they fail to open the heart and hand they have short-changed the student and misdirected a life. Whatever social program is advocated to improve the human condition, it will raise hopes only to smash them, if personal change is not the building blocks of social transformation.

Learn a lesson from the pyramid of Cheops at Giza. In Egypt

stands this monument to self-centeredness. A hundred thousand men laboring over twenty years erected this tomb at what today would cost half a billion dollars. It held food, spirit boats and slaves to serve the one man Cheops lest he become lonesome or lacking in any way (Herodotus). Learn a lesson from the cross of Christ at Calvary. Jesus acted always in his life and death with consideration for the needs of others. No wonder earth and heaven ring with his praises. Self-consideration is the first law of the jungle. Self-sacrifice is the highest rule of grace. It is the function of the Christian church to build the new race of men. Character building is the 100 level course in the school of Christ. "Repent" is one of the entrance requirements (Acts 2:38). Self-giving is the major field of study. "Well done" is the graduation speech for the class on commencement day (Matt. 25:21).

11

MONEY AND THE NATURE OF SALVATION

Bernard Baruch had a cure for the problem of excess spending by the populace. The solution he proposed was to pass a law changing human nature and making that law retroactive to the Garden of Eden. Will Rogers had an equally impractical fix for the snarled traffic of our big cities. He suggested that the streets allow only those cars that had been paid for. Jesus Christ on the other hand has a sane, sensible and Scriptural remedy for man's lost condition. It is a gospel that has "the power of God for the salvation of everyone who believes" (Rom. 1:16). It has the dynamic force to overcome "the cravings of sinful man, the lust of his eyes and the boasting of what he has and does" (1 John 2:16). The churches are filled with hosts of people ready to testify of the change that happened to them. Each, born blind to the needy ones around them, now confesses, "One thing I know. I was blind but now I see!" (John 9:25).

RESULTS OF SALVATION

Salvation comes in different dimensions. Followers of Jesus can say, "I have been saved, I am being saved, I will be saved." As far as forgiveness for all past sins, that happens at conversion (Acts 2:38). Regarding the return of Christ for his own, that is Biblically termed bringing "salvation to those who are waiting for him" (Heb. 9:28). The guilt of sin was removed in the past and the penalty of sin will be taken away in the future. In the present, believers are "being saved" (Acts 2:47) from the power of sin over their lives. One business man placed in the window of his store the sign "Open Under New Management." He explained to his curious neighbors, "I have accepted Jesus Christ as my Lord." His life, once regulated by commerce, was now free in Christ. With Paul he could say, "For to me, to live is Christ" (Phil. 1:21). That meant living for others rather than for self.

It is vital to note that all the money in the world could not save us and the domination of money over our lives is one of the evil powers from which we need rescue. Luke 8:26-39 is the account of a Gerasene man freed from his demon possession, while the community's pig owners, completely possessed by their possessions, turn the world's only Savior away. Their misplaced priorities evidenced their need for salvation from the enslaving power of things. They needed to read Ezekiel's message and that of Zephaniah, "Their silver and gold will not be able to save them in the day of the Lord's wrath" (Ezek. 7:19; Zeph. 1:18). They needed to hear Zophar's Amen!, "He cannot save himself by his treasure" (Job 20:20). They needed to listen to Bildad's counsel: "So perishes the hope of the godless. What he trusts in is fragile; what he relies on is a spider's web. He leans on his web, but it gives way; he clings to it, but it does not hold" (Job 8:13-15). They needed the gospel word of Isaiah, the evangelist of the Old Testament: "Without money you will be redeemed" (Isa. 52:3), "Come . . . you who have no money, come, buy and eat" (Isa. 55:1).

No one can "buy the gift of God with money" (Acts 8:20). No human "gifts and sacrifices" are "able to clear the conscience" (Heb. 9:9). No "perishable things, such as silver or gold," have redeeming power. "The precious blood of Christ" alone can save (1 Pet. 1:18,19). God will send "the rich away empty" (Luke 1:53), if they continue to say, "I am rich; I have acquired wealth and do not need a thing" (Rev. 3:17).

One result of salvation is freedom from "the love of money [which] is a root of all kinds of evil" (1 Tim. 6:10). One's wealth becomes gaining Christ. What earlier was listed as "profit" is moved from the asset column to the "loss" side of the ledger (Phil. 3:7,8). The walk and talk of the Christian — the behavior of the believer — reflect the dethroning of mammon and the enthroning of the Master. A salvation that does not affect the pocket-book and the bank account is no salvation at all. A new income without a new birth would bring an intensified debauchery.

STEPS OF SALVATION

It would be profitable to turn from what Soteriology has to say about salvation's means and power to its words regarding acquisition. In the New Testament instances of conversion recorded in the book of Acts, Jew and Gentile were brought to faith in Christ, repentance toward Christ and baptism into Christ (Acts 2:36-41). Each of these "steps" has a dollar-sign significance.

"Believe in the Lord Jesus," the Philippian jailer was told (Acts 16:31). "Be assured of this: God has made this Jesus . . . both Lord and Christ," was the message to the Jewish throng on Pentecost (Acts 2:36). What is this believing, or putting faith, in Jesus? When the Ethiopian Eunuch asked for baptism, Philip's response was, "If you believe with all your heart, you may" (Acts 8:37). To believe in Christ is to place your trust in him. The "important official in charge of all the treasury of Candace, queen of the Ethiopians" (Acts 8:27) declared, "I believe that Jesus Christ is the Son of God (Acts 8:37).

Saving faith is more than nodding the head to correct propositional statements about deity. "You believe that there is one God. Good! Even the demons believe that — and shudder" (James 2:19). "What good is it . . . if a man claims to have faith but has no deeds? Can such a faith save him?" James answers his own question by an illustration of a needy person being told kind words with no actual physical meeting of those needs. He calls such a faith "dead" (James 2:14-16).

A person professing to have faith, but yet possessing no confidence that God can supply his future needs, has *fides* but not *fiducea.* Saving faith is trusting reliance on the person of Christ and not simply agreeing to assertions about him. If I cannot trust him with the key to my saving's box, have I sufficient trust in him to save my soul? If I claim to believe in Jesus and make orthodox statements that will pass the scrutiny of theologians and yet do not trust him with my cash, you have a right to doubt my empty words. Should you hear me join in the statement of faith with other worshippers on Sunday and yet you notice I avoid the offering plate consistently, your suspicions may be justified.

Faith is joined in Scripture with repentance (Mark 1:15). The verb μετανοέω comes from the noun νοῦς meaning mind. Hence repentance is a change of mind that leads to a change in conduct. John E. Burkhart, a speaker at University of Southern California's chapel, was unimpressed with a religious boom of the time. He remarked that it was like "spiritual aspirin." He said it neither cost much, did much, hurt much nor was worth much.

Jesus' call for repentance was demanding. He offered no easy way. He called it "hard to enter the kingdom of God" (Mark 10:23). He insisted that he who would follow, would of necessity have to "deny himself and take up his cross daily" (Luke 9.23). The "cross" of which he spoke was no beautiful ornament to adorn a building or dangle as a jewel about one's body. It was a symbol of death to the self.

To shed tears profusely, while robbing Christ of what is rightfully his, cannot hide the lack of genuine repentance. Personal salvation is "purse-and-all" salvation. There is no option. "He who has been stealing must steal no longer" (Ephesians 4:28). "Produce fruit in keeping with repentance" (Luke 3:8). To repent is to change. Make the change. Keep the change. "Unless you repent, you too will all perish" (Luke 13:3,5).

The ten cases of conversion, preserved in Luke's account of Acts, conclude with the baptism of the converts. As death precedes burial, repentance is to come before baptism. To be buried with him through baptism" (Rom. 6:4; Col. 2:12) delcares to all who witness the initiatory rite that a death has occurred. How empty would be the arguments for total immersion from the lips of a person not living a life of total dedication.

Earl Hanson Fife recalled hearing his father describe the advocate of restoration, Benjamin Franklin, baptizing in Kentucky. When friends on the river bank offered to hold a convert's money and watch during his immersion, the new believer responded, "I'm going to be baptized all over — head, heart, time, money and all." An interesting theological issue is raised when some persons who have been sprinkled give to the Lord's work as though they have been immersed while a few of those who have been immersed give as though they had been sprinkled. Let the outer form express the full gospel of Christ's death and resurrection and our total surrender. Let the inner reality be complete and wholehearted faith, repentance and baptism.

What does baptism have to do with budgets? How does water relate to wealth and to wallets? Do praying and paying have any kinship? They can and must. In New Testament times they did. "All the people, even the tax collectors, when they heard Jesus' words, acknowledged that God's way was right, because they had been baptized by John. But the Pharisees and experts in the law rejected God's purpose for themselves, because they had not been baptized" (Luke 7:29). At Ephesus Paul preached Jesus and his hearers "were baptized into the name of the Lord Jesus" (Acts 19:5). Did it have any monetary consequence? Read on. "A number who had practiced sorcery brought their scrolls together and burned them publicly. When they calculated the value of the scrolls, the total came to fifty thousand drachmas" (Acts 19:19). The first of Jesus' disciples could say, "We have left all we had to follow you" (Luke 18:28). No cheap substitute for Christianity in our time by any name can slip by as the real thing. "What good is it for a man to gain the whole world, yet forfeit his soul" (Mark 8:36). Out of love for the Savior leave what was the object of your love before you met him. Turn from reliance on Mammon to dependence on Christ. Money will not buy your way to glory. Baptism as a work of merit to purchase God's favor won't pass approval by the President of the Bank of Heaven. But, baptism as an act of faith in the covenanted promises of God will bring his warm acceptance (Mark 16:16; Acts 22:16).

12

MONEY AND THE NATURE OF WORSHIP

"Spiritual worship" is defined by Paul as offering "your bodies as living sacrifices, holy and pleasing to God" (Rom. 12:1). Properly understood, to "worship in spirit and in truth" (John 4:24) may be more fittingly done when we reach our hands down into our pockets to help a poor man on Monday than when we lifted them up into the air on Sunday at the song-leader's request. To attach sacred significance to certain acts in certain places at certain hours may stem more from rubbing shoulders with quasi-religions than from reading Scriptures.

The etymology of our English word worship comes from *weorp,* which means worth or value. The Father of Jesus "seeks" as worshippers all who will hold him in highest regard. "Worth-ship" and "shipworthy" are relatives. Lives battered by contrary winds are able to reach their destination by the compass of "truth" and the motivating power of "spirit" (John 4:23,24). To think of Christian worship in the terms of an hour Sunday morning is to put asunder the sacred and secular that God has joined together. Worship is the Christian life-style. At no day nor hour is the believer to get out of character as one holding his God in highest worth. Worship has to do with "whatever you do, whether in word or deed." All is to be done "in the name of the Lord Jesus, giving thanks to God the Father through him" (Col. 3:17). Ethics is worship. Clothing the needy is worship. Meting out justice is worship. Telling the lost of a Savior is worship.

THE LORD'S DAY

Yet, from the beginning of the church, the daily private and family acts of adoration were encouraged at the corporate gatherings of the community. The church at Ephesus or Rome or Corinth could not be in assembly every day. The second and third century records of Lord's Day assemblies for the breaking of bread and apostolic teaching trace the roots of their practice to first century texts. Sunday was called "the Lord's Day" (Rev. 1:10). Luke gave the purpose of the Sunday gathering when he wrote, "On the first day of the week we came together to break bread" (Acts 20:7).

In Old Testament days the Jews gathered to worship on the seventh day. The very designation "sabbath" pointed out the fact that God did not want his people working all the time. Resting is legitimate. Not making money every day is all right. Time to consider what is really valuable is a good thing. The "seventh day" of Israel reminded the people of the fact of creation (Exod. 20:11). The "first day" of the church imbeds in the Christian the truth of redemption. "On the first day of the week" (Matt. 28:1; Mark 16:2; Luke 24:1; John 20:1) Christ was "raised to life for our justification" (Rom. 4:25).

THE LORD'S SUPPER

In the New Testament the "Lord's Supper" (1 Cor. 11:20) is

116

tied to the "Lord's Day" (Rev. 1:10). In these two texts we have the only New Testament instances where the word κυριακός is found. In the first instance it is κυριακόν δεῖπνον. In the second it is κυριακῇ ἡμέρᾳ. On the day in memory of Jesus' resurrection they shared a meal of memory recalling his sacrifice.

Beyond the elements of worship similar in synagogue and church, were the differences of day and dinner — of time and table. No corporate gathering pushed off center the drama of Jesus' sacrifice at Calvary. The point of the body's coming together was to celebrate "the grace of our Lord Jesus Christ, that though he was rich, yet for [their] sakes became poor, so that [they] through his poverty might become rich" (2 Cor. 8:9).

Romanism taught that a miracle of transubstantiation occurred when the priest said, *"Hoc est corpus meum"* or "This is my body." The Scripture rather marvels not over a change in the bread and the cup but in God's people. Through the physical elements on the table the worshippers are helped to remember a spiritual truth. Jesus died for them all. They must be "discerning" (ASV) or "recognizing the body of the Lord" (1 Cor. 11:29). They were each baptized into that "body" (1 Cor. 12:13). They must in thoughtful consideration of each member of that body "wait for each other" (1 Cor. 11:33). No rich believer is to come under judgment by ignoring the poor man at the family table. Would he, who washed the disciple's feet and called for "love" (John 13:34,35) at the Last Supper, accept the humiliation of "those who have nothing" (1 Cor. 11:20) by others at the Lord's Table?

Gnosticism may reject the material and plead for the spiritual. Christ rejects the dualism. Baptism in water is not denigrated by the Spirit's essentiality. Bread and the fruit of the vine do not lose importance in the spiritual communion of prayer. Rather at each occasion when bread is eaten and cup is drunk, the gathered church does proclaim the Lord's death until he comes" (1 Cor. 11:26).

THE LORD'S MONEY

In many congregations at the hour of worship, the Lord's Supper is followed by the offering. No pattern for the order of worship is so extensively given in the New Testament that it is made clear when in a service the collection should come. But our act of giving, as a response to the remembrance of Christ's gift to us, seems appropriate.

Giving prompted by gratitude for God's goodness makes the offering a doxology of praise. At the table of the Lord we heard answered the question, "What has Jesus done for you?" In the offering tray we respond to the inquiry, "What will you do for Christ?" If God "did not spare his own Son, but gave him up for us all" (Rom. 8:32), will giving only what we can easily spare be a worthy act of worship?

To the grateful children of God, praising the Lord is to "forget not all his benefits" (Psa. 103:2). The essence of worship is giving to the Father as an act of devotion from his grateful children. The fountain spring for giving is the thankful heart. In every appreciative disciple is the living sense of indebtedness to the Savior. With minds kindled afresh by Communion of God's supernatural love for us, the natural desire is to express our tangible love in return. The voice of the Crucified calls, "Freely you have received, freely give" (Matt. 10:8). The experience of the Macedonian Christians keeps being repeated where "overflowing joy" wells "up in rich generosity" (2 Cor. 8:2). And the Lord himself still watches "the crowd putting their money into the . . . treasury" and still sees both "the rich people" and the "poor widow" do their giving (Mark 12:41-44). He is present in large or minute gatherings in his name (Matt. 18:20).

Israel's worship had economic dimensions. Every spiritual relationship needs to be expressed in some material way. God's love shouted from the heavens or written in the sky would never have been grasped as clearly as it was when "the Word became flesh and lived for a while among us" (John 1:14). Christian adoration prays in social consciousness to "Our Father" about "our daily bread" (Matt. 6:11). Accepting the fatherhood of God opens the heart to the other members of the family. No child of God is alone. He worships with others and is strengthened by the sense of family solidarity. Family obligations are shared "on the first day of every week" during "the collection for God's people" (1 Cor. 16:1,2).

When Dan Kechel was preaching at Portland's First Christian Church a child volunteered to lead the national pledge of allegiance to the flag. He began, "I pledge my allowance to the flag. . . ." Not a bad improvement for a worshipper's commitment at the Lord's Table. "I pledge my allowance, my life, my prayers, my efforts and my all to Christ and his church." Once we see the love of the Giver, we seek to express our love with gifts to the Lover of souls. Shall all worshippers pray that they never give up in cowardice, give over in compromise, give in to surrender or give out in weakness. But may they offer supplication that they continue to give loving material support to the cause of the One whose nature is to give. The fire of God only falls on the sacrifice (Lev. 9:24).

13

MONEY AND THE NATURE OF MISSION

Will it be "butter or guns?" Shall the church budget provide food for the hungry or shall it meet the expenses of missionaries, who as "soldiers of the cross" are on foreign fields to capture the nations for Christ? To ask such questions is to hear the Lord of the church respond with clarity in the Bible. He commissioned the church to "Make disciples of all nations" (Matt. 28:19) by going "into all the world . . . to all creation" (Mark 16:15). That assignment alone calls for budgets of more than pee-wee size. But there is more. Jesus also said, "Give to the poor." (Matt. 19:21).

FOREIGN MISSIONS

For God's kingdom to come and his will to "be done on earth as it is in heaven" (Matt. 6:10) is not a prayer that will be answered by spare time and loose change. The extension of

God's reign calls for strategic planning and sacrificial support. It is hard to believe that an All-wise God would ask for the poor to be clothed, the orphans to be fed and the world to be informed with the gospel, while overlooking to explain how such a work was to be funded.

The Christian mission and Christian stewardship will advance together or not at all. At an ordination we say to our fledgling preacher "Go into all the world and preach the good news to all creation" (Mark 16:15). At an offering we must say the same to our dollars. There is no way to change the order. After preaching comes hearing. After hearing comes believing, then calling on God, then salvation. But prior to these comes sending and even before that the funding that launches all the rest (Rom. 10:15).

The outcome of our income can be the success of the gospel. Recall the story you heard in childhood of the King Midas and his golden touch. One modern writer suggests that King Jesus has reversed the story. Instead of the people touched turning to gold, our gold can turn the ones we touch into persons. There are boundless possibilities in Christian stewardship for the accomplishing of God's purposes of grace in the redemption of men.

You often read in religious publications that the universal observance of the tithe by Christians would supply all the money needed to evangelize the world. The American is well aware that the portion of his taxes going for war is likely to be many times as much money as the portion of his church offering going for missions. Plant seed in hard dry ground devoid of water. Irrigate that arid ground with an eye dropper and wonder why the crop fails to grow. Then look at the missionary on a difficult field undersupported and marvel that any converts are sprouting up at all. Perhaps we need to sing more often the hymn of

"O Zion haste, Thy mission high fulfilling,
To tell to all the world that God is Light;
That He who made all nations is not willing

122

One soul should perish, lost in shades of night . . .
  "Give of Thy sons to bear the message glorious;
  Give of they wealth to speed them on their way."[1]

LOCAL EVANGELISM

"Partnership in the gospel" (Phil. 1:4) and its spread is one side of our mission. "Sharing in . . . service to the saints" (2 Cor. 8:4) is another. Being "willing to share" (1 Tim. 6:18) with brethren is apostolic talk. Paul and the Twelve must never have heard the poor advice, "Never talk about money in the pulpit." Their teaching comes to grips with reality. They did not teach tossing coins into wishing wells, hoping that one's wish would come true. But they did champion placing offerings regularly in the treasury so God's desires for the world would come to pass (1 Cor. 16:1,2).

Lost souls are lost valuables and worthy of diligent search nearby in one's town as well as far off on some mission station. Operating the home church has its expenses as every congregation soon learns. We do not live in a police state where church doors are padlocked from without to prevent Chrsitian assembling. More dangerously we face the threat of indifference where complacency in outreach and failure in monetary support locks the church from within.

Christ wants his churches to mean business about his big business. He wants "his kingdom" to be "first" (Matt. 6:33). He would be pleased if every pay day the disciples would ask, "Now first of all, what shall we do for the church?" "His intent was that . . . through the church, the manifold wisdom of God should be made known . . . according to his eternal purpose" (Eph. 3:10,11). "Christ loved the church and gave himself up for

---

1. Mary A. Thompson, "O Zion Haste," *The New Church Hymnal* (Lexicon Music, Inc. 1976), Hymn 220.

her" (Eph. 5:25). He longs for his people not to save money but to save souls — the soul that Christian gifts may win and the soul of the Christian who gives the gift.

HUMAN CONCERN

If you and your congregation received a letter from an apostle today, it would probably carry similar practical urging as those of old: "Do everything you can to help Zenas the lawyer and Apollos on their way and see that they have everything they need. Our people must learn to devote themselves to doing what is good in order that they may provide for daily necessities and not live unproductive lives" (Titus 3:13,14). Here is no mysterious information about the meaning of signs in the sky, only down-to-earth practical concerns about people.

The pejorative "All the church cares about is money" is belied by the glorious truth that the church cares about men, women and youth. It cares about the sick and the dying. It cares about community morals and social justice. It cares because God cares. The believers do not wish to stick their noses in other people's business, but they stand ready to put their cash with their hearts in other people's problems.

Gospel proclamation and social improvement go together. Where the first is the other will follow. It would be shortchanging the world of need to provide things to keep the body alive and then fail to give the gospel that makes life worth the living. Any effort at restoring the Christian faith and practice of New Testament days will be concerned with caring for the poor — their spiritual as well as their physical needs. That effort will seek knowledge not only as to who the poor are but why they are poor. That effort will strive to treat the disease and not just the symptoms. That effort will call for giving not from the top of the purse but from the bottom of the heart.

You can't take it with you. You may not be able to keep it

while you are here, but you ought to channel all of it you can, while you can, into causes that "bear . . . the marks of Jesus" (Gal. 6:17). "Let us not become weary in doing good . . . as we have opportunity, let us do good to all people, especially to those who belong to the family of believers" (Gal. 6:9,10). When Robert Chapman was asked, "Would you not advise young Christians to do something for the Lord?" he replied, "No, I should advise them to do everything for the Lord."

14

MONEY AND THE NATURE OF THE CHURCH

Everything God said to Israel about money in the Old Testament, they understood in the light of the special covenant relationship the nation had to its Lord. In the New Testament is revealed the similarly unique relationship between Christ and the church. As people of the New Covenant, the church of Christ with the Christ of the church are the parties involved. The teachings of Jesus passed on by his apostles are the terms of the agreement with their accompanying promises. In the apostolic imagery of the people of God and the developing ministries in the community of believers our understanding of money is informed.

CONCEPTUALIZED FOR CLARITY

The figures — the imagery — Christ and his apostles used regarding the church show true Christianity to be ever personal but never private. That is, the believer is not in a one-to-one relationship with God in an exclusive way. He is joined to others in an intertwined social body, the church. Where in some religions the devotee goes privately to his shrine, in the Christian faith the community gathers. This social consciousness has financial consequences.

If we are "the body of Christ," then each member has concern "for the common good" (1 Cor. 12:7), in that "the body is a unit" with "all baptized by one Spirit into [that] one body" (1 Cor. 12:12,13). How can any individual think only of himself? Paul requests that each person in the church "have equal concern for each other. If one part suffers, every part suffers with it; if one part is honored, every part rejoices with it. Now you are the body of Christ, and each one of you is a part of it" (1 Cor. 12:25-27).

Do you sing, "I'm glad I'm a part of the family of God?" Do you read that elders are "shepherds of God's flock" (1 Pet. 5:2)? Do you recognize that you are "a chosen people . . . a holy nation" (1 Pet. 2:9)? "Family," "flock," "people" and "nation" are group words. That means we are "brothers" (Acts 6:3; 15:36; 1 Pet. 5:9). If we are admonished to "love the brotherhood" (1 Pet. 2:17), will words loudly uttered while wealth is tightly clutched fulfill the filial responsibility? James thinks not. He wrote, "Suppose a brother or sister is without clothes and daily food. If one of you says to him, 'Go, I wish you well; keep warm and well fed,' but does nothing about his physical needs, what good is it?" (James 2:15,16). Your brothers in rags and your sisters oppressed are also God's royalty. Joined in community with them, responsible concern is a must. Ananias and Sapphira violated the sharing principle inherent in family concept. Where the others in Jerusalem were acting as brothers and sisters ought (Acts 2:44,45; 4:32-37), this pair belied the family solidarity with its love attachment by their individualism (Acts 5:1-11).

Other cohesive images of the church are terms like "kingdom" (Rev. 1:9) and "The Israel of God" (Gal. 6:16). Citizens of any nation have privileges and responsibilities. The kingdom of God is no exception. Call the group "the twelve tribes scattered among the nations" (James 1:1) or "God's elect, strangers in the world" (1 Pet. 1:1), the body of believers carry obligations to each other. See them as a marching "army" (Rev. 19:19) girded for battle (Eph. 6:11-18; 2 Cor. 10:4; Rom. 13:12). They are a unit composed of many. They owe their lives to each other and they stand side by side a team. The word synagogue and the word *ecclesia* imply a gathered people — a community.

ORGANIZED FOR SERVICE

Jesus called himself "the way" (John 14:6), or the road to be followed to reach the destination of heaven. His church was called "the Way" (Acts 19:23), implying that the disciples had chosen Jesus' lifestyle. He had taken a route dealing with the things of the world different from most men. He chose not "to be served, but to serve" (Mark 10:45). As his church developed under the Spirit's guidance, ministries developed to continue Jesus' work in the world through his people.

Where apostles and prophets served the church universal, local needs called for local ministries. The work of deacons in Jerusalem had to do with "the daily distribution of food," where they were needed "to wait on tables" (Acts 6:1,2). Luke next tells us of elders. Their ministry likewise included the oversight of fund distribution to famine sufferers in Judea (Acts 11:29,30).

Requirements for "overseer" included both being "hospitable" and not being "a lover of money" (1 Tim. 3:2,3). Such a man would need the willingness to open his home and hand to offer hospitality. Such a servant, responsible for handling a congregation's money, would need to have the stamina of character enabling him to overcome the Judas tendency of putting his hand in the common purse (John 12:6). "Deacons, likewise are to be men . . . not pursuing dishonest gain" and "in the same way, their wives are to be . . . trustworthy in everything" (1 Tim.

3:8,11).

Whether an "evangelist" has brief ministries in a town or lengthy stays, like Philip in Caesarea (Acts 21:8), he can be a true shepherd or succumb to the flesh and be but a hireling. In Paul's day he knew of "many" who did "peddle the word of God for profit" (2 Cor. 2:17) and "exploited" people (2 Cor. 7:12; 12:18). He found it hard to conceive that man would consider preaching "a means to financial gain" (1 Tim. 6:5). One recent year the *Los Angeles Times* produced an article based on the U.S. Bureau of Labor statistics that surveyed the earnings of men in 321 occupations. Would it surprise you that doctors ranked first and preachers 245th? Truck drivers did better.

Some TV evangelists and flamboyant revivalists need to consider the false impression some parishoners are getting regarding preachers as a whole. All parishoners ought to support the local congregation of their community where fiscal responsibility can be readily known and faithfully corrected. Until time is no more there will be those false religionists "teaching things they ought not to teach . . . for the sake of dishonest gain" (Titus 1:11). "Balaam . . . loved the wages of wickedness" although he was a prophet (2 Pet. 2:16). Such "blemishes" by men "who feed only themselves" (Jude 12), should alert the believer of today to writers and speakers that preach the certain return of Christ in this decade while they accumulate affluent estates and drive fabulous cars. "The worker deserves his wages" (Luke 10:7). "The labourer is worthy of his hire" (KJV). And the hireling is worthy of our reproach. Thank God for the thousands of true shepherds who "feed" and "care" for Christ's sheep (John 21:15,16). Be in "partnership" with them (Phil. 1:5). Share with them in both giving and receiving" (Phil. 4:15). Encourage the true gospel proclaimer and "share all good things with [such an] instructor" (Gal. 6:6). He who makes the souls of men his concern, rather than the possessions of men, deserves backing.

15

MONEY AND THE NATURE OF LAST THINGS

In the light of eternity stewardship makes sense. Without life after death the believer would join the hopeless of the world who cry, "Let us eat and drink for tomorrow we die" (1 Cor. 15:32; Isa. 22:13). But, confident that Christ's resurrection guarantees a future for the disciple, the Christian calls out, "Always give yourself fully to the work of the Lord, because you know that your labor in the Lord is not in vain" (1 Cor. 15:58). At the final consummation of time the place of God's purpose for the world shines forth. The present gets its meaning from the future. How the Christian uses his money in this world is determined by how he views his mission in light of the pending judgment and his eternal destiny.

THE PENDING JUDGMENT

"Man is destined to die once, and after that to face judgment"

(Heb. 9:27). There will be no exceptions to that rule. Every Christian and every non-believer will be there. Every preacher, apostle and prophet will be included with every lay person, "for we must all appear before the judgment seat of Christ, that each one may receive what is due him for the things done while in the body whether good or bad" (2 Cor. 5:10).

Old Testament spokesmen warned, "The Lord Almighty has a day in store for all the proud and lofty" (Isa. 2:12). They raised the issue, "What will you do on the day of reckoning, when disaster comes . . . ? To whom will you run for help? Where will you have your riches?" (Isa. 10:3). The Gospels preserve Jesus' stories that announced such a coming day — a day of reckoning when God will say, "Give an account of your management" (Luke 16:2). Christ's promised return will be known as the time for "settled accounts" (Matt. 25:19). The stewardship issue will have high priority on that final day, for probing questions about aiding the "hungry . . . thirsty" and those needing "clothes" will prove or belie professions of faith in Christ (Matt. 25:35,36).

When will this accounting of our stewardship come? "At harvest time" (Mark 12:2). Will it really matter then if men have "devoured widows' houses?" Jesus' answer is, "Such men will be punished most severely" (Mark 12:40; Luke 20:47). Do rewards also come on that day for the faithful stewards? Again Christ's response is, "You will be repaid at the resurrection of the righteous" (Luke 14:14). Like Moses before them, the disciples of Jesus are "looking ahead to [their] reward" (Heb. 11:26). At a time, when all the rewards of earth have long vanished into dust, the follower on the path laid out by Jesus will enjoy the "inheritance that can never perish, spoil or fade" (1 Pet. 1:4). On the day of the final assize the rest will say to each other, "All your riches and splendor have vanished, never to be recovered" (Rev. 18:14). The end of all poor stewards will be the end of Korah's men: "They went down alive into the grave with everything they owned" (Num. 16:33). We, who brought nothing into the world and will take nothing out, will yet have destinies related to what we did as custodians of the wealth that was ours while here.

When we see our maker face to face, a millionare will be but a beggar begging for mercy. Money cannot buy salvation (Job 34:19; 36:19; Psa. 39:7,8; 52:7). The "books were opened" at the judgment throne (Rev. 20:12), possibly including the checkbooks that revealed our primary interests across the years. But, fortunately, because of God's forgiving grace, "another book was opened, which is the book of life" (Rev. 20:12).

THE ETERNAL DESTINY

David knew that there were "men of this world whose reward is in this life" (Psa. 17:14). He also sang of the others whose "inheritance will endure forever" (Psa. 37:18). Another Psalmist joined the chorus noting that a greedy "man, despite his riches, does not endure" (Psa. 49:12), neither will he take anything "with him when he dies, his splendor will not descend with him." The final line of that song rings out, "A man who has riches without understanding is like the beasts that perish" (Psa. 49:20).

"There are no pockets in a shroud," we say. That reality should make us wonder at the wisdom of spending more money in an endeavor to look young than we do in striving to live forever. We have the genuine option where we "store up . . . treasures in heaven" (Matt. 6:20). How can it be deemed unwise to part with what cannot be kept to invest in eternal treasures we cannot lose? The Bible gives the notion that the millionaires of eternity are the givers of time. The property we spend on ourselves perishes in the using. The valuables invested in God's kingdom become part of "the inheritance that can never perish" (1 Pet. 1:4).

The profound eschatological chapter of 1 Corinthians is the fifteenth. From the first to the last it argues for our hope of resurrection based on our historic faith in Jesus' victory over death. But, keep reading for the practical application that follows the final "therefore." "Therefore, my dear brothers, stand firm. . . . Always gives yourselves fully to the work . . . your labor in the Lord is not in vain. Now about the collection" (1 Cor. 15:58-16:2). Then follows the instruction as to when, who, how much and where the funds are to be given. Paul has given eternal significance to monetary and menial tasks for the church. You read of the transfiguration of Jesus in the Gospels. You read in 1 Corinthians of lowly stewardship's transfiguration by the light of eternity glowing through the seemingly insignificant act of putting "a sum of money in keeping with income" into the treasury.

The Bible points us away from "sin city," where self is crowned. It directs us to be "rich in good deeds, and to be generous and willing to share." It even gives the reason why such unnatural activity is the route to follow: "In this way [you] will lay up treasure . . . as a firm foundation for the coming age" (1 Tim. 6:18,19).

In parables, like that of the rich man and Lazarus, Jesus ties heaven and good stewardship together and unites hell and poor stewardship. In that story a beggar is carried by angels to "Abraham's side" and across a great chasm is earth's rich man in "hell" (Luke 16:19-31). Interpret the parables any way and the same bottom line remains that our life in this world is related to life beyond the grave. The present world is where each life is prepared for the future eternal world. The blessing of eternity is upon "the faithful and wise manager" (Luke 12:42). The prodigal most in need of forgiveness is he who has "squandered his wealth in wild living" (Luke 15:13). It is good news to be reminded that it is not too late. The "dead" can be made "alive again." The "lost" can become the "found" (Luke 15:32).

Part Three

Book by Book
(New Testament)

16

WHAT JESUS SAID ABOUT MONEY IN MARK AND JOHN

(The Gospels as preached by Peter and John who made their living at fishing)

MARK

Papias (70-155 A.D.) was an early Christian who is said to have been a disciple of the apostle John. He tell us that Mark wrote down accurately all that he remembered of both Jesus' teachings and life. This he had learned in his service as the "interpreter of Peter." Mark was the son of Mary (Acts 12:12) and a cousin of Barnabas (Col. 4:10). He was Peter's convert (1 Pet. 5:13) and a helper of Paul on the initial leg of the missionary journey that began in Cypress and concluded in Galatia (Acts 12:25).

The sermons of Peter, as recorded by Luke in his Acts of the Apostles (chapters 2, 3 and 10) have the same ring and follow the same outline as the story about Jesus recorded by Mark. In Mark's passion narrative that highlights the sacrificial self-giving of Jesus, what, if anything, is said about money?

One would not expect to find a great deal of information, since the Gospel of Mark is heavy regarding the deeds of Christ and light on his teachings. John's Gospel recalls the Lord's discourses as the other Synoptics preserve many of his parables, but Mark, the shortest account of Jesus' life, leaves us with but a limited knowledge of his words.

In the very first chapter, however, we meet men hard at work in the fishing business. Their investment in boats and nets has flourished to the point that Simon Peter, Andrew, James, John and Zebedee have "hired men" in their employ (Mark 1:16-20, cp. Matt. 4:18-22 and Luke 5:1-11). The first four named respond to Jesus' challenge to leave their trade that had met their families' needs in the years gone by and begin training as Christ's disciples for the exciting possibility of fishing for men. It had never entered their minds that God could envision their humble lives becoming no longer limited to plying their trade by the shores of Galilee. It seemed beyond belief that two pairs of brothers from Capernaum would be heaven's choice for casting the gospel net of redemption (by means of their preaching and writings) beyond the seven seas to draw humans of every kind into heaven itself. If there was monetary reward for the hard work of the earlier occupation, there would be satisfaction beyond description for the demanding tool of proclaiming God's Saviour to the lost world.

A similar call by Jesus early in his ministry is extended in Mark's second chapter to Levi (Mark 2:13,14). Here the invitation to discipleship is to one who takes money from people for the kingdom that is Rome in order to retrain him to offer to the people the riches of salvation from the kingdom of Heaven that Jesus is preaching. Like Simon and Andrew with James and John, Levi (Matthew) grasps at once the opportunity to be discipled by the Master Teacher.

Immediately catching the wonderful truth that God's salvation is for sinners, he turns the house he had purchased into a house of God where the lost men could hear good news beyond belief. At his own expense he has a feast prepared where other "tax collectors and 'sinners' " can eat with Jesus and learn that God's forgiveness and acceptance is offered even unto them. They hear God's Son make the coming church's purpose as clear as a cloudless sky, "It is not the healthy who need a doctor, but the sick. I have not come to call the righteous, but sinners" (Mark 2:15-17).

As the first two chapters of Mark contain some reference to possessions or wealth, all the remaining chapters but the last two have at least a minor verse or a major paragraph that must not be overlooked by one serious about finding what the Bible says about money.

In chapter three, where Jesus is proving by his power to cast out demons that he is mightier than Satan, he states, "In fact, no one can enter a strong man's house and carry off his possessions unless he first ties up the strong man. Then he can rob his house" (Mark 3:27, cp. Matt. 12:24-37). In other words, evil spirits are the valuables of the Evil One. Jesus, God's Holy One, by setting the demon-possessed people free, is robbing from the Devil's territory. And, thanks be to God, where once evil spirits held sway, now heaven's Holy Spirit rules (Mark 3:22-30). Chapter four contains the parables of the sower and the mustard seed. The first story is better called the parable of the soils, because the point being made is that while no flaw is to be found in Christ the sower or in his teaching which is the seed, the failure is clearly in the soil of human hearts into which the word of Jesus fails. Some minds, as hardened as beaten paths, will not open to let the seed of truth penetrate. Others are so shallow that in sheer emotionalism the initial response is quickly gone because the message was not rooted deeply enough. It is the third type of soil or heart, that deals with the money question. Money is compared to thorns that can and do choke life. Jesus teaches that some hearers are exposed to his life-giving message, "but the worries of this life, the deceitfulness of wealth and the desires for other things come in and choke the word, making it unfruitful" (Mark 4:19). This well-known parable has the happy ending that in spite of the bad soil problem that farmers and preachers face, there is enough good soil to make the effort worthwile. Then a crop "thirty, sixty or even a hundred times what was sown" can be found in many places (Mark 4:1-20 cp. Matthew 13:1-23).

While still dealing with the gospel hearers' responsibility, Jesus makes a parallel from the world of economics. He states, "With the measure you use, it will be measured to you — and even more. Whosoever has will be given more; whosoever does not have, even what he has will be taken from him" (Mark 4:24,25). We say that it takes money to make money. We know that getting depends on giving. The more one digs into the mines of heavenly truth or earthly goods, the more wealth of either kind is likely to be his.

The next comment on the wealth theme in this Gospel is an aside. A woman, who for twelve years had been chronically hemorrhaging, is reported to have "suffered a great deal under the care of many doctors and had spent all she had, yet instead of getting better she grew worse" (Mark 5:26 cp. Matt. 9:20-22 and Luke 8:43-48). In a day when medical costs seem to belie the axiom "what goes up must come down," a reader can relate to Mark's comment.

As we read on into chapter six, we find Jesus sending out the twelve on a limited tour. His instruction is aimed at turning their trust from reliance on the security offered by their drachma to that founded on his promise to provide. He informed his preachers on this training mission: "Take nothing for the journey . . . no money in your belts" (Mark 6:8 cp. Matt. 10:9 where Jesus orders, "Do not take along any gold or silver or copper in your belts").

By Mark 6:23 a foolish King Herod offers Salome, the dancing daughter of Herodias, whatever she might ask up to half his kingdom (cp. Matt. 14:1-12). By Mark 6:37 the confused disciples question how they can provide food for five thousand men and their families when such a command would break them financially. Their well-known protest to Jesus was, "That would take eight months of a man's wages! Are we to go and spend that much on bread and give it to them to eat?" When our survey of the Gospel takes us into the next chapter, we meet Jesus rebuking the Pharisees for scheming to save the money that God had designed for parental care. These religionists avoided their responsibility by devising a technicality, whereby the monies that should go to a father or mother from their children could be kept for self-use by the magic of the word "Corban." By that term, which means a gift devoted to God, they cancelled out God's plan to care for the aging (Mark 7:11-13 cp. Matt. 15:3-6). Such "theft" and "greed" is a heart problem, according to the penetrating eyes of the Great Physician (Mark 7:20-23).

Mark eight opens with the feeding of the four thousand (Mark 8:1-9 cp. Matt. 15:29-39), repeating the same problem and conversation that accompanied the feeding of the five thousand. The chapter closes with the prediction of Jesus' cross as the price he must pay for man's salvation and the revelation of a disciples' cross as the cost of discipleship. To avoid the accusation of "cheap grace," Christ called "the crowd to him along with his disciples." Both the in-group and the outsiders were to have no question: "If anyone would come after me, he must deny himself and take up his cross and follow me. . . . What good is it for a man to gain the whole world, yet forfeit his soul? Or what can a man give in exchange for his soul?" (Mark 8:34-37, cp. Luke 14:25-35). Mark 9:41 reminds us that the giving of the small gift, like a cup of water, brings a certain and great reward.

In the Perean ministry that immediately preceded the climactic week of Jesus' life on earth, we are introduced to a monied man. He is typical of so many in the modern world of the "have" rather than "have not" nations. This man was rich in the things of the world, "loved" by the Lord and in "lack" of the "treasure of heaven" (Mark 10:17-31 cp. Matt. 19:16-27 and Luke 18:18-27). Self-deceived that he was spotless in morality and faultless in keeping God's commands, he needed to have his ego deflated so that he might recognize that he like all others needed a

Saviour.

To the rich young ruler Jesus held up a mirror of truth so he could see himself. Calling for the sale of the great wealth he possessed so that the poor could be fed, Jesus quickly unbared the man's covetous heart. He could not turn to Jesus, for that would be turning from his mammon in which he trusted. How sad that a rich man allowed his riches to keep him from the true riches. He had a heaven on earth, but none in the sky.

At this point, Jesus sympathized with the rich for whom it is more than difficult to enter the kingdom of God. It is impossible without Divine help. In the Master's words: "It is easier for a camel to go through the eye of a needle than for a rich man to enter the kingdom of God." To soften the teaching some explain away the hard saying by suggesting that the changing of one letter in the Greek word would translate "rope." Then it would be a "rope" instead of "camel" that had to be threaded into the needle. Others, with no support from the days of Jesus for their optional concept, suggest that in the large gates into Jerusalem there was a smaller gate called the "needle's eye." Hence, when the gates were closed for business on such a day as a Sabbath, at least man with difficulty could squeeze through himself.

He who talked to his disciples about the rich man who sadly rejected his call to follow, did not say "difficult." He said "impossible." To their amazed cry, "Who then can be saved?", came the answer, "With men this is impossible, but not with God; all things are possible with God."

Upon hearing this, Peter reminded Jesus that he and the other disciples had "left everything" in order to become his followers. To this appeal the Lord held out more than the hope of "eternal life" in the coming age. He promised that "no one who has left home or brother or sisters or mother or father or children or fields for me and the gospel will fail to receive a hundred times as much in this present age," yet with the proviso "and with them persecutions" (Mark 10:28-30 cp. Matt. 19:27-30 and Luke 18:28-30). The Acts of the Apostles portrays the open-armed fellowship of the early church that offered family ties stronger and wider than the bonds of blood could provide.

On the Monday of the last week of Jesus' earthly ministry, he clears out the temple area of both buyers and sellers. Merchandise and tables for money changers made a house of prayer into a robbers' den. (Mark 11:15-17 cp. Matt. 21:12-17 and Luke 19:45-48). A religious setting, as a cloak for the corrupt business of fleecing religious pilgrims, is not limited to any ancient or modern faith. According to John 2:13-16 a cleansing of the temple took place at the beginning of Christ's ministry. Apparently it needed to be repeated. According to present day observation, the followers of the Messiah ought to remember what their Anointed One thinks about violating the sacred by commercializing it.

In the twelfth chapter of Mark are four places where reference is made to money or possessions. Mark 12:1 and 2 with verse 9 speaks of the rental of a vineyard and expectation of sharing in the profits (cp. Matt. 21:33-46). Verses 13-17 raise the question of paying taxes to the Roman Caesar (cp. Matt. 22:15-22 and Luke 20:20-26). Verse 20 is Jesus' condemnation of teachers of the law who "devour widows houses," while they cover their sinful greed by holy sounding "lengthy prayers." Verses 41-44 conclude the chapter picturing the Son of God studying the crowd of rich and poor putting money into the temple treasury. He finds the widow's "two very small copper coins" showing the highest commitment to God in that she had "put in everything — all she had to live on." Mark did not record this event so his readers would give a widow's mite, but that they would give with the widow's spirit.

The final references to our subject in Mark's sixteen chapters is found in Mark 14:1-11 (cp. Matt. 26:6-13 and John 12:1-8). In Bethany, at the home of Simon the Leper, some "very expensive perfume made of pure nard" is poured on Jesus' head by a woman. What Christ considered "a beautiful thing," others counted a "waste" to be rebuked. They saw "more than a year's wages" lost in a moment. Since their argument took on a religious sound (reasoning that such a sum could be better given to the poor), the Lord suggested that if they really cared about the needy they would have ample opportunities to fulfill their obligation. If Judas was behind the complaint, as the Gospel of John suggests, Mark's next paragraph strips off Judas' mask of religiosity by revealing his selling Jesus for "money." Side by side Mark has placed a story of extravagant love at its best and covetous greed at its worst.

JOHN

Peter had proclaimed Christ and his witness has been heard in the account recalled by Mark in his Gospel. John is another fisherman whose testimony has been saved in writing, but this time by his own pen. It may be that Mark's Gospel was the first of our four to be written and John's Gospel the last.

When John, the son of Zebedee, writes at a time after the incidents and teachings of the synoptic Gospels are known, he aims at supplementing those accounts. He tells of Christ cleansing the temple early in his ministry as it had been in the last week of that ministry. Jesus does this with the same concern that "selling" and "exchanging money" do not belong every place. He cries out, "Get these things out of here! How dare you turn my Father's house into a market!" (John 2:14-16). Yet, at other places and other times, it is appropriate for disciples to go "into town to buy food" (John 4:8). While the temple was an inappropriate place for commerce, it was an excellent place for "teaching" on every Biblical truth including money. This was the case when he was instructing near to "the place where the offerings were put" (John 8:20).

John writes of a beggar cured of his begging and turned into a productive human (John 9:8). John preserves the vital contrast Jesus made between pastors or religious leaders that enter the work to truly serve people and those who embarrass the true shepherds by only shearing the sheep for their own gain. In Jesus' words, false messiahs are "thieves and robbers" coming only "to steal and kill and destroy." Those who enter ministry must ever check their motives lest they be classed with the "hired hand . . . [that] cares nothing for the sheep" (John 10:8-13).

It is John who informs us of Jesus' seamless garment made of one piece. It was a robe so valuable that the soldiers crucifying him determine to "decide by lot who will get it," rather than tear it into four parts (John 19:23,24). It is John who records the words of Christ from his cross assigning the care of his mother into that disciple's hands (John 19:26,27). It also is John who remembers how Nicodemus provided "about seventy-five pounds" of a mix of "myrrh and aloes" for the anointing of Christ's body (John 19:39).

17

WHAT JESUS SAID ABOUT MONEY IN MATTHEW

(The Gospel written by Levi who made his living at taxation)

MATTHEW

The Gospel of Matthew relates many of the same incidents found in the Gospel of Mark. Believing the same Good News, the man Levi heralds the same story of Christ crucified and risen as proclaimed by Simon Peter. In addition, he supplements the story by giving material about the Savior's birth and includes five major sermons taught by him.

For our purposes we will not here retell the incidents that Matthew has repeated from Mark. Rather we will call to your attention the refences to wealth unique to this Gospel. Early-on the Magi bow down before the babe, laying before him "gifts of gold and of incense and of myrrh" (Matt. 2:11). By means of these treasures, Joseph and Mary can live in Egypt until the death of the tyrant Herod. God's royal Son at the age of thirty will, upon his baptism, resist the satanic idea of building God's kingdom in the way most earthly realms are established in power. The splendor of earthly governments is shown to Christ and promised to him, if like other rulers, he will bow down to the ways worldly kingdoms have ever been built (Matt. 4:8-10). Jesus knew that a man cannot live by either bread alone or money alone. Dough may be important but it is not primary.

Following the Lord's first battle with the tempter on the nature of the kingdom, he begins to gather disciples. He makes it clear to them what is different in the kingdom he is preaching. This sermon on the mount, delivered on the Horns of Hattin, is preserved in Matthew 5-7. While most every part of the message from the opening beatitudes to the closing illustration on home-building has financial implications, we will comment on only those lines that are specific in their mention of money.

Contrasting the Mosaic law that forbade killing with the law of love that roots out anger, the Master teacher calls for reconciliation with a brother before a "gift" to God be offered on the altar (Matt. 5:23-26). To fail to settle matters out of court may result in an imprisonment from which there is no escape "until you have paid the last penny." Here is reference to a debtor's prison.

The way of love exceeds the way of law. Before a lawsuit aims at getting your "tunic," volunteer "your cloak as well." Be of such a caring heart that you "give" when asked and you loan when it is needed (Matt. 5:40-42). It is to be expected that more shall come from a life in Christ's service than from a life that springs from a lesser religion. There is no "reward" for loving those who are lovely, loving and lovable. "Are not even the tax collectors doing that" (Matt. 5:46)?

Jesus knew that there was a place for alms-giving, prayer and fasting in every religion. He terms them "acts of righteousness" and then comments on the themes one by one. His emphasis is that our purpose should be doing these deeds for God's eyes alone. Giving to the needy is not because givers need to toot their horn and gain recognition. It is because men have genuine needs and Christ's followers both can and ought to do something about that. Such giving would best meet God's intention when you "do not let your left hand know what your right hand is doing" (Matt. 6:1-4).

Followers of Jesus are so conscious of the entire family of God rather than just themselves, their prayers begin "Our Father," not simply "My Father." Those interecessions continue, "Give us today our daily bread," which is several steps above the individualist's "Give me what is mine." This petition is for "bread," not cake. It is for necessities, not luxuries. This example of how to pray suggests we ask for "daily" bread, not for warehouse lots to hold sufficient supplies for weeks to come.

The entire second half of chapter six deals with money. If you want a bank where every dollar is safe and the interest is high, consider Jesus' suggestion to lay up "treasures in heaven." Moths can get at garments and metals can rust. Thieves are everywhere. But, every dime invested in eternal things is not only safe, it draws interest. In what company you invest, in that company you gain interest. Invest in the church and you get interested in its mission. "For where your treasure is, there your heart will be also" (Matt. 6:19-21). Note the words "will be." First comes the investment. Then comes the interest. First the money goes into the kingdom. Then follows the interest and excitement about its mission. In other words, the horse precedes the cart.

At this point in the sermon, Jesus makes evident that money is to be man's servant and not his God. "You cannot serve both God and Money." "Mammon," the word in most English translations, is the transliteration of an Aramaic word for riches. We will hold in highest regard either God or gold. It cannot be both. But anyone who prays with one eye open to the world's needs sees money as a potential servant of the omnipotent God. Wealth in the servant role is a blessing. Riches on the throne of a heart is the curse of all curses.

Once money is dethroned and God is enthroned, worry and ulcers pass away. Jesus' words, "do not worry" or "do not be anxious" (RSV), are not to be misunderstood as admonishing "take no thought" (KJV). To think of how adequately God cares for birds and flowers should expel any doubts that the Creator and Provider would neglect men. "Are you not more valuable?" is a good question. Can stewing and fretting "add a single hour to . . . life?" This is a theme worth thinking about. Such feverish anxiety is not the mark of a believer. It is rather "the pagans [who] run after all these things." Christ's disciples follow the higher path of giving priority attention to God's "kingdom and his righteousness" (Matthew 6:25-34). Those who take thought — serious thought — about God's love and care are free from sin and worry. To offer this kind of teaching to carnal, money-grabbing, self-serving humans in the rat-race of getting theirs is like throwing "pearls to pigs" (Matt. 7:6). Jesus' sermon on the mount shows a way of life that has meaning. Few may find the way, but how blest they are. Many in the world, possessed by their possessions, are poor in the midst of their wealth. The Son of Man with "no place to lay his head" (Matt. 8:20) knew the secret of happiness. He called people to live the joyous life of self-giving, where true contentment could be found. Those living in privation are not the only ones who become anxious. So do the rich who have so much to lose.

The second of the five sermons in Matthew's Gospel (chapter 10) could be called the ordination sermon for the twelve apostles. Christ's words describe their mission and give counsel: "Freely you have received, freely give." They are, on this mission which is both limited in scope and time, to take no "gold or silver or copper . . . for the worker is worthy of his keep" (Matt. 10:8-10). These men are to have full confidence that God will meet their basic needs. He has numbered each hair on their head. He provides adequately for the birds. So pose the question: "Are not two sparrows sold for a penny?" Then share the certainty: "You are worth more than many sparrows" (Matt. 10:29,30).

Mingled with the assurance of heaven's love and care for them is the awareness of the high cost of following the One who will pay the ultimate price for man's deliverance. The cost may be rejection by parents or children. Each disciple must be willing, if necessary, to follow without hesitation. "Anyone who does not take his cross and follow me," said Jesus, "is not worthy of me." The paradox is true: "Whoever finds his life will lose it, and whoever loses his life for my sake will find it" (Matt. 10:37-39).

This sermon to the twelve concludes by holding out reembursement for any who enter Christ's glad service. Jesus speaks of "a prophet's reward," then of "a righteous man's reward" and climatically of the big rewards awaiting all who render seemingly small service. He completes his message: "And if anyone gives a cup of cold water to one of these little ones because he is my disciple, I tell you the truth, he will certainly not lose his reward" (Matt. 10:41,42).

We often speak of the third sermon preserved in the Gospel (Matt. 13) as the parables of the kingdom. Prior to the record of these easy-to-remember illustrations, we catch a glimpse of phrases on our money theme. Jesus is said to be preaching "to the poor" (Matt. 11:5). John the Baptist is noted neither to be garbed "in fine clothes" nor dwelling in "king's palaces" (Matt. 11:8). Critics are calling the Son of Man "a friend of tax collectors" (Matt. 11:19) and Christ is teaching that a man is "much more valuable . . . than a sheep" (Matt. 12:12).

Comment has been given in our look at Mark's Gospel about the parable of the soils, where "the worries of this life and the deceitfulness of wealth" are mentioned (Mark 4:18,19). In Matthew's listing of seven parables, he begins with this story and its interpretation (Matt. 13:1-9,18-23). Among the other illustrations of the kingdom told by Jesus, he preserves two that speak of its value. In one case a "treasure" is accidentally found by a man as he routinely plows his field. In a second case a "pearl" is discovered at the end of a purposeful search by a pearl merchant. In both cases all previously held values are forfeited to gain this newly found treasure beyond all price. In incident number one, the farmer "sold all he had and bought that field" holding the treasure. In incident number two, the merchant "sold everything he had" to get the pearl of great price. The point of the stories is that whether you learn of God's kingdom unexpectedly like a Philippian jailer (Acts 16) or like a seeking Roman centurion named Cornelius (Acts 10), no previous value can compare to what the church of Christ offers.

And speaking of treasures, the Old Testament Scriptures, always held in high value by Israel, is found to have further riches when viewed through Jesus' eyes. "Therefore every teacher of the law who has been instructed about the kingdom of heaven is like the owner of a house who brings out of his storeroom new treasures as well as old" (Matt. 13:52).

After two years of living with Jesus and being instructed by him, the disciples have come to the unwavering conclusion that Jesus is the Christ, the Son of the living God. Now that the Master's marvelous words and miraculous works have shown Jesus to be God's Messiah, these disciples have it cleared up what kind of a Messiah he intends to be. Rather than the ruling earthly king his contemporaries hoped for, Jesus will choose to go to a cross as God's suffering servant. There is to be cross before crown.

At Caesarea-Philippi Jesus not only begins to clarify his role as crucified Saviour, but also his followers' role as sacrificing servants for the world's redemption. Each follower is to "deny himself and take up his cross and follow" (Matthew 16:24). There is no reference here to a cross forced onto them. Believers are to voluntarily look for opportunities to share in mankind's redemption. They "take up" the cross. And why not? To be a billionaire several times over is not to be compared to sharing salvation. "What good will it be for a man if he gains the whole world and forfeits his soul? Or what can a man give in exchange for his soul?" (Matt. 16:26).

Not long after his conversation with the disciples, the transfiguration experience and the healing of the epileptic boy, Jesus and Peter at Capernaum face the question of the "two drachma tax" paid to the temple. Even though king's sons are exempt from taxes in a realm, and therefore Jesus ought to be exempt as the Son of the King of Heaven in whose honor the temple was built, he will set example for others and make the contribution for both Simon and himself.

To show that he is related uniquely as Son to the God of the temple in Jerusalem, Jesus works a miracle. Peter is to cast a single line into the nearby lake. No net will be used to increase his chances. His omnipotence and omniscience will be there for all to see when "the first fish" caught will have "a four-drachma coin" in its mouth to fully pay the tax for both the Teacher and his learning pupil (Matt. 17:24-27).

As we enter the eighteenth chapter of Matthew we are in the fourth sermon of Jesus regarding his kingdom. The first had spoken to the demands of his kingdom (Matt. 5-7). The second had to do with the apostles as ambassadors for his kingdom (Matt. 10). Thirdly, we heard parables that illustrated the growth and value of the coming reign of heaven (Matt. 13). Now we arrive at the fourth message which speaks to the standard of greatness in the realm of God.

Chapter eighteen's final dozen verses (Matt. 18:23-35) deal with the generosity of God's forgiveness to men and to the sometimes stinginess of man in his treatment of a neighbor's wrongs against him. Jesus' story is about a man that owes the king a staggering sum beyond any person's ability to pay. This servant pleads for himself and his family that they not be sold into slavery. Generously and compassionately the king writes off the entire debt. But in stark contrast this very man harshly imprisons his own debtor who only owes him pocket change. Surely a man, whose sin obligation God has been ready to forgive (a debt comparable to ten million dollars) ought to more compassionately forgive another human who has wronged him (an I.O.U. of $17 by comparison). The bottom line of the parable is that we cannot expect to be forgiven unless we are forgiving.

The fifth and final message by Jesus, in Matthew's lessons from the Master Teacher, will be delivered on the Tuesday of Passion Week. Before Christ heads for the Holy City and his cross, he goes into Perea to await the Passover Season. While beyond the Jordan, the Lord told the familiar story of a "landowner hiring workers from early in the day until just before quitting time. To illustrate the unmerited grace of God who both offers salvation at the last moment of life to such as a dying thief on the cross and also to a child with a full life to live and serve, Jesus speaks of all the workers in his story getting the same wage. The parable has the monetary concepts of "pay," "wages," "money," "landowner," "foreman" and "workers." But it has the point that grace is not simply justice. As Paul would emphasize in his Roman epistle on grace, the landowner in Matthew replies to critics, "I want to give the man who was hired last the same as I gave you. Don't I have the right to do what I want with my money? Or are you envious because I am generous?" (Matt. 20:1-15).

After Jesus enters Jerusalem triumphantly on the Sunday of his last week, he highlights on Tuesday the same truth about grace. He does this in his parable of workers in the vineyard and the parable of the two sons. It concludes: "I tell you the truth, the tax collectors and the prostitutes are entering the kingdom of God ahead of you. For John came to show you the way of righteousness, and you did not believe him, but the tax collectors and the prostitutes did" (Matt. 21:31,32).

The next story, called the parable of the tenants, is told the same day. It takes the flip side of the coin of truth regarding salvation by grace. The sinners are reaching for a Saviour. The self-satisfied are pictured as rejecting the landowner's workers, both stoning and mistreating each one. They even kill his son when he is sent. It is obvious to all hearing the teaching that God is the landowner. The vineyard is the promised land. His prophets are the servants and His son is no less than Jesus, whom the Jews intend to destroy. Will they still remain God's chosen people? The answer of the story is, "He will bring those wretches to a wretched end . . . he will rent the vineyard to other tenants" (Matt. 21:33-41).

When the sun sets on this day, the public ministry of Jesus will be over and his final hours will be spent with his disciples. Matt. 23, 24 and 25 can be unified into a parting discourse. Chapter 23 contains the seven woes regarding Israel that justify in chapter 24 the three predictions that their temple will be destroyed, the gospel will go to Gentiles and then he will return.

The third woe speaks of the "gold" in the temple (Matt. 23:16-19). Woe four tells of Pharisees so religious that they give a "tenth" of even the garden vegetables, yet they fail in offering "justice, mercy and faithfulness" which humaneness alone would demand (Matt. 23:23,24).

One major prediction in the eschatological discourse of chapter 24 is that Jesus' second coming is a certainty but the time of it is unknown. That means in every following era of history good stewardship demands each of us to be a "faithful and wise servant" over that which has been charged to us by the "master." Dependability will be good for such a servant in that, at the return, the master "will put him in charge of all his possessions" (Matt. 24:45-47).

It is in chapter 25 of this discourse that money and what money will buy comes into prominence. In this section the three predictions of the former chapter are followed by the three illustrations of this chapter.

The ten virgins awaiting the bridegroom's coming are illustrative of disciples awaiting Christ's return. Some are wise and some are otherwise. Some are ready and some are not. Their lamps only will be ready for the glorious wedding day, if they go to those who sell oil and buy before the bridegroom arrives (Matt. 25:9,10).

Where being prepared is the message of the parable of the ten virgins, being faithful in our stewardship is the lesson of the parable of the talents. It is seen in these stories that we are both expected to work as well as to watch for the Lord. Each of us is entrusted with "property" and "money." Some have more than others ("five," "two" or "one" talent). These "talents" are not gifts which become ours to possess. They rather are a trust for us to use on behalf of the one who distributed them to us. He expects that proper use of that entrusted to us will bring increase. He leads us to expect that faithful stewardship will be rewarded. To do nothing for God with our wealth is shown to bring not the bright promise "Come and share your master's happiness!" but the gloomy prospect of being thrown as a "worthless servant outside, into the darkness" (Matt. 25:14-30).

The final parable in this chapter is that of the sheep and the goats. Feeding the hungry, visiting both the sick and imprisoned and clothing the naked determine who enters the eternal kingdom, while not doing these acts causes the final verdict "Depart from me." This might seem to suggest that salvation is by works. But this is far from the case. Faith is seen in action. Anyone can profess to believe, but the true people of faith are known by their fruit of their deeds. Such stewardship of one's time, talents, talk and treasures does not deserve or merit our salvation. Rather, such actions are the natural outpouring of gratitude from a life granted God's unmerited favor. "Eternal punishment" or "eternal life" is at the end of the road. Living selflessly or selfishly are the options (Matt. 25:31-36).

Matthew's Gospel follows the same chronology as Mark's both in Jesus' ministry and his last week. It not only relates Judas' bargain to sell Jesus for "thirty silver coins" (Matt. 26:15), it tells of his throwing the money into the temple and hanging himself in remorse. It explains what happened to the coins, since as "blood money," it could not be put into the temple treasury by the chief priests. Those silver coins were used in the purchase of a "potter's field" (Matt. 27:3-10). At the crucifixion we see Jesus dying between "two robbers" (Matt. 27:38). After the cross we find "a rich man from Arimathea, named Joseph" burying the body (Matt. 27:57-60). After the resurrection we find soldiers at the now empty tomb bribed with "a large sum of money" to falsify the fact of Christ's resurrection by uttering the fable that as Roman soldiers they had fallen asleep permitting the theft of the body they had been commissioned to guard. When the Matthean ac-count of the gospel story ends, the Risen Lord is commissioning his followers to teach "everything" he had "commanded" (Matt. 28:20). The Gospel penned by the former tax-collector makes the order one the church can fulfill, for it saves for posterity what Jesus taught including the many parables he gave about money.

18

WHAT JESUS SAID ABOUT MONEY IN LUKE

*(The Gospel written by Luke who made
his living at medicine)*

LUKE

The topic of riches has more space in the Gospel of Luke than in the other Synoptics: Matthew and Mark. No other topic is discussed so thoroughly as possessions. Nearly one fifth of Jesus' words in Luke regard possessions. There are in Luke 558 verses where Christ is teaching and 108 are on possessions. As the beloved "doctor" who had traveled with Paul, the Gentile Luke addresses his writing to the Gentile Theophilus and does not neglect to focus on money and what it can buy, for "after all these things do the Gentiles seek" (Matt. 6:32 KJV).

Where Matthew had inserted the Lord's teaching at five points into the narrative of Christ's deeds, Luke has preserved for us most of his unique material in the "major interpolation," which is basically chapters 10-18. He, like Matthew, also has started with the birth of Jesus, rather than like Mark commencing at the beginning of Jesus' ministry.

In the birth story material we hear the virgin Mary sing before Elizabeth in praise of God who "has filled the hungry with good things but has sent the rich away empty" (Luke 1:53). That Joseph and Mary were not included among the rich is evident at the census for taxing purposes in the day soí Caesar Augustus (Luke 2:1). That occasion brought this pair to Bethlehem where Jesus was born. When they presented this new offspring in the temple at Jerusalem, the offering of "a pair of doves or two young pigeons" (Luke 2:24) indicates they could not afford the lamb prescribed (Lev. 12:6-8).

Once we come to the time for the ministry of Jesus to begin, we learn, beyond what Mark had recorded, that the forerunner John the Baptist calls on his hearers to share "tunics" and "food" with the needy. Baptizing tax collectors and soldiers, he admonished the former to no longer "collect any more than . . . required to." To the latter he demanded, "Don't extort money and . . . be content with your pay" (Luke 3:10-14).

After Jesus is baptized and comes back from the temptation in the wilderness, he enters the synagogue at Nazareth where he had been brought up. There he read aloud the Isaiah prophecy that described the ministry he now was entering. That passage predicted how God's anointed one would "preach good news to the poor" (Luke 4:18).

Luke's Gospel has been called "the Gospel for the underdog." That is how Jesus' words sound to the ear as he teaches. He speaks: "Blessed are you who hunger now, for you will be satisfied. . . . But woe to you who are rich, for you have already received your comfort. Woe to you who are well fed now, for you will go hungry" (Luke 6.20-25). In the same chapter the teacher is calling for giving to those who ask (Luke 6:30,31) and for mercy in lending to those who cannot pay back (Luke 6:34-36). Instead of such a practice making them paupers themselves, Jesus assures, "Give and it will be given to you. A good measure, pressed down, shaken together and running over, will be poured into your lap" (Luke 6:38). If the Baptist hungering in the prison at Machaerus needs his faith bolstered that Jesus is the promised one, let his disciples report that they have witnessed "the good news . . . preached to the poor" (Luke 7:22). And let all the community appreciate John, a committed man, who neither "dressed in fine clothes" that were "expensive," nor did he "indulge in luxury" (Luke 7:25), yet even "tax collectors" came to be "baptized by him" (Luke 7:29).

At a meal, possibly following a synagogue service, Jesus is anointed by "a woman who had lived a sinful life in that town." The host, named Simon, could not imagine that a real holy prophet would allow himself to be touched by such a "sinner." This gave Jesus an occasion to illustrate the purpose of a Saviour. He told the parable of one debtor who was forgiven a debt of five hundred denarii he could not pay and a second debtor forgiven an obligation of fifty. The Lord's pointed question to Simon was, "Now which of them will love him more?" The answer, "I suppose the one who had the bigger debt cancelled," ought to have made even this legalistic Pharisee comprehend the sinful woman's appreciation for Christ's forgiveness.

The Lukan account immediately moves to explain how Jesus could afford to travel from town to town with the twelve. Other forgiven women (Mary Magdalene, Joanna, Susanna and others) in gratitude, "were helping to support them out of their own means" (Luke 8:1-3). To this day, as the church ministers in Christ's name across the world, the supporters are not deluded into thinking that their gifts are earning God's blessing. They know that someone has to foot the bill and they in genuine gratitude for their undeserved salvation make possible the telling of that love story to others.

We now come to the exclusively Lukan material. Much of it deals with Christ's Perean ministry that took him away from Palestine. We would expect the Gentile Luke to be appreciative of how even the earthly ministry of the Master allowed for his blessings to be shared also with non-Jews.

161

To prepare for his entry into Perea, Jesus appoints seventy-two to precede his coming by announcing the kingdom. If the earlier sending out twelve suggested that the new kingdom was for the twelve tribes of Israel, this commissioning likely foreshadows that the Gentile world is to be included, for seventy-two nations were thought, by a comparison to Genesis 10, to be the count of world governments at that time. The instruction of the seventy-two parallels that given to the twelve assuring that there will be no lack for their needs will be provided, since "the worker deserves his wages" (Luke 10:1-7).

The world-renowned Good Samaritan parable pictures humans and their different attitudes toward wealth. Some like the "robbers" set out to get, caring not who is hurt in the process. Others, pictured by Levite and priest have no place for meeting the needs of fellowmen, as their religion has much time for holy rites and holy places but little time for human hurts. The Samaritan, so often despised by pure-blooded Israelites, is chosen to typify true religion. He not only meets the immediate needs by bandaging wounds, but looks to the extended care required by offering "silver coins" to the innkeeper with further promise of reimbursement for "any extra expense" that might arise (Luke 10:30-36). Jesus suggests that pure religion lifts neighbors up. It never passes them up.

One of the most telling of all Christ's parables, that of the rich fool, is called forth by a man in the crowd soliciting Jesus to become an "arbiter," between him and his brother who are fighting over an "inheritance." Rather than become a judge in the specific instance, Jesus prefers to focus on the specific problem of covetousness that lies behind so many disputes between people. He speaks words that ought to be emblazoned on our minds as we live in a world marching to a different drum beat than that of Christ's followers: "Watch out! Be on your guard against all kinds of greed; a man's life does not consist in the abundance of his possessions" (Luke 12:13-15).

The following parable (Luke 12:16-21) describes success that would excite all persons who closely read the *Wall Street Journal* or dabble in stocks. The rich man's good crops demanded expansion in storage space to hold the burgeoning produce. Retirement in luxury seemed just around the corner. He talked to himself about that coming great day: "You have plenty of good things laid up for many years. Take life easy; eat, drink and be merry." These thoughts that have echoed across the years in mind after mind are labeled the words of a "fool" by God who knows both our mortality and our proneness to neglect preparing for eternity. The parable ends, " 'This very night your life will be demanded from you. Then who will get what you have prepared for yourself?' This is how it will be with anyone who stores up things for himself but is not rich toward God."

The fool was not called fool because of his honest attainment of wealth, his wise investment of his money, his good spending practices or his thought about retirement. What made him a fool was his self-centered greed, his blindness to the fact that time did not belong to him and his ignorance in thinking that food for his body held precedence over food for his soul. Retirement with wealth, but without purpose, would be empty. This fool left God out from the beginning with his myopic "my barns," "my grain" and "my goods."

Jesus follows this parable with words about unnecessary worry regarding things. The lesson is similar to what he taught in his sermon on the mount (Luke 12:22-34). When he points to the unexpectedness of his return, he ties with that coming the idea that then will be an accounting for each servant regarding his faithfulness as a steward (Luke 12:42-44).

How different is Jesus' value system to that of the world's! He advocates giving a "luncheon or dinner," where you do not invite "rich neighbors" who will repay you in some significant way. Rather, you reach out to "the poor, the crippled, the lame, the blind," anticipating no return on the investment until "the resurrection of the righteous" (Luke 14:12-14). Christ seemed to foresee, in the parable of the great banquet, that owners of fields and oxen might find no spare time to consider God's invitation. Such rejection explains why that gracious call to the heavenly feast has been echoing "into the streets and alleys," attracting "the poor" of this world (Luke 14:18-21).

Amplifying why Pharisees and teachers of the law turned a deaf ear to Jesus, but "tax collectors and 'sinners' " were coming in great numbers, he who spoke in the unforgettable parables told the three stories of lost valuable. A straying sheep was rescued after costly search (Luke 15:3-7). A "silver coin" had too much value to be ignored as being of little account. The careful search would not stop until the woman found the coin of such worth to her (Luke 15:8-10). A son, the treasure of all treasures, climaxes the stories about lost valuables. They illustrate God's search for lost men. This parable deals in estates, property, squandered wealth, hired men, robes, rings, etc. But these monetary items are simply the backdrop in the wordpainting that depicts the supreme value heaven places on the soul of a human being.

"Wasting . . . possessions" is the crime underlying Jesus' next story. We entitle it the parable of the unjust steward (Luke 16:1-15). It is about a shrewd manager who used his master's "worldly wealth to gain friends" for himself so that his personal future would be secure. In all his dishonesty the manager suggested that his master's debtors simply alter their books, trimming the full obligations to a much lesser fee ("eight hundred gallons" to "four hundred" or "a thousand bushels" to "eight hundred"). Those who serve the holy God of heaven and have a stewardship before Him, are never free to use the dishonest means of the unjust steward, but they ought to do some careful planning about their eternal future during the brief days thay have on earth. Teachers and preachers, entrusted with heaven's message, need also to learn from this story that to please men by cutting down to half any of God's requirements is the work of an unjust steward.

If, at this teaching, the "Pharisess, who loved money . . . were sneering at Jesus (Luke 16:14), wait until they hear his story about the rich man and Lazarus that follows (Luke

16:19-31). If anyone believes material worth is a signal of God's approval of a life and poverty is an evidence that the curse of heaven is its cause, let their ears open to this story. "Purple," "fine linen" and the every day "luxury" of the rich person are never once shared at his gate with the beggar. The parable uncovers the reality of God's discontent with any unbrotherliness worthy of "hell." The beggar Lazarus, with all his "sores" and physical needs, is the hero of the story for whom being in Paradise with Abraham is the happy ending ahead.

Another well-known parable in the teaching material preserved by Luke is that of the Pharisee and tax collector gone to temple worship. The former haughtily brags in prayer to God of his superiority to "robbers" and "tax collectors." He reminds God, as he probably did many others, that he did "give a tenth of all" received by him. The more ideal worshipper beats his own breast, rather than pats his own back, as he begs for a mercy God is anxious to extend to him (Luke 18:10-14).

At the border town of Jericho, as Christ passes from Perea toward Jerusalem, we are introduced to both poor and rich, who find blessing at the touch of Jesus. A blind beggar (called Bartimaeus in Mark's Gospel 10:46) receives the sight that he needed. A despised "chief tax collector" that had become "wealthy" was extended the acceptance that he longed for, when Jesus offered to stay in his house. This man named Zacchaeus was so transformed by such grace that he said to Christ, "Look, Lord! Here and now I give half of my possessions to the poor, and if I have cheated anybody out of anything, I will pay back four times the amount" (Luke 19:1-8). This is another evidence that the personal fellowship with Jesus has immediate and everlasting financial consequences. Page after page in the Gospels describe that the monies given under the Lord's influence are always overflows of appreciation and never purchases of expected favors.

Luke, giving the same chronology as Mark and Matthew, retells the last week of Christ's life from the triumphal entry into

Jerusalem to the triumphal exit from the world by ascension after his resurrection. A few additional words or lines that touch on the money theme are noted. The eschatological discourse, predicting the destruction of the temple, bears witness to how impressed the disciples were as they view "the temple . . . adorned with beautiful stones" (Luke 21:5). The message concludes with the warning, "Be careful, or your hearts will be weighed down with . . . the anxieties of life" (Luke 21:34).

We are indebted to Luke for including in his book of Acts a further word of Christ that no Gospel account had recorded. It is the line from Paul's sermon to elders that concludes, "help the weak, remembering the words the Lord Jesus himself said: 'It is more blessed to give than to receive' " (Acts 20:35).

After reading the four Gospels with an eye searching for their revelation about money, we conclude that Christ and those that followed him made use of money and spoke extensively about it. Jesus was not like Gautama Buddha who began life in the luxurious ease of a royal palace and then followed the pendelum swing to preaching austere renunciation. Jesus was never a beggar. He was reared in a carpenter's home, where he lived modestly on the minimum income of an artisan in the middle class of Galilean society.

We saw on the pages of the Gospel narratives a Messiah both ministering to the poor and dining with such as the wealthy Simon the Pharisee. He reflects sympathy toward a rich Zacchaeus and a Joseph of Arimathea, yet denounces a man of great means who had no concern for a beggar at his gate. He seems to distinguish in his mind the vast difference between the evil of living desparately and the value of living modestly. In other words, to lack life's necessities is bad, but to lack the world's luxuries is not per se an evil. To Jesus all people should become aware of what both money and the lack of it can do to people. For that reason Jesus spoke as much about wealth as he did about the danger of religious hypocrisy and the wonder of God's kingdom.

Jesus advocated no particular political system or economic

theory. He rather gave his followers a glimpse at how this world's goods can contribute to the advancement of the next world's goals. His parables in the Synoptics are thirty-eight in number. Of these, sixteen speak to a disciples' use of money. The focus of the stories is on attitude. Money must not be a rival in the heart to the rule of God. The Lord must be first even before family. And no disciple is to forget that men are of more value than dollars. Rather than the dictum, "Every man for himself," Jesus called for becoming the servant of all. The life of Christ, as much as the words of Christ, is the norm of our stewardship.

Since the Gospels give us only what "Jesus began to do and teach" (Acts 1:1), we turn to the writings of his Spirit-guided Apostles for Jesus' further teaching on our subject.

19

WHAT JESUS' APOSTLES SAID ABOUT MONEY IN PAUL'S EARLIER EPISTLES

In the New Testament Epistles from Romans to Revelation the bulk of the letters are from the Apostles Paul, Peter and John. We are wise to start with the letters from one who made his living at tent-making because of the quantity and quality of that material.

ROMANS

The great theological Roman epistle heralds that God's salvation comes by man's trusting in this completed work of Christ, rather than by relying on his own perfect living of the law of Moses. This single purpose, of clarifying Paul's gospel, trims from this letter many references to money but there are a few. "Greed" is classified as "wickedness" (1:29) and gaining wealth by "stealing" or in setting out to "rob temples" is condemned (2:21,22).

The commandment, "do not covet," is credited with making Paul and others aware of the evil of "covetous desire" (7:7,8). "Famine or nakedness," as possible hardships to be faced in the service of Christ, are not considered capable of separating the believer from the love of Christ" (8:35).

The tenth chapter holds up both good and bad news. That "everyone who calls on the name of the Lord will be saved," (10:13) is the good news. The bad news is that this calling on God for salvation depends on believing, believing on hearing, hearing on preaching and preaching on the sending out of the preachers (10:15). That sending implies financial support as well as ordination by elder's hands and prayers in congregational gatherings.

Another pertinent passage is where the use of God's many gifts "is contributing to the needs of others," that contribution should be given "generously" (12:8). Love demands that all of us "share with God's people who are in need" and that we "practice hospitality" (12:13). Whatever the price, love requires even the giving of food and drink to an "enemy" (12:20).

Where Romans 1-11 makes clear what God has done to save sinners, chapters 12-16 shows how men so redeemed ought then to live. One obligation is toward governments of earth. "Taxes" are to be paid to the authorities, considering them God's servants" (13:6,7). "No debt [is to] remain outstanding, except for the continuing debt to love one another" (13:8), while we ever obey the commands to "not steal" and to "not covet" (13:9).

As the Roman epistle concludes, Paul promises a later visit on his way to Spain. He seeks that the church "assist" him on his journey (15:24). At present he is on a trip bearing "a contribution for the poor among the saints in Jerusalem." Paul is happy that Macedonians and Achaians were "pleased" to share as Gentiles with Jews. They recognize that "they owe it to the Jews" from whom has come their spiritual blessings (15:25-28). The long list of names in the last chapter include Priscilla and Aquila in whose "house" the church meets (16:5) and that of "Erastus, who is the city's director of public works" (16:24), (or, according to the KJV, "the city treasurer").

CORINTHIANS

The letter we call 1 Corinthians tackles one question at a time from the problem of congregational division to doubt regarding the resurrection. It is the ninth chapter that raises the issue of financial reimbursement for those who preach the gospel. On the way to that significant chapter only some side-remarks deal with riches and rags. Preachers who follow Paul to Corinth, where Christ was proclaimed as the foundation of God's temple, are advised to build "on this foundation" only the revealed truths of God. These are comparable to "gold, silver [and] costly stones." The opinions of men are more like "hay or straw" only to perish in "the flames" of coming judgment (1 Cor. 3:12). Stewards of the heaven-given gospel "must prove faithful" (1 Cor. 4:2). Where undependable workers "have become rich," true apostles, like Paul, have been content while wearing "rags" and being "homeless." They ever work hard with their own hands (1 Cor. 4:11,12). More than the Christian herald need to beware of avarice that can corrupt life. So must one "who calls himself a brother" and yet becomes "greedy" and a "swindler." It is hoped that disassociation from such a sham disciple will bring about his repentance (1 Cor. 5:9-11).

Proper perspective on the things of this world is maintained by remembering "that the time is short." Let "those who buy something," act "as if it were not theirs to keep; those who use the things of the world, as if not engrossed in them. For this world in its present form is passing away" (1 Cor. 7:29-31).

In the heart of this epistle (chapter nine), we hear the heartbeat of Paul. He reasons that all ministers of the gospel have a right to the finanical support of the church, yet he is willing to forego that right in the advancement of the message.

His logic runs that such monetary support should be adequate not only for a preacher but for a wife and family. He points to married gospel heralds, even naming "the other apostles and the Lord's brothers and Cephas." If every "soldier" plus every one dealing in field or with flock is rewarded for his efforts, why not the preachers? The Law of Moses is quoted to prove the point and "plowman" and "thresher" are held up as illustrations of workers enjoying "the hope of sharing in the harvest" (1 Cor. 9:3-12).

Strong advocates of tithing for the church of New Testament days take firm hold of the next verses where Paul notes that in Old Covenant times "those who serve at the altar share in what is offered on the altar." The conclusion is drawn, "In the same way, the Lord has commanded that those who preach the gospel should receive their living from the gospel" (1 Cor. 9:13,14). The Greek word οὕτως is an adverb of manner. Some twentieth century tithers remind us that the manner of support for Old Testament priests and Levites was the tithe and so they see Jesus as ordaining the tithe of the church for the support of her ministry. Other believers find the point of comparison not in the amount (a tenth) but in the fact that support should come to the workers on whose behalf such work is done. Paul makes clear that he did not demand his right but voluntarily chose to offer the gospel "free of charge" (1 Cor. 9:15-18). If the Gospels had preserved for us the exact wording of Jesus' command referred to in 1 Corinthians 9:14, we might be more dogmatic on the topic of tithing, but they did not.

Concern for the poor, as they gather for the "Lord's Supper," gets attention in Chapter eleven. To not share food with the less fortunate at the love feast keeps it from being a feast of love. To "humiliate those who have nothing" is not a proper way to recognize the body of Christ which consists of all baptized into that body (1 Cor. 11:20-22, cp. 12:12). Love should guide every action, because even to "give all . . . to the poor" yet not be motivated by love would "gain nothing" (1 Cor. 13:3).

Such love lies behind the appeal for "the collection for God's people" at the end of the epistle. Each Sunday each member is to "set aside a sum of money in keeping with his income." The monies coming from basically Gentile churches, like those in Galatia and Corinth, will communicate to the needy in Jerusalem that the church is one great family throughout the earth. Love also for the good name of the church will counsel the believers to approve men to travel with the gift, so the cause will not be defamed by some false accusation that not all of the money reached its destination (1 Cor. 16:1-4).

The letter concludes with an announced opportunity for the church to share in hosting Paul on a "stay" in their town and on his "journey" that will follow (1 Cor. 16:6). Such backing had been shown in the coming of "Stephanas, Fortunatus and Achaicus," as it ever had been evident in the "house" of Aquila and Priscilla that was always open to the meetings of the congregation from day one of its existence (1 Cor. 16:17-19).

The second Corinthian epistle contains two full chapters on money. Thirty-nine verses from 2 Cor. 8:1-9:15 all speak to the subject. Elsewhere in the letter Paul contrasts his true apostleship with his defamers, who aim only at enriching their purses by fleecing God's flock.

"Unlike so many," the apostle wrote, "we do not peddle the word of God for profit" (2 Cor. 2:17). "We have exploited no one" (2 Cor. 7:2), he argues. After reminding them that he preached "free of charge," and still intends to not be "a burden . . . in any way," he lays bare that his motive is "to cut the ground from under those who want an opportunity to be considered equal" to true apostles (2 Cor. 11:7-12). Hirelings exploit and take advantage of their flock. Paul and his co-workers care for every sheep. That should be evident to any one noting how "often [Paul has] gone without food," or been "cold and naked" in carrying out his mission (2 Cor. 11:20,27).

Did the false teachers ever write "what I want is not your possessions but you?" Did they ever say, "I will very gladly spend for you everything I have and expend myself as well?" Could they ever meet the challenge to find one case of exploitation by any representative of Paul (2 Cor. 12:14-18)?

Never did the apostle regret his sacrifices. Though he knew "hunger" and was by men's standards "poor," he gloried that he was "making many rich" and that in reality he was "possessing everything" that genuinely mattered (2 Cor. 6:5,10).

We are reading a letter that at the periphery contrasts at every opportunity those who preach to save souls and those who are in religion to make a financial killing. That letter at its core is encouraging sacrificial giving as a "grace." Chapters eight and nine need more to be read than exegeted. The "rich generosity" of the Macedonian congregation is told to the Corinthians for the purpose of encouraging similar giving on their part. If "overflowing joy" can motivate magnanimity in the face of "extreme poverty" at Philippi; it can do the same in Corinth. People will plead for "the privilege of sharing," when they give themselves "first to the Lord" (2 Cor. 8:1-7).

The giving Paul seeks does not rise because of harsh commands but from remembering tender love. The incarnation story is the highest stimulus to sacrificial giving where "the grace of our Lord Jesus Christ" left the riches of heaven to make us truly rich. That memory alone should spark the completion of their last year's willing participation. That beginning now waits completion (2 Cor. 8:8-12). There is something right about the "equality" idea. To give to others in need while you have something to give, makes likely the reverse action when the shoe of need is on the other foot. (2 Cor. 8:13-15).

"Enthusiasm," "initiative," "eagerness" and "zeal" mark workers like Titus and the others who will carry the funds to their destination. Such quality "representatives of the churches" ought to encourage participation in such a project. No church should make a member's regular offerings a test of membership, or ought to consider tithing a test of orthodoxy. Yet, all ought to recognize that the apostle sees giving as a test of love. He admonishes the

Corinthians, "show . . . the proof of your love" (2 Cor. 8:16-24).

Paul belives his "boasting," about the Corinthian "eagerness to help," will "not prove hollow." He rejoices that their "generous gift" will not be "grudgingly given" (2 Cor. 9:1-5). He reminds them all of a fact of life down on the farm, where sparse sowing leads to sparse reaping. Yet since "God loves a cheerful giver," no contribution should be made "reluctantly or under compulsion." Will God reward the sharing? He not only is "able to make all grace abound to you," he will make you "rich in every way so that you can be generous on every occasion" (2 Cor. 9:6-11).

Many blessings flow from gifts to the needy. Toward heaven flow "expressions of thanks to God." Toward the needy runs the answer to their cries for help. Toward you will rush their heartfelt love, as the recipients lift your name in prayer. Toward Jesus on the cross will flow faith in "his indescribable gift" (2 Cor. 9:12-15).

What the whole Bible says about the giving of money is summarized in these chapters penned by Paul to the saints in Corinth. In overview they call for giving to be considered a "grace." When it is that, the giving is sacrificial (8:2,3). It is willing (8:4,10). It is wholehearted (8:5) and consistent (8:6,11). It is loving (8:8,24), appreciative (8:9, 9:15) and proportionate (8:12-15). It is careful (8:16-23), exemplary (9:2) and actual (9:2-5). It is to be pledged (9:5), business-like (9:6-10) and purposive (9:7,11-14). It, above all, is to be cheerful (9:7). Yet, it would be none of these without guidance and stimulation. As the Corinthians can be grateful for this teaching from Paul, every congregation will be the better that has a teacher that arouses it to its potential by teaching the whole counsel of God on every Bible topic including this one.

GALATIANS AND THESSALONIANS

The Roman and Corinthian letters were written in the mid-fifties. About five years or so earlier Paul had sent correspondence to churches in Galatia reminding the Gentile converts that becoming followers of Christ did not require them to follow the Jewish ways of circumcision and law keeping. Not long after that the apostle wrote two brief epistles to Thessalonian converts of his second missionary journey. These brethren needed instruction regarding the second coming of Christ. None of these letters give primary attention to a Christian's relationship to money. Yet, what is said is in no way insignificant.

The Galatian letter shows the unanimity of all the church leaders that Paul was to reach Gentiles as surely as Peter was to preach to Jews. The only counsel the Jerusalem "pillars" had given Paul and Barnabas was that they "should continue to remember the poor." Paul writes that he was "eager" to do exactly that (Gal. 1:10).

In refutation of the Judaizers' claim that a convert from the Pagan world would need to become a Jew on the route to becoming a Christian, Paul argues that the Law of Moses was binding only until Christ (chapters 3-4) but freedom in Christ from that Mosaic Law did not mean lawlessness. It rather meant living by Christ's Spirit (chapters 5-6). In the last chapter two vital points are made regarding money.

Paul, in his authoritative position as an apostle of Christ, instructs, "Anyone who receives instruction in the word must share all good things with his instructor" (Gal. 6:6). "All good things" refer to more than food, lodging and clothing, but by no means can these material benefits be omitted.

The very next line reminds the reader that "a man reaps what he sows." The believer, like a farmer, knows that after investing seed in the ground his toil and patient waiting will bear certain harvest. Therefore, the hardworking Paul admonishes all who labor in the kingdom to "not become weary in doing good, for at the proper time we will reap a harvest if we do not give up." This doing of good should be our desire at every opportunity. Those good actions should be offered "to all people, especially to those who belong to the family of believers (Gal. 6:7-10). While the

Galatian Epistle is generally listed with Paul's doctrinal works, it like the others has its strongly practical applications.

The short Thessalonian letters show us that the earliest Christians not only looked back to Jesus' first coming but lived in anticipation of his second advent. As in Galatians, so in these letters, the importance of doctrine does not erase the essentiality of standards for daily life. Let all converts know Paul's reasons for laboring in gospel preaching. He had no "impure motives" and did not "put on a mask to cover up greed." His evangelistic team was never "a burden" to them. Any recollection of the facts will bring to their memories that all of those that came preaching with Paul "worked night and day in order not to be a burden to anyone," as they "preached the gospel of God" (1 Thess. 2:3,5,7).

Neighbors and friends will be more easily reached for the church when suspicion of monetary motives cannot be placed on those who are in ministry. Such an "ambition . . . to work with your hands, just as we told you" should mark every member. And why is that so essential? "So that your daily life may win the respect of outsiders and so that you will not be dependent on anybody" (1 Thess. 4:11,12).

The "idle" are to be warned because of the harm that such a life-style causes to the reputation of Christianity (1 Thess. 5:14). This single verse in the first letter to Thessalonica grows into a large paragraph in the second letter. Idlers are to be shunned. They violate the clear apostolic teaching and go against the translucent apostolic example. Paul says his workers did not "eat anyone's food without paying for it." Their self-sacrifice was not because they had no right for support but to give a "model" to follow. The rule Paul gave was, "If a man will not work, he shall not eat" (2 Thess. 3:6-12). Could the readers of the letter but have seen the caloused hand of Paul as he signed "the greeting in [his] own hand," they would know that hand to belong to a laborer and not a man of idleness (2 Thess. 3:17).

20

WHAT JESUS' APOSTLES SAID ABOUT MONEY IN PAUL'S LATER EPISTLES

PAUL'S PRISON EPISTLES

Out of the Roman imprisonment told of in the last chapter of Acts come four brief but potent letters. Called "prison epistles," because written while Paul was in bonds, they nevertheless have set free many a reader's spirit. The epistles contain devotional material indeed.

The key word of Ephesians is "walk," admonishing the followers of the Way to walk in love, in light and in wisdom. Those in the church are expected to change life-styles. If their baptism is to be more than an empty rite, their old ways, old words and old attitudes must be left buried to rise no more. The converts raised to walk in newness of life must consider even their pocket books to be included in the ceremony that calls for total surrender. Paul lays it down for all eyes to see, "he who has been stealing must steal no longer, but must work, doing something useful with his own hands, that he may have something to share with those in need" (Eph. 4:28).

There must be no misunderstanding, "greed" is as evil as "sexual immorality" and not even a hint of it is proper for God's people. Greed is labeled "idolatry" and is named as a barrier to "any inheritance in the kingdom of Christ." Some consider avarice at worst a misdemeanor of little consequence. Paul knows it by any name to be a soul damning crime. He warns, "Let no one deceive you with empty words, for because of such things God's wrath comes on those who are disobedient" (Eph. 5:3-7). The Colossian letter delivered at the same time as Ephesians and by the same letter-bearer, Tychicus, likewise in its only monetary reference, calls "greed . . . idolatry" (Col. 3:5). Since the Colossian church met in the home of Philemon, where the Colossian letter was read to the gathered church, it is well to give a glance at the apostle's private words to this brother. As Paul returns his prison-convert Onesimus, who had run away from Philemon, he states his willingness to pay that slave-owner any amount deemed owed by his son in the gospel. He writes, "If he . . . owes you anything, charge it to me . . . I will pay it back" (Phile. 18-19).

Toward the end of the imprisonment at Rome that produced the Prison Epistles, Paul writes a thank you note to the church at Philippi. To the responsible leaders, called "overseers and deacons," whose encouragement brought the support referred to, Paul expresses gratitude for their "partnership in the gospel from the first day until now" (Phil. 1:5). The ASV renders the passage more accurately explaining Paul's thanksgiving to be for their "partnership in the furtherance of the gospel." His praise is not here for the common κοινωνία he has with all believers, but for the specific fellowship he enjoyed with Lydia's household, the Jailor's household and the rest of the original church from "the first day."

The Anglo-Saxon "fee-lay-ship" carries the idea where the "fee" of various individuals pooled together constitutes the partnership of sharing. Later in the letter, Paul refers to the partnership that congregation "shared with [him] in the matter of giving and receiving" (Phil. 4:15). "Fellowship" comes from "fee" referring to a price of money or life and "lay" describing the placing down of that fee as a payment.

The bearer of the Philippian gift was Epaphroditus, who had been "sent to take care of [Paul's] needs" (Phil. 2:25 cp. 4:18). The gifts Epaphroditus bore spoke of the church's concern for him. Paul, refusing to admit he was really in need, expresses the secret of handling all adversity. He writes, "I have learned to be content whatever the circumstances. I know what it is to be in need, and I know what it is to have plenty. I have learned the secret of being content in any and every situation, whether well fed or hungry, whether living in plenty or in want. I can do everything through him who gives me strength" (Phil. 4:11-13).

Wife abuse and child abuse are nothing compared to the textual abuse of that last sentence. Taken out of context by some modern day "miracle-workers," the passage has been used to imply that any believer can perform wonders and signs of every kind in every circumstance. In context, the verses rather remind us that a Christian's economic condition, positive or negative, can not destroy him. Where sudden wealth is more than some people can handle and abject proverty is more than others can bear, the believer can manage in either financial condition with Christ's help.

Let the givers know that their giving is "credited" to their "account." The missionary Paul's needs are met and God is pleased with the donor's sacrifice. That guarantees that in the future "God will meet all [their] needs according to his glorious riches in Christ Jesus" (Phil. 4:14-19).

The apostle to the Gentiles was so single-minded he only lived for the success of the gospel. What the world counted "profit," he "considered loss for the sake of Christ." Others may spend their lives in the amassing of riches. He will spend his days amassing souls. By comparison with the valuables of eternity, Paul considers worldly wealth as "rubbish" (Phil. 3:7,8).

PAUL'S PASTORAL EPISTLES

Paul was not one to leave any base uncovered. Planning to go West to evangelize Spain, after his three year imprisonment in Rome, he first marshals Timothy and Titus to strengthen the churches in some earlier fields of his endeavor. Timothy is delegated to "straighten out" any unfinished work in Asia, as Titus is to do on the isle of Crete.

The tack of Titus included appointing of "elders in every town . . . as directed." These functionaries must be qualified. One such requirement was that they not be men "pursuing dishonest gain" (Titus 1:7). There already were too many false teachers to the detriment of the church. A man "entrusted with God's work" must stay on the course chartered by the apostles. The reason behind the erroneous teaching "of the circumcision group," was that it tickled the ears of the hearers to the deceiver's personal profit. Whole households were being taught the wrong doctrine "for the sake of dishonest gain" (Titus 1:10,11). Titus was to watch out for every group in the several congregations of the island. Former "slaves" were to be reminded that no longer was stealing from a master an option (Titus 2:10). Fellow workers were to have their needs met and all members were "to devote themselves to doing what is good, in order that they may provide for daily necessities and not live unproductive lives" (Titus 3:13,14).

It is in the first letter to Timothy that we find a rich source of information regarding Paul's teaching on money. After learning that he wanted women at worship "to dress modestly" without "gold or pearls or expensive clothes" (1 Tim. 2:9) and that he desired the "overseers" and "deacons" be men who are neither "lovers of money" nor pursuers of "dishonest gain" (1 Tim. 3:3,8); we find him speaking at length about the support of widows.

Not every woman who has lost a husband needs to be thrown on the financial responsibility-list of a congregation. "Children or grandchildren . . . should learn first of all to put their religion into practice by caring for their own family and so repaying their parents and grandparents" (1 Tim. 5:3-5). It would be worse than atheism for a believer to "not provide for his own relatives, and especially for his immediate family." Paul also stipulates that those worthy of receiving aid from the church should be "over sixty" and beyond the likelihood of a remarriage meeting the need, as well as having shown her own true religion in the past by the showing of "hospitality" and "helping [others] in trouble" (1 Tim. 5:6-10). Since the church's resources are limited, the other sources of support are to be tapped, before "the church be burdened." Those "really in need" can then get the help they must have (1 Tim. 5:16).

Next Paul addresses the issue of a paid ministry. He is careful to protect the right to support for those true men of God who preach the gospel, but he is quick to condemn those who enter ministry with a profit motive. Quoting the same Old Testament passage of Deuteronomy 25:4, that he had quoted in the 1 Corinthian letter that says an ox is not to be muzzled while working at treading out grain, he argues that "the worker deserves his wages." He reasons that this includes the "elders who direct the affairs of the church" and "work" at "preaching" (1 Tim. 5:17,18).

But not all teachers are worthy by virtue of office. Some teach false doctrines and "think that godliness is a means to financial gain." This is a temptation that Timothy and all other men of God ought to "flee" at all cost (1 Tim. 6:5,11).

Having warned of following religion for "financial gain," Paul rejoices at the genuine "gain" to be found in "godliness with contentment." He remembers that at birth we enter the world with nothing and will leave in the exact same way. Everybody knows this, but not many act like they do. Paul calls for contentment with but food and clothing and then utters the words that the world has had burned into their memories over the two thousand succeeding years.

He observes that waiting to get rich becomes a "temptation and a trap" that has brought "ruin and destruction" to many. Those words are as applicable to the poor as to the wealthy. It is the desire or wanting of riches and not the having or not having of them that "plunge man into ruin." This is true because "the love of money is a root of all kinds of evil" (1 Tim. 6:6-10).

How often this truism is falsely understood. Money itself can be a root of much good as the dedicated gifts of believers have proven. Many days we observe the lack of money appearing to be the root of many social ills. The King James Version translates in a way untrue on the face of it by the wording "the love of money is the root of all evil." It is not money but the love of it that Paul addresses. That love of money is not "the root of all evil" but is certainly "a root" of evils of all kinds. The Greek word for evil is in the plural.

The love of money is one of the roots of social evils of many kinds. Behind slavery and war is that love. Behind graft in politics and income from pushing alcohol, tobacco and drugs is that love. Prostitution, gambling and smut for sale at the theater or book store find their root in the desire for riches. Wanting to keep people of certain races from your neighborhood or your job, likely stems from the consequence feared in the drop in property value or competition for the labor market.

When money becomes one's purpose for living, he is "pierced . . . with many griefs." Losing one's soul should be of greater concern than losing one's money. That being true "those who are rich in this present world" are "not to be arrogant nor to put their hope in wealth, which is so uncertain." All in the church can and should be "rich in good deeds . . . and willing to share." Paul echoes what Jesus had taught. The sharers are laying up "treasures for themselves . . . for the coming age" (1 Tim. 6:17-19). One can only conclude after reading the Pauline letters that wealth is not that relevant to the true issues of life, but those who have it in any degree should take advantage of their opportunity to serve others.

21

WHAT JESUS' APOSTLES SAID ABOUT MONEY IN PETER AND JOHN'S EPISTLES

1 AND 2 PETER

Turning from the letters penned by a Christian tentmaker to those written by Christian fishermen is to walk the same familiar road. The big fisherman, Simon Peter, exalts in the pricelessness of the believer's "faith" and God's "promises" which are "precious" beyond imagination (2 Pet. 1:1,4). Christ's apostle to the circumcision is set back by the "greed" of false teachers who "exploit" their hearers. He defines them as "experts in greed," like Balaam "who loved the wages of wickedness" (2 Pet. 2:3,14-16).

Where 1 Peter contrasts truth and error — the teaching that is apostolic and that which is apostate — 1 Peter is a letter to give encouragement to believers under pressure. Yet it, too, looks at the believer's faith as "of greater worth than gold" and at his hope as "an inheritance that can never perish, spoil or fade" (1 Pet.

1:4,7). How could it be otherwise, when the redeemed were purchased "with the precious blood of Christ," rather than "with perishable things such as silver and gold" (1 Pet. 1:18-19).

Men so redeemed are to rid their hearts of all "deceit" and "envy," as they build their new lives in Christ the "precious cornerstone" (1 Pet. 2:1,6,7), whether they be "free men" or "slaves" (1 Pet. 2:16,18). Wives are to reflect a beauty beyond that which is set off by "gold jewelry and fine clothes." The Christian women have the "unfading beauty of a gentle and quiet spirit, which is of great worth in God's sight" (1 Pet. 3:3,4). All are to be hospitable using their possessions faithfully (1 Pet. 4:9,10). None are to stoop to theft, no matter how great their need (1 Pet. 4:15). Each is to "cast all . . . anxiety on him (God) because he cares" (1 Pet. 5:7). The example is to be set by the elders who are not to be "greedy for money, but eager to serve" (1 Pet. 5:2).

1, 2 AND 3 JOHN

One of Peter's partners in the earlier fishing business on the shores of Galilee was John. He, too, left all to follow Christ, and to become a fisher of men. Now in distant Ephesus we find him at his new trade, mending spiritual nets and gathering in the souls of men for which Jesus had prepared him henceforth to fish.

In two of his little letters, he admonishes about the perils and opportunities afforded by our possessions. 2 John does not deal with the subject, but 1 John warns against falling in love with "the world or anything in the world." Satan has lures that appeal to "the cravings of sinful man," such as "boasting of what he has." To avoid becoming a catch for the Devil, the reader is told to remember that "the world and its desires pass away" (1 John 2:15-17). Let the believer recall that the anointing he received from God is "not counterfeit" (1 John 2:27). The genuine religion is so down-to-earth that a "brother in need" is to find willing assistance from "anyone" in the church who "has material possessions" (1 John 3:17,18). Any Gnostic spiritualizing of the faith, that turns God's practical love for the world in an exclusively other-world direction, is not the faith Jesus left to his followers. Hear the apostolic warning, "Dear children, keep yourselves from idols" (1 John 5:21). Not all idols are whittled out of wood. Some false gods and false ideas are whittled out of the imagination of the human mind.

Diotrophes was such a false teacher. He is warned against in 3 John, a letter addressed to Gaius. The KJV translates the wish that he "mayest prosper . . . as [his] soul prospereth" (3 John 2). John is appreciative of the support this believer is giving to Christian workers. These in turn have reported about Gaius' generosity that sent "them on their way in a manner worthy of God." The gospel workers "for the sake of the Name . . . went out, receiving no help from the pagans." Giving hospitality to such men made the donors partners in the work for truth (3 John 5-8).

REVELATION

In the Bible's final book, the Revelation or Apocalypse of John, the spiritual values of heaven are described in the coinage of earth. We read of "golden lampstands" (Rev. 1:12,20; 2:1) and a robe with "a golden sash" (1:13; 15:6). We see "crowns of gold" (4:4; 9:7; 14:14), "cups" of gold (17:4) and "cargoes of gold" (18:11). The Holy City "of pure gold" (21:18) is measured by a "rod of gold" (21:15) and has streets of "pure gold" (21:21).

As God's New Jerusalem is evaluated, precious metals of earth are used to illustrate its worth. We read of "jasper," "saphire," "chalcedony," "emerald," "sardonyx," " carnelian," "chrisolite," "beryl," "topaz," "chrysoprase," "jacinth," "amethyst" and "pearls" (Rev. 21:11,18-21). But God's despised "Babylon," the unholy city which is to be destroyed, had held out earthly riches to attract the damned to her ways. She is considered a "prostitute" and is described as "dressed in purple and scarlet, and was glittering with gold, precious stones and pearls" (Rev. 17:4). "Merchants of earth grew rich from her excessive luxuries" (18:3) and sea captains "became rich through her wealth" (18:19).

Material wealth, although often corrupting the persons who become slaves in its pursuit, is used to contrast the true riches of the people who in the service of God use money as a servant rather than a master. Upon the collapse of the Babylon built by man, you hear mourning over the loss of that in which the deceived put their trust. The list is almost endless. It includes "gold, silver, precious stones and pearls; fine linen, purple, silk and scarlet cloth; every sort of citron wood, and articles of every kind made of ivory, costly wood, bronze, iron and marble; cargoes of cinnamon and spice, of incense, myrrh and frankincense, of wine and olive oil, of fine flour and wheat; cattle and sheep; horses and carriages" and the list goes on (Rev. 18:12-21).

The stark contrast between heaven's wealth and earth's riches runs throughout the book. The suffering Christians in Smyrna were known to be experiencing "poverty," yet were truly "rich" (Rev. 2:9). The foolish Laodiceans were duped by the Deceiver to brag, "I am rich; I have acquired wealth and do not need a thing." But they were admonished by Jesus, "buy from me gold refined in fire, so you can become rich" (Rev. 3:17,18). Better off is the poor follower of Christ, who must buy "a quart of wheat for a day's wages, and three quarts of barley for a day's wages" (Rev. 6:6), than worshippers of "demons, and idols of gold, silver, bronze, stone and wood — idols that cannot see or hear or walk" (Rev. 9:20).

To hear Jesus speak on material possessions and then to hear his apostles teach on the same topic is to know you are hearing an echo ringing from Galilee across the Roman world. The ascending Christ ordered his followers to teach what he commanded. Their writings evidence that the Sanhedrin's observation was accurate. Luke had said, regarding "Peter and John," that the Jewish leaders "were astonished and they took note that these men had been with Jesus" (Acts 4:13). There is no other way to account for their harmonious teachings on money.

22

WHAT JESUS' DISCIPLES SAID ABOUT MONEY IN ACTS, JAMES, JUDE AND HEBREWS

ACTS OF THE APOSTLES

The term "disciple" is a broader term than the word "apostle." Every follower of Jesus is and was a disciple of Christ. Out of the vast group of "disciples," Jesus hand picked "twelve of them, whom he also designated apostles" (Luke 6:13). Peter and John were apostles of Christ from the days of Jesus' earthly ministry. Paul was chosen as a special apostle to the Gentiles much later. Perhaps comparing disciples to citizens and apostles to ambassadors will help our thinking. There are responsibilities and opportunities afforded every citizen. Those chosen to be ambassadors serve the citizenry but have special responsibilities and powers that automatically go with the office. We have just examined the epistles by apostles in our New Testament and now turn to the writings penned by significant church leaders who were disciples indeed, but not apostles. We start with the doctor who had given us the Gospel of Luke and then wrote the Acts of the Apostles.

In the pages of this book on the early history of Christ's church, we meet more than a dozen personalities that are interested in money. The first chapter, reviewing some of the facts Luke had revealed in his Gospel, finds him recalling Judas who bought a field "with the reward he got for his wickedness" (Acts 1:18). We soon meet a beggar that from birth was hitting up worshippers for a handout, as they entered the temple courts. Asking Peter and John "for money" brought out of Peter the now famous response that few modern preachers honestly could give, "Silver or gold I do not have, but what I have I give you" (Acts 3:1-6). The healing in Jesus' name that followed resulted in another gospel sermon with astounding conversion results.

As the story of the church spreads from Jerusalem to Rome, we hear Stephen remind the Sanhedrin of the old historic fact of Abraham buying a burial plot "from the sons of Hamor at Shechem for a certain sum of money" (Acts 7:16). We see Simon the Sorcerer bring the new world "simony" into the vocabulary of Christendom. He had observed the apostles lay hands on Philip's converts and give to them gifts of the Spirit, enabling the newly founded church in Samaria to carry on. Wanting to get in on what appeared to have future great financial potential for him, Simon offered money to Peter and John, seeking to buy the secret of their power. The ecclesiastical office of apostle was not for sale, so Peter uttered a stinging rebuke that ought permanently to have stopped such a practice in its tracks. He spoke, "May your money perish with you, because you thought you could buy the gift of God with money" (Acts 8:18-20).

Before the record ends, we have met an Ethiopian "official in charge of all the treasury of Candace, queen of the Ethiopians" (Acts 8:27) and a Roman centurion in Caesarea named Cornelius, whose generous gifts to the needy caught the eye of God (Acts 10:1-4). In both cases their conversion stemmed from their serious interest in God's will. The Ethiopian was searching for the meaning of Isaiah's prophecies and the centurion had an angel inform him, "Cornelius, God has heard your prayer and remembered your gifts to the poor" (Acts 10:31). We have read also about a prophet, Agabus, predicting famine severe enough to affect the entire Roman world (Acts 11:28) and a "slave girl" who by a demonic spirit could predict the future, earning "a great deal of money for her owners by fortune-telling" (Acts 16:15,19). We have been introduced to the good guys like Aquila and Priscilla, whom Paul worked with as tentmaker (Acts 18:1-3). We have become acquainted with the bad guys, like the silver smith Demetrius, who reminded "the craftsmen" and "workmen in related trades" how their "good income from this business" was threatened by the preaching that Artemis and other idols were not real gods at all (Acts 19:23-27). Teaching that "we should not think that the divine being is like gold or silver or stone" (Acts 17:29), is hard on the religion of the populace and fatal to the income of those whose living is based on the tourist trade to the sacred shrines. Conversion is costly for idolaters and sorcerers, like those at Ephesus, whose repentance was shown to be real when they publicly burned scrolls valued at "fifty thousand *drachmas*" (Acts 19:19) or $10,000.

We pass by the tribune Claudius Lysius, who "had to pay a big price for his citizenship" (Acts 22:28), and Felix the Governor, who hoped for a "bribe" from Paul who had brought "gifts for the poor" of Jerusalem (Acts 24:17,26). We come to Luke's heavy stress on early genuine Christian sharing.

The first Christian congregation in all the world was that founded in Jerusalem on Pentecost of 30 AD. Luke in the brevity of one sentence pointed out the distinctives of a Christian assembly. In addition to "the apostolic teaching" and the "breaking of bread" (the Lord's Supper) with "prayer," is named "the fellowship." This κοινωνία has both the sound and the sense of a "coin." It can be translated partnership. The Lukan interpretation includes in its definition of fellowship the being "together" and having "everything in common." He writes that the believers were "selling their possessions and goods," giving "to anyone as he had need" (Acts 2:42,44,45).

Describing the happy, spontaneous giving that flowed from each life in those early days, Luke declares that "all the believers were one in heart and mind" with none claiming "that any of his possessions was his own." Because of their willingness to share everything they had, "there were no needy persons among them" (Acts 4:32-34).

The general rule is first stated, "from time to time those who owned lands or houses sold them, brought the money from the sales and put it at the apostles' feet, and it was distributed to anyone as he had need" (Acts 4:34,35). Then follows a specific good example. Barnabas is chosen because he will be joined later in the book with Paul on his first missionary journey (Acts 4:36,37). Immediately follows a specific bad example. Ananias with his wife Sapphira want to be considered as generous as the rest, who like Barnabas would sell a field and bring the entire amount to the apostles for distribution to the needy. However, the pair have agreed that they will pretend to have given more than in reality they want to give. It is the pretense or lie to the Holy Spirit that is condemned.

Peter's rebuke reminds the couple that the property was theirs to do with as they pleased. God desired all living of love's commandment to be spontaneous and voluntary. The Essenes by the Dead Sea may carry out their benevolence by fixed laws and strictly devised plans. Communism may put all ownership in the hands of the State, so that a common man may have nothing to say about who receives what. The heart warming actions of the early church are falsely labeled Christian communism. No human government is involved, only human heart-beats for brethren in need. No sales of property were compulsory and no effort was made to put every Christian on the same financial level. No imprisonment was threatened against any choosing not to share. The phenomenon told by Luke is the natural response of the

Spirit of Christ coming into lives open to him. It is not the outcome of State demands to be enforced by guns. A new spirit of
brotherhood is rising naturally and spontaneously to the genuine
spiritual experience of receiving Christ as Lord.

The sin of Ananias and his wife was not in the giving of a particular amount but in desiring to gain the prestige of other
believers by wanting to be credited with a more generous gift than
they were willing to make. The words of Jesus tell us that "it is
more blessed to give than to receive" (Acts 20:35). The example
of Ananias could be saying "it is more blessed to give than to
deceive," because lying to the Holy Spirit is the name Peter gives
to Ananias' sin.

You might think that such generosity as exemplified in Acts
2-5 would dissipate all church problems. However the vast sums
of benevolent money for apostolic distribution became a problem
in itself among such a growing church. "The Grecian
Jews . . . complained against those of the Aramaic-speaking
community because their widows were being overlooked in the
daily distribution of food" (Acts 6:1). Apparently language differences were behind the confusion. The apostolic solution was to
keep such unintended unfairness from rising again. Seven
qualified men were to be chosen to take over the responsibility of
food distribution.

True to the same loving spirit of brotherhood that marked the
gathering of the resources, it marked balloting for the seven. An
examination of the names of the selected men shows them to be
all of Greek names. There was no power bloc seeking to get at
least four of the seven from one linguistic group to control future
decisions. If the complaint came from the Grecian Jews, who felt
an injustice was done, let a unanimous selection from that body
show that love can conquer all. The apostles in Jerusalem now
have what some call "deacons" to assist them. In later times
famine relief was administered through men in Judea called
"elders" (Acts 11:29).

The latter half of the book of Acts records the missionary victories of Paul, the special apostle to the Gentile world. The tesimony regarding Paul's motivation for preaching is unanimous. The "city clerk" in Ephesus denies that Paul ever "robbed temples" (Acts 19:37). The apostle himself told the elders of that city that he had "not coveted anyone's silver or gold or clothing." Rather by his own hands he had met his "own needs" plus those of all his "companions" (Acts 20:33-35). The Jewish elders knew he would be willing "to pay . . . expenses" for men ready to make a vow in Jerusalem's temple (Acts 21:24). Even at the end of the story Paul is paying his own way. He is renting a house with help from Philippi "for two whole years." There he will abide and carry on his ministry until his trial is over (Acts 28:30). While it was Paul's intention to make his own way, he occasionally accepted assistance from others. He had allowed the appreciative people of Malta to furnish needed supplies for those sailing with him (Acts 28:10), as he had friends at Sidon there to "provide for his needs" (Acts 27:3).

JAMES AND JUDE

It is a certain fact that Paul had made his living at tent-making and his traveling companion Luke was known to be a physician. It is but an assumption to suggest that Jesus' half-brothers James and Jude were carpenters. The foundation for the guess is that Jewish boys most often followed in the trade of their fathers and Joseph had been a carpenter in Nazareth. However they provided for their families as married men (1 Cor. 9:5), their epistles make comment on the theme of possessions.

Jude, who is thought to have written after the deaths of Peter, Paul and James, is alerting the believers that what those giants in the faith had predicted was coming to pass. False teachers were arising and they were led to their destructive ways by the lure of riches. He writes, "Woe to them . . . they have rushed for profit into Balaam's error." He exposes them as "shepherds who feed only themselves" and they do that "without the slightest qualms" (Jude 11,12).

James had become a leading figure in the fast-growing Jerusalem church. When this flock that he pastored was "scattered throughout Judea and Samaria" by the great persecution that followed Stephen's martyrdom (Acts 8:1), James wrote to them in loving pastoral concern. His letter has much to say about both the poor and the rich. The wise Christian will keep his priorities straight. Money is not everything. It is not to be one's highest pursuit.

The readers now "scattered among the nations" and facing "trials of many kinds" are not to forget what James had taught them while they were still under his care in Jerusalem. He often said then and writes now, "The brother in humble circumstances ought to take pride in his high position. But the one who is rich should take pride in his low position, because he will pass away like a wild flower." James reminds them what scorching heat can do in withering beautiful plants and concludes, "in the same way, the rich man will fade away even while he goes about his business" (James 1:9-11).

It is easy for one who is in the "have not" group to long to be in the "have" grouping. Such desire, while natural, needs to be restrained by the facts of the case. Have not many persons, who have amassed wealth, undergone a negative transformation? Are not some in their acquaintance now less rather than more humane? James asks, "Is it not the rich who are exploiting you? Are they not the ones who are dragging you into court? Are they not the ones who are slandering the noble name of him to whom you belong?" (James 2:6,7).

James' condemnation of the uncaring rich sounds like the voice of Amos that long ago cried out for justice and mercy. His biting condemnation reveals a possible, but not essential, end of the road for those who follow the trail to endless wealth. "Now listen, you rich people, weep and wail because of the misery that is coming upon you. Your wealth has rotted, and moths have

197

eaten your clothes. Your gold and silver are corroded. Their corrosion will testify against you and eat your flesh like fire. You have hoarded wealth in the last days. Look! The wages you failed to pay the workmen who mowed your fields are crying out against you. The cries of the harvesters have reached the ears of the Lord Almighty. You have lived on earth in luxury and self-indulgence. You have fattened yourselves in the day of the slaughter" (James 5:1-5).

It is not that an abundance of things has to callous the heart. But, it often does. The Christian defense against the hardening of the heart, that money as a first-place goal of life can bring, is to bring it off the god pedestal and robe it in servant's garb. As an instrument by which God's will can be done, money can enter into the realm of "religion" that is "pure and faultless." The believer with monetary means can "look after orphans and widows in their distress" (James 1:27). Religion, that tied you to the God above you and loosed you from the man in need beside you, would not be the religion Jesus taught. It would be a hollow faith indeed that spoke well wishes to "a brother or sister . . . without clothes and daily food" and yet did zero about "his physical needs." Such a religion is worse than worthless (James 2:15,16).

The healthy view toward wealth will show at a church assembly in the way greeters at the door and ushers at the aisles treat the guests. That God wants the hearts of all men equally would be negated by giving princely service to those with "a gold ring and fine clothes" but grubby treatment to a "poor man." If numbers prove anything, are not more of the poorer classes responsive to God's gospel than the self-sufficient well-to-do? "Has not God chosen those who are poor in the eyes of the world to be rich in faith and to inherit the kingdom he promised those who love him?" (James 2:1-5).

When you get right down to it, money can be a blessing. But, due to man's weakness, it is often a blight. "Fights and quarrels" stem from wanting something you do not get. It is coveting that is behind praying "with wrong motives." Self-centered prayer asks for items so that "you may spend what you get on your pleasures" (James 4:1-3). The wise Christian will remember whose he is and why he is here. He will be conscious of his stewardship and his mortality. He will not say, "Today or tomorrow we will go to this or that city, spend a year there, carry on business and make money." He will rather recognize that, since life is as fleeting as "a mist that appears for a little while and then vanishes," he must as a steward accomplish in the days he has his "Lord's will" (James 4:13-15).

HEBREWS

It may be a mystery who authored the epistle to the Hebrews, but there is no doubt that the original Christian recipients had a rich appreciation of their Jewish past. Using the tools of history and typology, the writer holds up Christ and his teaching to be superior in every way to the revelation of Old Testament times. The New Covenant days, that were ushered in by Jesus, are compared to a last will and testament. Such a will, while made during a man's life-time, became effective after his death. This very important point makes clear how Christ could live and die under the Old Covenant and yet his New Testament not be fully in place until after his cross. The writer of Hebrews illustrates that, "in the case of a will," it is "in force only when somebody has died; it never takes effect while the one who made it is living" (Heb. 9:16,17).

If the date of this letter is shortly prior to the destruction of the Jerusalem temple in 70 AD, the covenantal distinction is vital to grasp. With the Jews scattered, the temple and its priesthood gone, living by the sacrificial system of yore becomes an impossibility. Let the ancient heroes and practices be seen as types foreshadowing the reality that Jesus came to bring.

Abraham as a man of faith is typical of believers. Melchizedek foreshadows the priesthood of Jesus, who is the true "king of righteousness," as the name of that man implies and the genuine "king of peace," as the name of his city of Salem suggests. The tithe, later given to mortal Levites, is early in Genesis said to be given to Melchizedek concerning whom there is no death record. It was not difficult for the Hebrew writer to see the parallel between the Christians bringing their money gifts to the everliving Jesus and Abraham giving "a tenth" to Melchizedek (Heb. 7:4-10).

Jesus was also seen to be typified by the later high priests "appointed to both gifts and sacrifices" (Heb. 8:3,4). The tabernacle of the wilderness days foreshadowed the Christian system by all its details including "the golden altar of incense and the gold-covered ark of the covenant" containing "the gold jar of manna" (Heb. 9:4).

Beyond the types in Hebrews, with their eternal significance, we see the temporary plight of the believers in the author's day. As the heroic figure Moses "regarded disgrace for the sake of Christ as of greater value than the treasures of Egypt, because he was looking ahead to his reward" (Heb. 11:26), some of the letter's recipients, for the sake of imprisoned believers were said to have "joyfully accepted the confiscation of . . . property" because they knew they "had better and lasting possessions" (Heb. 10:34).

The last chapter of the letter calls for loving as brothers during this time of opposition, when many were finding it necessary to flee for their lives. Opening one's home to fellow Christians in flight called for heroism in "entertaining strangers." There would be no time to check for credentials. Some may have opened their homes to "angels without knowing it." I understand the word ἄγγελος to be best translated messengers and refer to the fact that some evangelists of the evangel might have been amongst the ones helped (Heb. 13:1,2).

The warning is appropriate that one on the run, with no promise of a sure source for the next meal, needs to be resistant to the temptation of theft. There is real lack of appreciation for a free night's lodging, if the donee steal from the donor some item to secure his next day's needs. Hear the plea "keep your lives free from the love of money and be content with what you have, because God has said, 'Never will I leave you; never will I forsake you.' " That kind of confidence in God's help should keep any believer from helping himself to another man's belongings (Heb. 13:5,6).

The persecution being faced at the time was not against the Jews but specifically aimed at the followers of Christ. This presented the Jewish believers with a tempting option. They could hold to faith in God, plus their ancient Scriptures and traditions; and yet avoid the fires of persecution by simply dropping Jesus. Yet, to find momentary relief at the price of losing the salvation only Christ could bring, would be as foolish as "Esau, who for a single meal sold his inheritance rights as the oldest son" (Heb. 12:16,17). At no time should the things that money can't buy be lost in the saving of our own necks or the holding on to that which money can buy.

Part Four

Book by Book
(Old Testament)

23

WHAT JESUS' BIBLE SAID ABOUT MONEY IN THE LAW (GENESIS-LEVITICUS)

The followers of Jesus have a desire to know what the Old Testament Scriptures say in all their parts because those writings constituted Jesus' Bible. Out of a rich background "in the Law of Moses, the Prophets and the Psalms" (Luke 24:44), Jesus came forth teaching. Can we find money dealt with in Moses, profits in the Prophets or dollars in David? The eight hundred and eighty-eight pages of material in the New International Version of the Old Testament before me are burgeoning with data on the theme of money that must here be only lightly touched. From the second chapter of the first book of Moses and its reference to the "land of Havilah, where there is gold" that is "good" (Gen. 2:11,12) to the next to last chapter of the final prophetic writing and its plea to not "rob God" by withholding "tithes and offerings" (Mal. 3:8), there is revelation on riches.

GENESIS

Of course Genesis begins with the announcement that God is Creator of the world. No farmer is to forget that the grains and vegetables with which he deals are the work of his Creator. No rancher is to ignore that animal life came from God. Every business man should keep in mind that both sellers and buyers owe their very life to the common source of all being. By putting all things at man's disposal, God has revealed his love for man and the human's obligation to use that which has been entrusted to him as God wills (Gen. 1:1,11,24,26).

To relate the beginnings of the Jewish people — the covenant people of God — Genesis introduces its readers to Abraham, then Isaac and finally to Jacob from whom sprang the twelve tribes. Abram, later called Abraham, is a man blessed of God in the accumulation of many "possessions." He came to acquire "sheep and cattle, male and female donkeys, menservants and maidservants and camels" (Gen. 12:5,16). He had become so "very wealthy in livestock and in silver and gold" that the land could not sustain the animals of both him and his relative Lot (Gen. 13:2,5,6). We read of Lot and his possessions being captured by four kings, only to have them recovered by Abram who then tithed all that was taken to Melchizedek. At that point, Abram swore to the king of Sodom never to take a thing belonging to him so that the king could never be able to say "I made Abram rich" (Gen. 14:11,12,16,20-24).

God, in the chapters that follow, promises Abraham an "heir" (Gen. 15:3,4) and predicts that his descendants, after an enslavement of four hundred years, would leave that enslavement "with great possessions" (Gen. 15:13,14). Those possessions are increased in his shady dealings with Abimelech king of Gerar. He took from him "sheep and cattle and female slaves," plus "a thousand shekels of silver" (Gen. 20:14,16,17), and later made a treaty with him concerning the well at Beersheba for the payment of sheep and cattle (Gen. 21:27,28).

At the death of Abraham's wife, Sarah, the purchase of "property for a burial site" is described at length (Gen. 23:3-20). Abraham insists on paying "the full price," while the Hittite prefers to "give it." After the dickering goes back and forth, the land is valued at "four hundred shekels of silver" and that amount is "weighed out . . . according to the weight current among the merchants." It is not long until Abraham dies leaving "everything he owned to Isaac" (Gen. 25:5).

Since the blood line of the coming Messiah will pass from Abraham through Isaac, Genesis details how Isaac received Rebekah for a wife. The story is preserved in Genesis 24. There we read of "a gold nose ring weighing a *beka* and two gold bracelets weighing ten *shekels*" being given by Abraham's chief servant for her hand in marriage. In addition to putting "the ring in [Rebekah's] nose and the bracelets on her arms," additional gold and silver jewelry and articles of clothing" were given to her, plus "costly gifts" were passed to her brother and mother (verses 22,29,30,34,35,47,53).

Details about Isaac are slim in Genesis, but as his father Abraham was "blessed" by God and became "wealthy" (Genesis 24:35), so Isaac his son reaps crops "a hundred fold" and "his wealth continued to grow until he became very wealthy. He had so many flocks and herds and servants that the Philistines envied him" (Genesis 26:12-14). On his death bed Isaac blesses Jacob by praying for him to experience from the "earth's richness — an abundance of grain and new wine," while omitting Esau from the blessing "of earth's richness" (Genesis 27:28,39). This was the bitter outcome of the bargain Esau had made with Jacob (Gen. 25:31-33). Yet Esau's loss of the birthright did not keep him from also gaining great possessions (Gen. 36:6,7).

As the Genesis story begins to focus on Jacob, we find him at Bethel vowing to God, "of all that you give me I will give you a tenth" (Gen. 28:20-22). The account reflects the blessing of material wealth falling upon Jacob, as it had poured forth upon Abraham and Isaac before him. Some of those riches came to

Jacob from Laban the father of Leah and Rachel. The "wages," for which Jacob worked fourteen years, were the two girls for wife (Gen. 29:15,18,20,27,30). That proved not to be the end of the business relationship as Laban begs Jacob to stay, offering whatever he might ask. He said, "Name your wages, and I will pay them" (Gen. 30:27,28).

Crafty Jacob, having been cheated by Laban in the earlier years, devises a clever stratagem. Since sheep are usually white and goats black or brown, he proposes that Laban keep these, while he takes the speckled and spotted ones. By controlling the breeding practices, it turned out that wise Jacob "grew exceedingly prosperous and came to own large flocks, and maidservants and manservants, and camels and donkeys." This caused Laban's sons to observe, "Jacob has taken everything our father owned and has gained all this wealth from what belonged to our father" (Gen. 30:31-33,43; 31:1). Jacob justified his questionable methods to his wives by reminding them that Laban their father had changed his "wages ten times" (Gen. 31:7,41).

By the time Jacob flees from Laban, he leaves with "wealth" and "all the goods he had accumulated in Paddan Aram" (Gen. 31:14-16,18). The extent of his holdings is seen in the gift he offers to Esau in seeking to pacify him. He gave "two hundred female goats and twenty male goats, two hundred ewes and twenty rams, thirty female camels with their young, forty cows and ten bulls, and twenty female donkeys and ten male donkeys" (Gen. 32:12-15,18,20,21; 33:10,11). His wealth is evident also in his ability to buy for "a hundred pieces of silver" a plot of ground in Shechem for pitching his tent (Gen. 33:19). That wealth grows as his sons loot the city and carry off "all their wealth . . . taking as plunder everything in the houses" (Gen. 34:27-29) until soon Esau and Jacob are forced to separate in that "their possessions were too great for them to remain together" (Gen. 36:6,7).

The latter chapters of Genesis turn attention to Jacob's son Joseph, whose significant leadership will bring Jacob's sons into

Egypt and set the stage for the Israelite exodus recorded in the book of Exodus. Joseph is the eleventh son of Jacob but the first born of Rachel. Favoritism toward him is seen in the giving to him the "richly ornamented robe," which his brothers strip from him as they "sell him to the Ishmaelites . . . for twenty sheckels of silver." The Ishmaelites, in turn, offer him for sale to Potiphar in Egypt (Gen. 37:3,23,25,27,28,36). Under the providence of God, Potiphar entrusts "to his care everything he owned" (Gen. 39:1-5). This small beginning leads to Joseph predicting "seven years of abundance" to be followed by "seven years of famine." With sage preparations in Egypt, the consequence was "all the countries" buying "grain from Joseph . . . in all the world" (Gen. 41:27,29-31,34-36,42,47,48,50,53-57).

Joseph's brothers are sent to Egypt to buy grain twice. By maneuvering, Joseph gradually gets his father and brothers into the land of Egypt (Gen. 42:2,3,5-7,10,19,25,27,28,35; 43:1,2,8-10,25; 44:1,2,8-10,25: 45:6,20-23; 46:6; 47:5,6,11). By shrewd business acumen throughout the famine years, "Joseph bought all the land in Egypt for Pharaoh." In the years that followed, his contracts made with the Eypgtian people for grain kept them paying in the succeeding years "a fifth of the produce . . . to Pharoh" (Gen. 47:14-26). At the same time "the Israelites settled in Egypt" and "acquired property" (Gen. 47:27). Before Joseph dies and the Genesis scroll concludes, he has joined his brothers in mourning their father buried in the land of Canaan where Abraham, Isaac and Jacob will lie in the "burial place" which Abraham "had bought" (Gen. 49:30; 50:12,13).

We must conclude that, in the first book of Jesus' Bible, we find the God who made the material world become the God of Abraham, Isaac and Jacob. These chosen ones, through whom the Messiah will come to bring the spiritual riches of redemption, are also men who experienced material prosperity.

EXODUS

Israel's enrichment under Joseph is turned upside down by

the Pharaoh who subjects Jacob's sons and their families to "forced labor" under "slave masters" (Exod. 1:11,13,14; 2:23; 3:7; 5:4-6,10,13,14; 6:5,6). But God is already at work to bring them the release for which they pray. He causes Moses to be born, and guides Pharaoh's daughter to order Moses' very own mother in these words, "Take this baby and nurse him for me, and I will pay you" (Exod. 2:9). After forty years in the palace and another forty in the wilderness, Moses is called of God at the burning bush to deliver Israel. He is promised that the years of slave labor would be rewarded. God said, "I will make the Egyptians favorably disposed toward this people, so that when you leave you will not go empty handed. Every woman is to ask her neighbor and any woman living in her house for articles of silver and gold and for clothing, which you will put on your sons and daughters. And so you will plunder the Egyptians" (Exod. 3:21,22; 11:2,3; 12:35,36).

Even during the ten plagues, the destruction harmed God's enemies and not God's people. When the plague hit the livestock, God made "a distinction between the livestock of Israel and that of Egypt," so that "all the livestock of the Egyptians died, but not one animal belonging to the Israelites died" (Exod. 9:2-4,6,7). So it was when the hail fell in Egypt. The "hail struck everything in the fields — both men and animals; it beat down everything growing in the fields and stripped every tree. The only place it did not hail was the land of Goshen, where the Israelites were" (Exod. 9:25,26,31,32). After the devastating plague of locusts (Exod. 10:4,5,12,15), came that on the firstborn, which made the Egyptians ready to give all the "silver and gold" asked in order to be rid of the Israelites (Exod. 11:2,3). That looting became a topic worth singing about (Exod. 15:9).

In commemoration of the deliverance of their first-born from the death their captors suffered, Israel is given the Passover feast as a memorial. The financial implications of that celebration is that "no work at all" is to be done on the first and seventh days, placing the gaining of money in a secondary place (Exod. 12:16).

Also, allowing purchased slaves who have been circumcised to "eat" of the passover meal, has a cost to it (Exod. 12:44,45). Growing out of the rescue of Israel's firstborn, came at this time, the redemption of all firstborn males, both man or animal (Exod. 13:1,12,13; 22:30; 34:19,20).

When the exodus has become a fact, the nation is formed at Mount Sinai into God's covenant people. Many of the laws God gives, show a concern for man's welfare. The Sabbath law protects any man, animal or alien from being a slave to his work. Other regulations on the tables of stone forbid stealing and discourage coveting that which belongs to others (Exod. 20:9,10,15,17; 23:12; 31:14,15; 34:21; 35:2). Unbending rules with financial obligations are given to protect Hebrew servants from abuse (Exod. 21:2-11). Still other laws call for fairness, when personal injuries are caused (Exod. 21:16,18-22,26,27,29-36) and when property changes hands (Exod. 22:1-17). Special care is taken toward widows and orphans (Exod. 22:22-27,29). That the poor be given justice and mercy is thoroughly spelled out (Exod. 23:3,4,6,10,11). No one of God's people is to "accept a bribe" as a means of fund acquisition and no one is to "appear . . . empty handed before God in acts of adoration (Exod. 23:15). Each is counselled to "bring the best . . . to the house of the Lord" (Exod. 23:19; 34:26).

The first house of worship for this newly-formed nation was to be the portable tabernacle. Its rather plain appearance from the outside hides the splendor of the interior. Perhaps its greatest beauty radiated from the hearts of the people, who voluntarily brought the items from which it was to be constructed. "The Lord said to Moses, 'Tell the Israelites to bring me an offering. You are to receive the offering for me from each man whose heart prompts.' " Then follows a list of metals, cloths, oils and fragrances to be used in the building or its services (Exod. 25:1-7,11,13,17,18,23-29,31,36,38,39; 26:6,11,18-21,25, 29,32,37; 27:2-4,6,10,11,17,19; 28:5-9,11,13-15,17-20, 22-24,26,27,31,34,36; 30:3-5,12-17,22-25,34,35; 31:4-6,8;

35:4-9,21-29,32-34; 36:12,13,18,23-26,30,34,36,38; 37:1-4, 7,10-13,15-17,22-28; 38:1-6,8,10-12,17,19.20). Most every item, if not pure gold, was covered with gold. To worship a golden calf was "a great sin" (Exod. 32:2-4,24,31), but to use gold in the adoration of the true God was a great pleasure to Him. Each person, who was "willing and whose heart" was moved, brought the materials (Exod. 35:4,21,22) in such abundance that all had to be "restrained from bringing more, because what they already had was more than enough to do all the work" (Exod. 36:3-7).

A staggering list of the shekels and talents of gold, silver and bronze used in the construction is given in Exodus 38:24-30. If the tent of meeting is elaborate, so will be the garb of the ones ministering there (Exod. 39:2,3,6,8-13,15-17,19,20,25,30).

LEVITICUS

As the name Leviticus implies, Moses' third book of the Torah has to do with instructions to the Levites regarding their priestly ministries. We early on learn how God provided for the tribe which has been anointed for the work that related to the movable tabernacle and the permanent temple that would succeed it. A portion of the offerings were for "Aaron and his sons" (Lev. 2:3,10; 7:31-36; 10:12-15). The provision must have been adequate, for we read that some could even afford to buy "a slave with money" (Lev. 22:11).

These priests were to accept lesser prescribed sacrifices for sin from a person "that cannot afford a lamb." When the worshipper "cannot afford two doves or two young pigeons, he is to bring as an offering for his sin a tenth of an ephah of fine flour for a sin offering" (Lev. 5:7,11). The same concern for the needy will show in the laws telling harvesters to leave "the edges of the field" and some "gleanings" of every crop "for the poor and alien" (Lev. 19:9,10; 23:22).

The Levites were to see that all guilt offerings were to be made by "a ram . . . of the proper value in silver, according to the sanctuary shekel." Should the sinner intentionally fail to do as instructed, "a fifth of the value" was to be added and given to the priest (Lev. 5:15,16,18). Restitution, plus a fifth of the value, was likewise required where there has been theft or extortion (Lev. 19:11,13,15,35,36).

To keep the pursuit of things in perspective, times were set aside when no labor was allowed. There were annual feasts, like Passover (Lev. 23:7,8), Trumpets (23:25), Tabernacles (23:34-36), Pentecost (23:21) and the Day of Atonement (23:28-31) when all work was to cease. Every week there was the Sabbath of the seventh day (Lev. 23:3), every seven years the Sabbatical year (Lev. 25:4,6) and after seven cycles of seven years there was to be the Year of Jubilee (Lev. 25:10,11,13-17, 23,25-34,44-54). In the consecrated fiftieth year family property was to be returned. That being true, the sale price of a land purchase was to reflect how long the property could be useable to the purchaser. Houses in walled cities could belong permanently to the buyer and were not affected by the Year of Jubilee.

Regulations are given that discourage loans to their own poor at interest. The laws encourage the release of some of the poor at Jubilee. These by poverty had been forced into slavery (Lev. 25:35-41).

To encourage willing obedience to the rules, God promised reward for compliance and punishment for disobedience. To the responsive, God gives his word, "If you will follow my decrees . . . I will send you rain in its season, and the ground will yield its crops . . . your threshing will continue until planting, and you will eat all the food you want . . . You will be eating last year's harvest when you will have to move it out to make room for the new" (Lev. 26:3-5,10). The opposite of material abundance awaits the nation, if it disobeys. Seed planting will be "vain, because . . . enemies will eat it." The people will become "so few in number that . . . roads will be deserted." It will be so bad that "ten women will be able to bake . . . bread in one oven, and they will dole out the bread by weight" (Lev. 26:14,16,20,22,26).

The final chapter of Leviticus from beginning to end is monetary. It teaches how vows and tithes can be substituted by a money payment. In the trade-offs for human life there is variation by sex and age. A male age twenty to sixty is redeemed at "fifty shekels of silver" and a female at "thirty shekels." At ages five to twenty, the same are "twenty" and "ten" and at ages one month to five years, "five" and "three." When reaching one's sixtieth year, the values drop to "fifteen" and "ten" (Lev. 27:2-8). Itemized information is given for the redemption of animals, houses and fields (Lev. 27:9,12-28).

The climax of the last chapter is the "tithe of everything" the Israelite was required to pay. Those who worked in fields and those who worked with flocks were to know that this tenth of the increase "belongs to the Lord." That was true of the land itself (Lev. 25:23) and is true as well of all that comes from the land (Lev. 27:30-33). No farmer or shepherd is to think of himself as the owner of his field in any absolute sense. Tithing recognized a partnership with God. The payment of the tithe was considered a business transaction with God and not a gift given.

24

WHAT JESUS' BIBLE SAID ABOUT MONEY IN THE LAW (NUMBERS-DEUTERONOMY)

The longest chapter in all the Bible is in the book of Numbers. It is the seventh chapter of Numbers and contains nearly two thousand words. That trivial fact ceases to be trivial, when we learn that it has to do with money or more specifically with offerings at the dedication of the tabernacle.

Numbers covers the forty years of Israel's wandering in the wilderness and gets its name from the numbering or census taken at the beginning and end of the trek (Num. 1:3; 26:2). As in Moses' earlier writings, we read again of "the gold altar" (Num. 4:11), "the lampstand . . . made of hammered gold" (Num. 8:4) and "trumpets of hammered silver" (Num. 10:1). We hear again also of the firstborn males, for whom redemption money was to be paid. This was to be "five shekels for each one, according to the sanctuary shekel, which weighs twenty gerahs" (Num. 3:47-51; 18:15,16). Rules we have heard before are echoed here, such as full restitution for a wrong plus one fifth is to be given to the harmed party. If that person or a close relative cannot be found, the priest is to be the recipient. The regulation reads, "All the sacred contributions the Israelites bring to a priest will belong to him. Each man's sacred gifts are his own, but what he gives to the priest will belong to the priest" (Num. 5:5-10). Further repeated are the stipulations regarding the share of the offerings that is to go to the priests and Levites (Num. 18:8,9,11), especially their ownership of "all the tithes in Israel" (Num. 18:21).

That last quotation raises a problem that seeks solution. When we come to Deuteronomy (especially 26:1-11; 14:24-26), we will read of the tithe being for the worshippers, rather than the priests. That tithe was for consumption in Jerusalem at the temple by the household of the worshipper (Deut. 12:5-19; 14:22,23). The answer to the dilemma is in discovering that there were actually three tithes. The first was annual and was exclusively for the Levites, as Numbers 18 claims. A second annual tithe, established after Israel settled in the Promised Land, was that for the worshipper's consumption in the time of thanksgiving in the temple. A third tithe replaced the second each third and sixth year of the Sabbatical cycle. It had charity for the poor as its purpose.

It is the first tithe for the priests to which Numbers 18 speaks. That tithe is said to be "the Levites' . . . inheritance in return for the work they do while serving at the Tent of Meeting" (verses 21,23,24). The Levites themselves are to tithe their tithe (verse 26). All tithes are to be more than just any tenth, they are to be "the best and holiest part of everything" received (verses 28-30). It is right for the Levites to receive the tithe, for God said "it is your wages for your work" (verse 31).

As the tithes, so the gifts, are to be "freewill offerings" (Num. 15:3; 29:39). This would be a good time to open your Bible and read Numbers 7 from beginning to end, where is recorded the bringing of the offerings by the heads of families at the dedication of the tabernacle. For twelve days a tribal head in turn brought generous gifts from his people that were itemized for all to see (verses 1-83). Totaled there were freely given "twelve silver plates, twelve silver sprinkling bowls and twelve gold ladles. Each silver plate weighed a hundred and thirty shekels, and each sprinkling bowl seventy shekels. Altogether, the silver dishes weighed two thousand four hundred shekels, according to the sanctuary shekel. The twelve gold ladles filled with incense weighed ten shekels each, according to the sanctuary shekel. Altogether, the gold ladles weighed a hundred and twenty shekels." Then are listed the number of animals given for the burnt offering totalling "twenty-four bulls, sixty rams, sixty male goats and sixty male lambs" (verses 84-88).

Once the tabernacle is dedicated, the preparations for the journey are over (chapters 1-10). Numbers 10:11 to 22:1 takes us from Sinai to Moab. During the journey Moses faces rebellion from men like Korah, Dathon and Abiram, causing him to beg God not to accept their offerings saying to himself "I have not taken so much as a donkey from them" (Num. 16:15). Shortly the earth opens up to swallow not only the men and their households, but "all their possessions as well," including "everything they owned" (Num. 16:31-33). During the journey money is paid for water (Num. 20:19) and a "bronze snake . . . on a pole" is the means of rescue from snake-bite (Num. 21:9).

The third section of Numbers (chapters 22-36) tells of events in the plains of Moab. Of interest in our investigation is Balaam. The Moabite king Balak for a fee seeks to hire Balaam to put a curse on the Israelites only to find Balaam responding, "Even if Balak gave me his palace filled with silver and gold, I could not do anything great or small to go beyond the command of the Lord my God" (Num. 22:18; 24:12,13). Another set of characters, the five daughters of Zelophehad seek from Moses "property as an inheritance," leading to stipulations for the passage of the inheritance when there is no son (Num. 27:4-11). The Midianites, who contributed to the Israelite's apostasy in Moab, are plundered of their possessions (Num. 31:9,11,12,

21,22). The spoils are divided between the soldiers and the rest of the community. The loot is extensive, amounting to "675,000 sheep, 72,000 cattle, 61,000 donkeys and 32,000 women who had never slept with a man." Soldiers, citizens and Levites receive their allotment (Num. 31:25-40,43-47). The army officers, in gratitude for victory, offer to God "gold . . . armlets, bracelets, signet rings, earrings and necklaces" weighing "16,750 shekels" (Num. 31:50-54). Land is distributed fairly (Num. 32:54) and arrangement is made that by marriage "No inheritance in Israel is to pass from tribe to tribe" (Num. 36:7).

DEUTERONOMY

Laws given at intervals in Exodus, Leviticus and Numbers were rehearsed and expounded in Deuteronomy. The title of this fifth book of the Torah means second law or repetition of the law. As Israel prepares to end its nomadic life for a settled one, a restatement of the covenant and its parties, terms and promises is in order.

Deuteronomy is at core three addresses by Moses given over a period of about forty days. The time extends from the end of their forty years in the wilderness to their crossing over Jordan to possess their promised land. The first speech (Deut. 1:1-4:43) surveys their entire journey from Sinai to the Jordan under God's care and pleads for obedience to God's law. In Moses' oration, they are reminded how in passing through the territory of others they followed the Lord's instruction "to pay . . . in silver for the food . . . and the water" (Deut. 2:6). This advice they followed, saying to the people of the lands, "Sell us food to eat and water to drink for their price in silver" (Deut. 2:28). When battles ensued from every defeated city, "all the livestock and the plunder were carried off" (Deut. 3:7).

The last speech of Moses, also a brief one, is Numbers 29:1-30:20, where the covenant is renewed and enforced with promises and threats. Moses warns, "Carefully follow the terms of this covenant, so that you may prosper in everything you do" (Deut. 29:9). He reminds of the "detestable images and idols of wood and stone, of silver and gold" that were in Egypt and throughout the wilderness (Deut. 29:16,17) and promises that upon repentance from sin and idolatry "the Lord your God will restore your fortunes" (Deut. 30:2,3).

The major address by Moses covers Deuteronomy 4:44 to 28:68 and starts with the repetition of the decalogue with its commands of financial consequence — not working every day and neither stealing nor coveting — (Deut. 5:13,14,19,21). Obedience is stirred by the remembrance that God was about to fulfill his promise made to Abraham, Isaac and Jacob, giving to their seed cities they "did not build, houses filled with all kinds of good things [they] did not provide" (Deut. 6:10,11). It was the Lord's intent that they "always prosper" (Deut. 6:24) with crops . . . calves . . . and lambs" (Deut. 7:13). But the "silver and gold" of images were to be burned and not to be taken for themselves, as Moses warns, "you will be ensnared by it" (Deut. 7:25).

Gold and other possessions can become a snare and threat to the people of faith. God has brought them to a "good land," where they "will lack nothing." Should they not "praise the Lord," or should their "flocks grow large and [their] silver and gold increase and all [they] have is multiplied," there is the danger of a pride in which God could be forgotten (Deut. 8:7-10,12-14). They might even say to themselves, "My power and the strength of my hands have produced this wealth for me." They, with all other humans, needed to remember it is God "who gives . . . the ability to produce wealth" (Deut. 8:17,18). The same God expects the blessed to be a blessing — the men of means to consider others without means — for the Lord "defends the cause of the fatherless and the widow, and loves the alien, giving him food and clothing" (Deut. 10:18).

As the speech turns to the covenant people and worship (chapters 12-16), they are informed that God will choose the place where he wants them to bring their "tithes . . . and . . . freewill offerings" (Deut. 12:5,6,11,17,18,26). Seven verses are given of guidance in how tithing is to be practiced by the Israelites and how it is to be used by the priests (Deut. 14:22-29). Eleven verses explain that debts of brother Israelites are to be cancelled after seven years, as a means of eliminating poverty (Deut. 15:1-11). Prosperity is God's will for the nation. He has promised this and has added, "you will lend to many nations but will borrow from none." Let no person in the covenant "be hardhearted or tightfisted." Let each one "give generously . . . without a grudging heart." Seven verses call for releasing Hebrew slaves and then to send such away with liberal supplies and never empty hands. "Give to him as the Lord your God has blessed you," speaks Moses (Deut. 15:12-15,18). At no religious feast is a worshipper "to appear before the Lord emptyhanded: Each . . . must bring a gift in proportion to the way" he has been blessed (Deut. 16:10,16,17).

The address turns to officials. It calls on judges to refuse bribes (Deut. 16:19) and kings to "not accumulate large amounts of silver and gold" (Deut. 17:17). Priests are not to hesitate to "live on the offerings made," as "the share due the priests from the people" (Deut. 18:1,3,4,6,8).

In conducting business, no neighbor's boundary stone "set up by . . . predecessors," is to be moved (Deut. 19:14). In conducting warfare, it is permitted that "the plunder the Lord your God gives you from . . . enemies" can be used (Deut. 20:14). A beautiful woman captured could be had for a wife, but not later sold as a slave (Deut. 21:14).

A variety of laws follow. One secures the right of the first-born as heir, although the man might prefer to give it to the son of the favorite of his two wives (Deut. 21:15,16). Another fines a new husband "a hundred shekels of silver" for lying about his bride's virginity (Deut. 22:19) or fines a rapist "fifty shekels of silver for his vile deed" (Deut. 22:28,29). Still another forbids the bringing of a male or female prostitute's earnings into God's house (Deut.

23:18), while the next rule forbids usury (Deut. 23:19,20).

One law follows another and many affect both borrowers and lenders. Those who "make a vow" are not to "be slow to pay" (Deut. 23:21). Those who take security for a debt are not to "take a pair of millstones — not even the upper one — . . . because that would be taking a man's livelihood as security" (Deut. 24:6). The lender is not to enter the borrower's house to get a pledge. A poor man's cloak must be returned "by sunset so that he may sleep in it" (Deut. 24:10-13). The poor and needy, when hired, is to be paid "his wages each day before sunset, because he is poor and is counting on it. Otherwise he may cry to the Lord against you, and you will be guilty of sin" (Deut. 24:14,15). God's concern for those in poverty is further seen in the prohibition against taking "the cloak of the widow as a pledge" and in the order to leave "remains" from grain, olive and grape harvests for any in want (Deut. 24:17-22). Even animals are to be given compassionate care, so that no ox treading grain is to be muzzled (Deut. 25:4). It follows then that in dealing with men there must be total honesty in business transactions: "Do not have two different weights in your bag — one heavy, one light. Do not have two differing measures in your house — one large, one small. You must have accurate and honest weights and measures, so that you may live long in the land the Lord your God is giving you. For the Lord your God detests anyone who does these things, anyone who deals dishonestly" (Deut. 25:13-16).

Further instruction is given about both firstfruits and tithes (Deut. 26:2,10,12-14). The tithe here is the one brought to the Levites "in the third year, the year of the tithe." Its exclusive purpose was that "the alien, the fatherless and the widow . . . may eat . . . and be satisfied."

Moses' extended speech is heavy at the end with blessings and curses. The curse falls upon a man who would move "his neighbor's boundary stone," who would withhold "justice from the alien, the fatherless or the widow," or who would accept "a bribe to kill an innocent person" (Deut. 27:17,19,25). Full obedience brings promise of the Lord sending "a blessing on [their] barns and on everything [they] put [their] hands to." Ahead of them will be "abundant prosperity." They as a nation, will be made "the head, not the tail" (Deut. 28:4,5,8,11,12).

One might wish that the message by Moses would end with the fourteen verses of blessings (Deut. 28:1-14). It rather ends with fifty-four verses of warning against disobedience (Deut. 28:15-68). If the people with whom God has covenanted break the bargain, they will be "unsuccessful" in all they do and will suffer the loss of all their possessions. The verdict will be, "Because you did not serve the Lord your God joyfully and gladly in the time of prosperity, therefore in hunger and thirst, in nakedness and dire poverty, you will serve the enemies the Lord sends against you." The final sentence of the speech is, "There [in Egypt] you will offer yourselves for sale to your enemies as male and female slaves, but no one will buy you" (Deut. 28:15,17,18,29-31,33,43,44,46-48,68).

25

WHAT JESUS' BIBLE SAID ABOUT MONEY IN THE PROPHETS (FORMER PROPHETS)

JOSHUA

In the Jewish arrangement of the Scriptural writings the Law of Moses is followed by the Prophets. The Former Prophets (Joshua, Judges, Samuel and Kings) precede the Latter Prophets (Isaiah, Jeremiah, Ezekiel and the Twelve). The book of Joshua tells the conquest of Canaan. The story begins with Joshua being promised, "You will be prosperous and successful" if you do "not let this Book of the Law depart from your mouth." He is assured of victory in taking "possession of the land" as God's gift (Josh. 1:8,11), Toward the end of the account, the Eastern tribes are sent beyond the Jordan with the blessing, "Return to your homes with your great wealth — with large herds of livestock, with silver, gold, bronze and iron, and a great quantity of clothing — and divide with your brothers the plunder from your enemies" (Josh. 22:8).

In between the opening promise and the concluding fulfillment are accounts of plundering (Josh. 8:27; 11:14) and instruction that "all the silver and gold and articles of bronze and iron are sacred to the Lord" and hence are to go into his treasury" (Josh. 6:19,24). The latter regulation is disobeyed by Achan to whom the temptation of wealth was more than he could handle. He confesses to Joshua, before his stoning, "When I saw in the plunder a beautiful robe from Babylonia, two hundred shekels of silver and a wedge of gold weighing fifty shekels, I coveted them" (Josh. 7:21,22,24).

JUDGES

The book of Judges covers the earliest three centuries in the Promised Land when God raised up deliverers or judges to meet his people's needs. Plundering of others continues (Jdgs. 2:14), but that no king can plunder Israel is a topic for singing in the song of Deborah and Barak (Jdgs. 5:19,30). Not all the accumulation of plunder was for the good. Gideon, after the routing of the Midianites, asked each Israelite for "an earring from [his] share of the plunder." The weight of them all "came to seventeen hundred shekels, not counting the ornaments, the pendants and the purple garments worn by the kings of Midian or the chains that were on their camel's necks." The evil result of the amassed riches was that Gideon "made the gold into an ephod, which he placed in Ophrah, his town." The consequence of that act was all Israel worshipped it instead of God and "it became a snare to Gideon and his family" (Jdgs. 8:21,24-27). To name a few others who succumbed to the lure of wealth, we mention Abimilech who used "seventy silver shekels from the temple of Baal-Berish . . . to hire reckless adventurers" (Jdgs. 9:3,4) and Micah's mother who had a silversmith make an idol of "eleven hundred shekels of silver" (Jdgs. 17:1-4,10; 18:4,7).

Two well-known persons, whose stories are told in Judges,

are Samson and Delilah. Garments of value are to change hands from Samson to thirty Philistine companions at his marriage feast to a woman of Timnah if they can solve his riddle (Jdgs. 14:12,13,15,19). Delilah later is offered "eleven hundred shekels of silver" by each of the five Philistine tyrants, if she will find for them the secret of Samson's strength (Jdgs. 16:5,18,21).

SAMUEL

The two books of Samuel and the two books of Kings give the history of the rise and fall of a nation. 1 and 2 Samuel cover roughly a hundred years and 1 and 2 Kings the following four centuries. Samuel, who anoints Israel's first kings, Saul and David, gives his name to the first two of the four historical records. His mother's prayer rejoices in the Lord who "sends poverty and wealth," delighting to see her God raise "the poor from the dust" and lift "the needy from the ash heap" (1 Sam. 2:5,7,8). Samuel in the judgment of all never "cheated" or "accepted a bribe" (1 Sam. 12:3,4), but his sons as judges are a disappointment. They are said to have "turned aside after dishonest gain and accepted bribes" (1 Sam. 8:3), faring no better than Eli's sons (1 Sam. 2:36). Samuel is well aware that the clamor for a king may result in deeper disappointment for a divine theocracy changing to a human monarchy. Taxation and enslavement could be the price (1 Sam. 8:14-17).

Saul, the one to be Israel's first king, comes in contact with Samuel. He will anoint him by a strange circumstance. Having lost some donkeys in his care, Saul seeks out the prophet and makes an offer to him as a "seer" to show him what path to follow. He suggests "a quarter of a shekel of silver" for the fee (1 Sam. 9:7,8). During his reign as king, we find Saul paying out money for the sharpening of crude weapons. "The price was two thirds of a shekel for the sharpening of plowshares and mattocks, and a third of a shekel for sharpening forks and axes and for repointing goads" (1 Sam. 13:20,21). Saul found satisfaction in the plunder of the Philistines against the counsel of God. This disobedience lead to his replacement (1 Sam. 14:32,36; 15:19,21). The high price the Philistines had to pay for taking the ark as a trophy is told in 1 Samuel 6 (especially note verses 4,8,11,15,17 and 18).

While Saul still lives, David shows himself worthy of the future kingship by the slaying of Goliath. Saul offers "great wealth" to whoever kills the giant. But, more than that, he extends the exemption of "his father's family from taxes in Israel" (1 Sam. 17:5,6,25). Saul offers his daughter Michal to David for wife at "no other price . . . than a hundred Philistine foreskins," which he paid in duplicate (1 Sam. 18:25,27). He later marries Abigail. Her "very wealthy" husband Nabel was saved from David's anger by her "gift" of appeasement, which is described as "two hundred loaves of bread, two skins of wine, five dressed sheep, five seahs of roasted grain, a hundred cakes of raisins and two hundred cakes of pressed figs." Her marriage to David follows her husband's death leaving possible credence to the theory that a man's heart can be reached by way of his stomach. The accumulation of riches by David is often accounted for by his practice of plundering enemies (1 Sam. 27:9; 30:18-20,22,26). With the booty, the king ingratiates himself to tribal leaders assuring their future loyalty.

The heart of David's reign is the burden of 2 Samuel. We hear him lament his predecessor who clothed the people "in scarlet and finery . . . with ornaments of gold" (2 Sam. 1:24 cp. 13:18) and the "richly ornamented robe" of Tamar. We hear him relate victories that resulted in great quantities of plunder "of silver and gold and bronze." These he dedicated "to the Lord, as he had done with the silver and gold from all the nations he had subdued" (2 Sam. 8:7-12, see also 12:29,30). We hear him lament the slaughter of Gibeonites by his predecessor. This act he believes to be behind the three year famine his land was suffering. The offer of making amends brings the Gibeonite response, "We have no right to demand silver or gold from Saul or his family" (2 Sam. 21:1,4). We hear him offer to buy Araunah's threshing floor and refuse to take it for an outright gift for it was to serve as an altar. His final and well-remembered words are, "I insist on paying you for it. I will not sacrifice to the Lord my God burnt offerings that cost me nothing" (2 Sam. 24:21,24).

The best remembered incident in the book of 2 Samuel is David's sin with Bathsheba leading to the king's causing the death of Uriah her husband. This black incident brought the rebuke of Nathan's parable about a rich man and a poor man. To entertain a traveler, the rich man took the single ewe lamb from a poor man for the meal rather than use one from the abundance of his own sheep or cattle. Before David grasped the truth that the villain in the story was himself, he blurted out that the guilty party deserved to die and ought to first "pay for the lamb four times over" (2 Sam. 11:8; 12:1-6). The other money passages in 2 Samuel show money being used to hire mercenaries (10:6), buy information from informants (2 Sam. 18:22) and acquire hit men (2 Sam. 18:12).

KINGS

1 Kings presents the glory of Solomon's reign. At Gibeon, Solomon had received in a dream an offer from God. He could ask for whatever he wanted. Since he chose wisdom above "wealth" for himself, God moreover gave what he did not ask "both riches and honor" (1 Kgs. 3:10,13). The fulfillment of that promise was seen in his rule "over all the kingdoms from the River [the Euphrates] to the land of the Philistines, as far as the borders of Egypt. These countries brought tribute and were Solomon's subjects all his life" (1 Kgs. 4:13,21).

The glory that was Solomon's is reflected in the magnificent temple and palace he built. He ordered Hiram to cut cedars of Lebanon for him, offering to pay the workmen "whatever wages

[he] set." For the logs Solomon paid generous amounts in "wheat" and "olive oil." He did ths "year after year" (1 Kgs. 5:6,11). Each item in the inner sanctuary of the temple was overlaid with "pure gold" (1 Kgs. 6:20-22,28,30,32,35). Fine bronze work was in the temple's furnishings (1 Kgs. 7:14-16,27,30) along with golden ones (1 Kgs. 7:48-51).

At the temple's dedication, Solomon made a costly sacrifice of "twenty-two thousand cattle and a hundred and twenty thousand sheep and goats" (1 Kgs. 8:62-64). Hiram, king of Tyre, who had "supplied him with all the cedar and pine and gold he wanted" was further paid by the gift of "twenty towns in Galilee" (1 Kgs. 9:11,14). The Queen of Sheba had heard of Solomon's splendor but was overwhelmed with what she saw (1 Kgs. 10:2,10,11). When your eyes read the sixteen verse description of his wealth (1 Kgs. 10:14-29), you too will find it mind-boggling.

The rest of I Kings mentions several individuals who use money for a variety of purposes. King Jeroboam tries to stop a man of God on his mission with a fee. It was to no avail, as the prophet responded, "Even if you were to give me half of your possessions, I would not go with you" (1 Kings 13:7,8). King Shishak of Egypt sacks Jerusalem carrying off "the treasures of the temple . . . including all the gold shields Solomon had made" (1 Kgs. 14:25-27). King Asa of Judah purchased help from Syria with gifts of "silver and gold" (1 Kgs. 15:15,18,19). King Omri of Israel buys Samaria for his capital for "two talents of silver" (1 Kgs. 16:23,24). King Ben-Hadad of Aram demands Ahab to submit and further requires all Israel's "gold and silver" (1 Kgs. 20:3-7). When defeated in battle, Ben-Hadad offers not on-ly to return all captured cities, but he further tells Ahab "You may set up your own market areas in Damascus" (1 Kgs. 20:34). This Ahab, "who sold himself to do evil in the eyes of the Lord," tries to force the sale of Naboth's vineyard and brings about Elijah's judgment (1 Kgs. 21:2,6,15,16,28,20,25). King Jehoshaphat of Judah invests in "a fleet of trading ships to go to Ophir for gold, but they never set sail" (1 Kgs. 22:48).

Early in 2 Kings we read of the Syrian commander-in-chief, Naaman, being cured of leprosy through the prophet Elisha. In seeking the prophet's aid, Naaman brings "ten talents of silver, six thousand shekels of gold and ten sets of clothing" (2 Kgs. 5:5). Whatever the value set on the clothing, the silver and gold offered would be an impressive amount estimated at $80,000. God's prophet refuses any money at all, but Gehazi, his servant, greedily asks "a talent of silver." "Two talents" are freely given by the cured Syrian. Elisha's rebuke contains the question, "Is this the time to take money, or to accept clothes, olive groves, vineyards, flocks, herds, or manservants and maidservants?" The rebuke also includes the curse of receiving Naaman's leprosy (2 Kgs. 5:15,16,20,22,23,26,27).

Elisha's being offered remuneration for his ministry continues. King Ben-Hadad of Aram, when ill, offered through his servant Hazael "a gift [of] forty camel-loads of all the finest wares" for information as to his chances of survival (2 Kgs. 8:8-9). Ben-Hadad is the king whose extended siege of Samaria lasted so long that it caused famine so great "that a donkey's head sold for eighty shekels of silver, and a fourth of a cab of seed pods for five shekels" (2 Kgs. 6:25; 7:1,8,16,18).

During the 2 Kings account of the divided Kingdom, from eighty years after the division to the captivities — of Israel by Assyria and Judah by Babylon — there are instances of plunder, taxation and temple repair. There was extensive temple repair under king Josiah (2 Kgs. 12:4,5,7-16,18). It is pleasing to read that "the money brought into the temple was not spent for making silver basins, with trimmers, sprinkling bowls, trumpets or any other articles of gold or silver for the temple of the Lord; it was paid to the workmen, who used it to repair the temple. They did not require an accounting from those to whom they gave the money to pay the workers, because they acted with complete honesty." The stories of plunder are thorough (2 Kgs. 14:14; 15:19,20; 16:8,14-18; 17:3,4,20; 18:14-16; 20:12,13,15-17;

21:14; 23:33,35), meaning that temple repair will be necessary again under king Josiah (2 Kgs. 22:4-7,9).

The unknown writer of 1 and 2 Kings has taken his readers from the golden age of Solomon to the destruction of Jerusalem in 587 BC. The account of a nation, from stability to complete collapse and deportation, carries the moral that prosperity stems from following God's way and judgment flows when God is forgotten. The sad words near the end of the book are that "Nebuchadnezzar removed all the treasures from the temple of the Lord and from the royal palace, and took away all the gold articles that Solomon king of Israel had made for the temple of the Lord" (2 Kgs. 24:13,14; 25:13-17). After thirty-seven years of exile there is seen a small glimmer of future hope. The new king in Babylon puts the exiled king of Judah on a daily "regular allowance" as long as he should live (2 Kgs. 25:30).

26

WHAT JESUS' BIBLE SAID ABOUT MONEY IN THE PROPHETS (MAJOR PROPHETS)

ISAIAH

Isaiah heads the list of the major prophets. He is sensitive to Judah's emptiness before God, which foreshadows her judgment. Her rituals are not hiding her wretchedness. In Isaiah's discourses from chapters 1-12, he cries out for God to the nation, "Stop bringing meaningless offerings" (Isa. 1:13). He calls for them to "seek justice, encourage the oppressed. Defend the cause of the fatherless, plead the case of the widow" (Isa. 1:17).

Because the rulers have become "companions of thieves . . . and chase after gifts," they neglect their mission of defending the weak (Isa. 1:22,23). The judgment of God will turn the people of the land "full of silver and gold" and endless "treasures" (Isa. 2:7) into a populace crying out, "I have no food or clothing in my house" (Isa. 4:7). Why the change from God's blessing of wealth to his condemnation to penury? The Lord responds, "the plunder of the poor is in your houses. What do you mean by crushing my people and grinding the faces of the poor?" (Isa. 3:14,15). What lies ahead for a people tight-fisted toward the needy? "In that day the Land will snatch away their finery, the bangles and headbands and crescent necklaces, the earrings and bracelets and veils, the headdresses and ankle chains and sashes, the perfume bottles and charms, the signet rings and nose rings, the fine robes and capes and cloaks, the purses and mirrors and the linen garments and tiaras and shawls. Instead of fragrance there will be a stench; instead of a sash, a rope; instead of well-dressed hair, baldness; instead of fine clothing, sackcloth; instead of beauty, branding" (Isa. 3:18-24).

The people's "idols of silver and gold, which they made to worship" (Isa. 2:20), will be of no help. Their "house to house" and "field to field" holdings "until no space [was] left" (Isa. 5:8-10), will not keep "men of rank" from "dying of hunger" or the masses from being "parched with thirst" (Isa. 5:13). Their failure to use their wealth compassionately toward the needy, promises "in that day, in every place where there were a thousand vines' worth and thousand silver shekels, there will be only briars and thorns" (Isa. 7:23). The clenched fist of greediness will become a beggar's open hand reaching out in distress and hunger (Isa. 8:21) caused by the king of Assyria's plundering (Isa. 8:4; 10:1-3,6,13). God expects the standards of justice and mercy from his covenant people. He will accept no less from others or similar judgment will fall eventually on them (Isa. 11:14).

Judgment is announced in Isaiah 13-23 against the surrounding nations, in chapters 24-27 against the entire world and in chapters 28-32 especially against Egypt and Syria. Concerning Babylon it is predicted that men will be "scarcer than pure gold," as they face the "Medes, who do not care for silver and have no delight in gold." That devastation will mark her "luxurious palaces" (Isa. 13:12,17,22). Concerning the Philistines "famine" is foreseen (Isa. 14:30). Regarding Moab "the wealth they have acquired and stored up" is visualized being carried away (Isa.

15:7). In Egypt, how will it be? "Every sown field along the Nile will become parched, will blow away and be no more. The fishermen will groan and lament, all who cast hooks in the Nile; those who throw nets in the water will pine away. Those who work with flax will despair, the weavers of fine linen will lose hope. The workers in cloth will be dejected, and all the wage earners will be sick at heart" (Isa. 19:7-10). It will be no better for the people of Tyre (Isa. 23:1-3) nor for the rest of the earth (Isa. 24:1-2).

While man is to face condemnation for his lack of humanitarian kindness, the Lord is to be praised for he has "been a refuge for the poor, a refuge for the needy in his distress" (Isa. 25:4). Worshippers will sing that God "humbles those who dwell on high, he lays the lofty city low . . . feet trample it down — the feet of the oppressed, the footsteps of the poor" (Isa. 26:5,6; 29:19). When judgment does strike, gold and silver idols will be proven to be of no aid and will be thrown away "like a menstrual cloth" (Isa. 30:22; 31:7).

One day there will be a golden age under God himself, when the plunder of the nations wil be erased and "a rich store of salvation and wisdom and knowledge" shall be enjoyed by those who have "the fear of the Lord" which "is the key to this treasure" (Isa. 33:4-6,15,18,19). In that future day "an abundance of spoils will be divided and even the lame will carry off plunder" (Isa. 33:23).

In the final twenty-six chapters of Isaiah, we catch the spirit of undying hope in the heart of the exiles in Babylon. The loss in the days of Hezekiah, so that "nothing" was "left" (Isa. 36:16; 39:1,2,4-6), is seen to be because of idolatry (Isa. 40:19,20; 41:7; 44:9,11; 46:6) and sin. When the question is asked, "Who handed Jacob over to become loot, and Israel to the plunderers," the answer is confident, "Was is not the Lord against whom we have sinned?" (Isa. 42:22-24; 50:1). The bitter fires of the adverse captivity will refine Israel, "though not as silver" (Isa. 48:10) and the story will not end until she is redeemed "without money" (Isa. 52:1,3).

It was comfort indeed for the captives to be told of a future for their "afflicted city," when the "stones of turquoise . . . foundations with sapphires . . . battlements of rubies . . . gates of sparkling jewels and . . . walls of precious stones" would be part of their New Jerusalem (Isa. 54:11,12). Into that city will come "the wealth on the seas . . . the riches of the nations" (Isa. 60:5-7,9,11,17; 61:6-8,10; 63:1; 65:21,22; 66:12). Seen through Christian eyes, this glorious future is seen to come through the ministry of God's suffering servant. He, as substitutionary sacrifice for man's transgressions, "was assigned a grave with the wicked and with the rich in his death" (Isa. 53:9). His invitation is to "come with neither money or cost" and to "delight in the richest fare," which God offers to any who want to be in "everlasting covenant" with him (Isa. 55:1-3). Those who seek their "own way" or "gain" or are filled with "sinful greed," need not apply (Isa. 56:11; 57:17).

JEREMIAH

Isaiah spoke to his nation under the threat of Assyria. Jeremiah about 100 years later speaks out in Jerusalem, as it faces the invasion of Babylon. The prophet weeps as he recalls the Jews' glorious exodus from Egypt now becoming exile to Babylon. It is a one hundred and eighty degree turn from Israel's reception of "a fertile land . . . and rich produce" to experiencing bitter "plunder" (Jer. 2:7,14). The reason? God replies, "Does a maiden forget her jewelry, a bride her wedding ornaments? Yet my people have forgotten me, days without number" (Jer. 2:32). To forget God is to forget his concern for the poor (Jer. 2:34; 5:4,27-29; 7:6-7; 20:13; 22:16; 49:11). To not remember God is to not remember his holiness. Can a righteous God send "showers" on a nation that has "defiled the land with . . . prostitution and wickedness" (Jer. 3:2,3) or bless a populace that "from the least to the greatest all are greedy for gain; prophets and priests alike" (Jer. 6:12,13,15; 8:9,10,13; 22:15,17-19)? To push the true God aside in one's mind in order to make room for gold and silver idols, is to fall out of God's grace (Jer. 3:23; 10:3,4,9,14; 51:17). It is to become "rejected silver" by the Refiners of souls (Jer. 6:30).

To "dress . . . in scarlet and put on jewels of gold" will not hide Judah's dreadful condition (Jer. 4:30). God laments, "I supplied all their needs, yet they committed adultery and thronged to the houses of prostitutes. They are well-fed, lusty stallions, each neighing for another man's wife" (Jer. 5:7,8). Their lowest act is prostituting temple worship, making the house of God a "den of robbers" by the way they gain their possessions (Jer. 7:9-11). Jeremiah compares those who "gain riches by unjust means" to "a partridge that hatches eggs it did not lay" (Jer. 17:11). He warns, "Woe to him who builds his palace by unrighteousness, his upper rooms by injustice, making his countrymen work for nothing, not paying them for their labor" (Jer. 22:13). The truly wise "rich man" will not "boast of his riches," but will boast in knowing God's "kindness, justice and righteousness on earth" (Jer. 9:23,24).

The Book of Jeremiah is filled with the awareness of "famine" (Jer. 11:22; 14:12,15,16,18; 15:2,13; 16:4; 18:21; 21:7,9; 24:10; 27:8,13; 29:17,18; 32:24,36; 42:13,16,22; 44:27; 52:6). It also knows of "plunder" (Jer. 17:3,6; 20:5; 30:16; 49:9,29,32; 50:37; 51:13; 52:15-20), including that by Nebuchadnezzar king of Babylon that made of Judah "an empty jar" (Jeremiah 51:34). The prophet is aware of "disaster" of every kind (Jeremiah 39:16). But the book also knows consolation. Even in Babylon the exiles can "build houses and . . . plant gardens," for the Lord promises, "I have for you . . . plans to prosper you and not to harm you, plans to give you hope and a future" (Jer. 29:4,7,11,28; 31:5,12,14). Jeremiah himself buys a field in Jerusalem to express hope in their future return. The business transaction is described at length (Jer. 32:7-12,14,15,25,43,44; 33:11,13,26).

The relationship between prosperity and security and keeping covenant with God reverberates across the lengthy Book of Jeremiah. The Babylonian captivity would never have happened, if Judah had been true to its commitments to the Lord.

EZEKIEL

Ezekiel, a young contemporary of Jeremiah, preaches to the captives in Babylon a similar message to what Jeremiah had preached in Jerusalem. Ezekiel first paints the black picture of Israel's sins and God's judgment (chapters 1-24). Then he draws the dark picture of the surrounding nations' sins and their judgment (chapters 25-32). Finally he sketches the bright scenes of Israel's restoration (chapters 33-48).

Ezekiel prophesies "famine" (Ezek. 4:10; 5:12; 6:11; 7:15; 12:16; 14:21) and "plunder" (Ezek. 7:21; 23:26,40; 25:7; 26:12; 29:19; 34:8; 36:5; 38:12,13) until nothing will be left — "no wealth, nothing of value." It will neither be a time for "the buyer [to] rejoice nor the seller [to] grieve," for "the seller will not recover the land he has sold as long as both of them live" (Ezek. 7:11-13). In that hour "they will throw their silver into the streets, and their gold will be an unclean thing. Their silver and gold will not be able to save them in the day of the Lord's wrath." This wealth of theirs is said to have "made them stumble into sin" and to have made them "proud of their beautiful jewelry" (Ezek. 7:19-21).

An itemized list of Judah's sins that relate to money would include:

(1)   sorcery for the profit of "a few handfuls of barley and scraps of bread" (Ezek. 13:19),
(2)   male idols for prostitution (Ezek. 16:17,29,31,33, 34,36,39,41),
(3)   greed (Ezek. 16:27),

(4)   dishonest business practices (Ezek. 45:10-12; 28:18),

(5)   the practice of taking usury and "excessive interest" to "make unjust gain from . . . neighbors" (Ezek. 22:12,13,19,20,25,27) and

(6)   lack of concern for the poor (Ezek. 16:49; 22:7,29).

This sin with the previous one is highlighted as Jeremiah defines a "righteous man" in contrast to a "violent son." The righteous "does not oppress anyone, but returns what he took in pledge for a loan. He does not commit robbery but gives his food to the hungry and provides clothing for the naked. He does not lend at usury or take excessive interest." The violent son "oppresses the poor and needy. He commits robbery. He does not return what he took in pledge. . . . He lends at usury and takes excesive interest" (Ezek. 18:7,8,12,13,16-18).

Guilty of such sins, judgment must come from the hand of God. It was that very hand that earlier had dressed them "in fine linen . . . costly garments," adorned them with "jewelry . . . bracelets . . . necklace . . . earrings . . . crown . . . fine linen and costly fabric and embroidered cloth" (Ezek. 16:10-13). It is that same hand that in the future will guide them back to Zion "accept them" and their "choice gifts" (Ezek. 20:39,40).

The blessing of the coming restoration is the theme of Ezekiel's final fifteen chapters. In that day the fields will be fruitful (Ezek. 34:27,29; 36:29,30,34,35; 47:12), the streams filled with fish (Ezek. 47:9,10) and the people will have security (Ezek. 34:28). At that time property holdings will be adequately allotted to all (Ezek. 45:1,4,5; 46:16-18; 47:13,14,22,23; 48:14,17,19; 28:25,26). Such a destiny awaits people for whom the Lord is their greatest wealth. An opposite scene follows. An elaborate description of people, who gain the whole world and lose their souls, is given in the dirge against Tyre. Tyre was the outstanding example of trade and commerce. All caravan routes came to Tyre and freighted ships filled her harbor. Ezekiel describes the city's glory in 27:1-24 and its destruction in 27:25-28:19.

27

WHAT JESUS' BIBLE SAID ABOUT MONEY IN THE PROPHETS (MINOR PROPHETS)

HOSEA

Of the twelve minor prophets that conclude the section of the Hebrew Bible called "the Prophets (Luke 24:44), Hosea heads the list, as Malachi concludes it. To term them "minor prophets" is not to speak of their importance but only of their size in comparison to the lengthy works of Isaiah, Jeremiah and Ezekiel.

Hosea was one of the eighth century prophets. He did his preaching to Israel in the last period of the Northern Kingdom. The first three chapters tell the domestic tragedy of the prophet himself that is illustrative of the deathless love of God for Israel in spite of that nation's unfaithfulness to her covenant promises. The rest of the work, chapters 4-14, contain separate oracle-poems based on the experience of Hosea with the infidelity of his wife Gomer and its application to the wayward nation that can either suffer penalty or confess her sin and experience God's grace.

Israel has acted like a prostitute. She breaks God's heart, but is thinking only of the wealth that would be coming to her as she sold herself. Her thoughts are, "I will go after my lovers, who give me my food and my water, my wool and my linen, my oil and my drink" (Hosea 2:5). Like a harlot decking "herself with rings and jewelry" (Hosea 2:13), she sells herself "among the nations" (Hosea 8:10), for she loves "the wages of a prostitute at every threshing floor" (Hosea 9:1).

Hosea's wife Gomer and God's wife Israel were blind to the provisions their true covenant-partner had provided. The crushed husband laments, "She has not acknowledged that I was the one who gave her the grain, the new wine and oil, who lavished on her the silver and gold — which they used for Baal" (Hosea 2:8). For Israel to turn from the monotheism of the past, and "with their silver and gold . . . make idols for themselves" (Hosea 8:4), is spiritual adultery at its worst.

How can there be anything but judgment ahead? "Even if they escape from destruction . . . their treasures of silver will be taken over by briars" (Hosea 9:6) and every "storehouse will be plundered of all its treasures" (Hosea 13:15).

There is but one way out. To continue in spiritual adultery leads only to destruction. That way of doom is to use "dishonest scales" and to "defraud." The road to disaster is to boast, "I am very rich; I have become wealthy. With all my wealth they will not find in me any iniquity or sin" (Hosea 12:7,8). The single channel of escape is to remember the love of God. Recall that Jacob "served to get a wife and to pay for her he tended sheep" (Hosea 12:12). Call to mind that it was the God of Israel that instructed Hosea, "Go, show your love to your wife again, though she is . . . an adultress" (Hosea 3:1). As the offended husband bought Gomer back for "fifteen shekels of silver and about a homer and a lethek of barley" (Hosea 3:2), God stands ready to forgive wayward Israel, if she only will repent.

JOEL

We know next to nothing about the prophet Joel. We cannot be certain even regarding when he lived. But there is left no doubt that God's justice and mercy are to be trusted. The locust plague that called for fasting and prayer, also forewarned of the coming day of the Lord and foretold an outpouring of God's Spirit that would lead to a harvest of souls. Very little in Joel deals with our theme of money in the Bible, but what it does say is consistent with the rest of the Scripture.

After corrective judgment that leads to repentance, better days will come when the disciplined people of God "will have plenty to eat" (Joel 2:26). While mercy ever is available to the penitent, judgment ever is certain for the wicked. Let "Tyre and Sidon and all . . . regions of Philistia" know that condemnation will fall on the heads of those to whom the Lord speaks, "You took my silver and my gold and carried off my finest treasures to your temple" (Joel 3:4-8). Can God let go unpunished a people concerning whom he can say they "cast lots for my people and traded boys for prostitutes; they sold girls for wine that they might drink" (Joel 3:3)?

AMOS

The message of Amos, given to Israel in the Eighth Century BC, is relevant reading to all affluent nations in the Twentieth Century AD. This contemporary of Hosea points to the rottenness that is hidden beneath the affluence of the nations. The corruption of the surrounding pagan peoples is equally prevalent in God's Israel. Is Gaza guilty of selling captives (Amos 1:6)? Does Tyre commit the same crime (Amos 1:9)? Can the Ammonites be charged with extending their borders at the price of ripping "open the pregnant women of Gilead" (Amos 1:13)? Shall the Lord wink at equal iniquities in his own nation? His people "sell the righteous for silver, and the needy for a pair of sandals. They trample on the heads of the poor as upon the dust of the ground. . . . They lie down beside every altar on garments taken in pledge" (Amos 2:6-8). "They do not know how to do right . . . who hoard plunder and loot in their fortresses" (Amos 3:10).

What should God do to a nation that wears his name and yet has even "women who oppress the poor and crush the needy" (Amos 4:1)? What shall be the Almighty's attitude to men who "trample on the poor and force him to give . . . grain" (Amos 5:11)? Or, what shall the Holy One of Israel feel toward a people that "oppress the righteous and take bribes and . . . deprive the poor of justice in the courts" (Amos 5:12)? Can God remain God and not judge those "who trample the needy and do away with the poor of the land" (Amos 8:4)?

The answer of Amos lays bare the masked religionist, who deceives himself into thinking that religious ceremonies on a Holy Day hides his activities on a work day. In satire, Amos has the Lord declare: "Go to Bethel and sin. . . . Bring . . . your tithes every three years . . . brag about your freewill offerings — boast about them, you Israelites, for this is what you love to do" (Amos 4:4,5). Let the truth be known, says God, "Even though you bring me burnt offerings and grain offerings, I will not accept them" (Amos 5:22). The Omniscient God of heaven is aware of the thoughts in the mind of every formalist. Such worship goes through the right rituals at the desired locations. He attends feasts on the correct days. Yet he has his heart wholly on the business opportunities of the next day. Instead of hearing a sincere prayer of gratitude from the man's lips, the ears of God hear the worshipper's heart ask, "When will the New Moon be over that we may sell grain, and the Sabbath be ended that we may market wheat? — skimping the measure, boosting the price and cheating with dishonest scales, buying the poor with silver and the needy for a pair of sandals, selling even the sweepings with the wheat" (Amos 8:5,6).

OBADIAH, JONAH, MICAH

Obadiah, the shortest of all the Old Testament books, announces the judgment of Edom. That people had placed all confidence in their amassed wealth and had shown no concern for their brother Jacob's plight. They "stood aloof while strangers carried off his wealth" (verse 11). Things will soon be different for "Esau will be ransacked, his hidden treasures pillaged." (verses 5,6). At that time, however, Jacob is not to "seize their wealth in the day of their disaster" (verse 13). The story about the prophet Jonah — other than the line saying he had paid "the fare" for his boat ride — has no information on the issue of a man and his money (Jonah 1:3). With Micah it is otherwise. This so-called Minor Prophet is in the major leagues when it comes to ethical concerns. As an eighth century contemporary of Hosea, Amos and Isaiah, Micah denounces Samaria and Jerusalem for their ill-gotten gain and their lack of compassion for the oppressed.

Samaria is to become "a heap of rubble" for moral reasons. She has "gathered her gifts from the wages of prostitutes" (Micah 1:7). Like an incurable venereal disease spreading now even to Jerusalem, "the beginning of sin to the daughters of Zion" has resulted in a situation of no hope. Judah can write off its earlier possession to Assyria for Judah will "give parting gifts to Moresheth Gath" (Micah 1:13,14), meaning Judah will be obliged to relinquish that which was once her possesssion, as if it were a wedding gift.

Contaminated by heathen practices round about, now Jerusalem shows the infection of greed. The prophet cries out, "Woe to those who plan iniquity, to those who plot evil on their beds! At morning's light they carry it out because it is in their power to do it. They covet fields and seize them, and houses, and take them. They defraud a man of his home, a fellowman of his inheritance" (Micah 2:1,2). God will neither forget their "ill-gotten treasures" nor their "short ephah, which is accursed" (Micah 6:10). He inquires, "Shall I acquit a man with dishonest scales, with a bag of false weights?" (Micah 6:11). He informs the "rich men" that are "violent," "you will store up but save nothing, because what you save I will give to the sword" (Micah 6:12,14).

As guilty as the rulers are in demanding "gifts" and judges in accepting "bribes" (Micah 7:3); or as culpable as the robber gangs are "who strip off the rich robe from those who pass by without a care" (Micah 2:8); the false prophets are worse. They deceive the people for a price. God laments such pseudo-teachers, when he ironically says, "If a liar and deceiver comes and says, 'I will prophecy for you plenty of wine and beer,' he would be just the prophesy for you plenty of wine and beer,' he would be just the prophets who lead my people astray, if one feeds them, they proclaim 'peace' " (Micah 3:5). If God were describing modern clergymen, could he ever in any place or time say, "Her leaders judge for a bribe, her priests teach for a price, and her prophets tell fortunes for money" (Micah 3:11)?

Such injustice brings this "mournful song: 'We are utterly ruined; my people's possession is divided up. He takes it from me! He assigns our fields to traitors' " (Micah 2:4). Lest Micah's truthful judgment lead to despair, he offers, like all true messengers of heaven, the repentance option. At repentance would come better days, when "every man will sit under his own vine and under his own fig tree" (Micah 4:4) and the "ill-gotten gains" and "wealth" of evil nations will be devoted "to the Lord of all the earth" (Micah 4:13).

NAHUM

The graphic poetry of Nahum predicts the destruction of Assyria's capital Ninevah, as Jonah, about one hundred fifty years earlier, had told of the city's reprieve. Ninevah has "increased the number of . . . merchants till they are more than the stars of the sky, but like locusts they strip the land and then fly away" (Nahum 3:16). The very ctiy that has despoiled her captors is now become rich spoil for others. The order is: "Plunder the silver! Plunder the gold! The supply is endless, the wealth from all its treasures! She is pillaged, plundered, stripped!" (Nahum 2:9,10). The moral God of Israel predestines that uninhibited militarism and uncaring materialism go down. He wills that ethical people, like "Jacob" that has been laid waste, experience a restoration "like the splendor of Israel" (Nahum 2:2).

HABAKKUK

Habakkuk wrestles with the problem of theodicy in his time as have men of every time. Why does the righteous God over all allow such injustice as is evident most anywhere one turns? Here is a man "who piles up stolen goods and makes himself wealthy by extortion!" (Hab. 2:6). There is a nation that has "plundered many nations" (Hab. 2:8). Over there is a person "who builds his realm by unjust gain" (Hab. 2:9). Next to them is a people "who builds a city with bloodshed and establishes a town by crime!" (Hab. 2:12).

Fidelity to God will bring its own reward. Let believers trust in God and find strength in him. In the meantime, learn from centuries of history that those who "have plundered many nations" find that "the peoples who are left will plunder" them (Hab. 2:8). God is sovereign and there appears to be moral order in the universe. Even when visible signs of God's presence may seem dim, Habakkuk says, "Though the fig tree does not bud and there are no grapes on the vines, though the olive crop fails and the fields produce no food, though there are no sheep in the pen and no cattle in the stalls, yet I will rejoice in the Lord, I will be joyful in God my Savior. The Sovereign Lord is my strength; he makes my feet like the feet of a deer, he enables me to go on the heights" (Hab. 3:17-19). Do the wicked appear to swallow up the righteous? Not in the end. The "righteous will live by his faith" (Hab. 2:4).

ZEPHANIAH

The ethical idealism of the prophets is continued in Zephaniah. He, too, knows that God has a conscience and men ought to so live as persons who will give account of their actions to their Maker on the final day. This coming day of the Lord is nearing. His words "on that day" will include the cry, "Wail, you who live in the market district; all your merchants will be wiped out, all who trade with silver will be ruined" (Zeph. 1:10,11). Does one trust in his bank account or real-estate holdings? These will be of no aid, for "their wealth will be plundered, their houses demolished" (Zeph. 1:13). Only God has power to save the people on "the great day of the Lord." Neither their silver nor their gold will be able to save them on the day of the Lord's wrath" (Zeph. 1:18). There are things that money cannot buy. Salvation is one such commodity. The final sentence of the book holds out the promise of a day " 'when I restore your fortunes before your very eyes,' says the Lord" (Zeph. 3:20; 2:7,9).

HAGGAI

After the Jews return from the Babylonian captivity, as recorded in the books of Ezra, Nehemiah and Esther, the prophet Haggai comes on the scene calling for the rebuilding of God's temple in Jerusalem. Where is their sense of priority? The people say, "The time has not yet come for the Lord's house to be built." Yet they themselves live in "paneled houses, while this [God's] house remains a ruin" (Hag. 1:2,4). Let every Israelite remember God's truth: " 'The silver is mine and the gold is mine,' declares the Lord Almighty" (Hag. 2:8).

Shall making their own living take precedence over erecting the house of God? The Lord calls for the people to "give careful thought" to their ways. Let them observe that they "earn wages, only to put them in a purse with holes in it" (Haggai 1:6). Let them be advised by God, " 'You expected much, but see, it turned out to be little. What you brought home, I blew away. Why?' declares the Lord Almighty. 'Because of my house, which remains a ruin, while each of you is busy with his own house' " (Hag. 1:9). Haggai, colleague of Zechariah, was the right man for the job of giving heart and hope to the Jews at a critical time in their history.

ZECHARIAH

Using the tools of symbols and visions, the priest Zechariah continues the work of his lay-contemporary Haggai. Both work at dispelling the discouragement of God's people and calling for the completion of the temple. Zechariah's words are words of hope and promise, for God had given the assignment, "Proclaim further: This is what the Lord Almighty says: 'My town will again overflow with prosperity' " (Zech 1:17). The good days prophesied will be so bountiful that "Jerusalem will be a city without walls because of the great number of men and livestock in it" (Zech. 2:4). Where will some of this riches come from? "The wealth of all the surrounding nations will be collected — great quantities of gold and silver and clothing" (Zech. 14:14). What a contrast the envisioned future will be to some earlier times, when "there were no wages for man or beast" (Zech. 8:10). What a comparison it will be to the better days "when Jerusalem and its surrounding towns were at rest and prosperous" (Zech. 7:7).

A contingent to blessing from God is purging from sin. Not all will bathe in the fountain to be "opened to the house of David" (Zech. 13:1). But some false teachers convicted of their deception will admit, "I am not a prophet. I am a farmer; the land has been my livelihood since my youth" (Zech. 13:5). A remnant of the people is promised, "This third I will bring into the fire; I will refine them like silver and test them like gold" (Zech. 13:9). Each of the redeemed, like the high priest Joshua, will hear the angelic order, "Take off his filthy clothes. . . . See, I have taken away your sin, and I will put rich garments on you" (Zech. 3:4).

Symbols in the book include "a solid gold lampstand" (Zech. 4:2), "two gold pipes that pour out golden oil" (Zech. 4:12) and "two mountains — mountains of bronze" (Zech. 6:1). Messianic prophecies include the infamous "thirty pieces of silver" and its hurling "into the house of the Lord to the potter" (Zech. 11:12,13).

The rest of the book reflects an awareness of buyers and sellers feeling "rich" (Zech. 11:5) and nations suffering "plunder" (Zech 2:9). We read of cities as wealthy as Tyre heaping up "silver like dust and gold like dirt of the street," only to have God take their possessions away (Zech. 9:3,4). We learn of "silver and gold from the exiles" being made into a "crown" for Joshua (Zech. 6:10,11). We hear the consistent prophetic call, "Administer true justice; show mercy and compassion to one another. Do not oppress the widow or the fatherless, the alien or the poor" (Zech. 7:9,10).

MALACHI

The twelve prophetic books that we call "minor," as a quantitative description, conclude with Malachi. To the Christian, Malachi's voice is the last prophetic voice to be heard before the prophet John the Baptist announces the Messiah and his kingdom to be at hand. By the question and answer dialogue, Malachi reasons with a disobedient nation. If the people feel God is indifferent to them, they should see in fact how indifferent they have been to him.

Malachi tells the priests either to bring to God the best in offerings or to lock the temple doors, close down the services and resign from the ministry. Things had become so bad spiritually that the Lord declares, "I will accept no offering from your hands." The priests say, "What a burden!" (Mal. 1:10,13). Let the people know that God cannot smile on an offering to him by one who breaks covenant with his wife (Mal. 2:13,14). True religion demands right relations with people beside us as well as correct rituals for the God above us. The promised Messiah will both purify and judge. "He will sit as a refiner and purifier of silver; he will purify the Levites and refine them like gold and silver" (Mal. 3:3). In judgment he "will be quick to testify against . . . those who defraud laborers of their wages, who oppress the widows and the fatherless" (Mal. 3:5).

Malachi is probably best known in religious circles for his labelling the withheld tithe "robbing God." Many a missionary has been robbed of needed funds to do his work effectively and many worshippers have been robbed of the blessing that comes in sharing, but Malachi says even God is robbed. The prophet accuses "the whole nation" (Mal. 3:8,9). The command is, "Bring the whole tithe into the storehouse, that there may be food in my house" (Mal. 3:10).

Every word of the prophetic command has significance. "Bring" gets the donor there. "The whole tithe" implies a lesser portion to be unacceptable. "Into the storehouse" suggests no options for individual preferences. The clear order is followed by a motivating promise, " 'Test me in this,' says the Lord Almighty, 'and see if I will not throw open the floodgates of heaven and pour out so much blessing that you will not have room enough for it. I will prevent pests from devouring your crops, and the vines in your fields will not cast their fruit,' says the LORD Almighty" (Mal. 3:10,11).

28

WHAT JESUS' BIBLE SAID ABOUT MONEY IN THE WRITINGS (PSALMS, JOB)

PSALMS

Jesus had a special knack at opening the Old Testament Scriptures to his disciples. He gave new insights on every teaching occasion, whether he instructed from the Mosaic Law, the Prophets or the Sacred Writings (Luke 24:32,44). The *Hagiographa*, which included the poetical books (Psalms, Proverbs, Job), the five scrolls (Song of Solomon, Ruth, Lamentations, Ecclesiastes, Esther) and history (Daniel, Ezra-Nehemiah, Chronicles), was sometimes referred to by the single title Psalms.

Many of Jesus' words in the Gospels are quotations or reflections from that individual book of the Sacred Writings called Psalms. Its richness as a devotional book does not keep its practical teaching on money from shining through. As Moses' books of law are five in number the Psalms are arranged into five books (chapters 1-41; 42-72; 73-89; 90-106; 107-150). For conven-

251

ience sake, we will look at the Psalter by following the five divisions.

In Book One no doubt is left that the righteous man is blessed so that "whatever he does prospers" (Psa. 1:3). He can sing "I shall lack nothing" (Psa. 23:1). The invitation is God-given "Ask of me, and I will make the nations your inheritance, the ends of the earth your possession" (Psa. 2:8). The God-fearer is told "he will spend his days in prosperity, and his descendants will inherit the land" (Psa. 25:12,13). He is further assured that "those who fear him [God] lack nothing. The lions may grow weak and hungry, but those who seek the Lord lack no good thing" (Psa. 34:9,10). It is the people "who hope in the Lord" that will "inherit the land" (Psa. 37:9-11,22,29). It is the persons who "delight . . . in the Lord" that will receive "the desires" of their hearts (Psa. 37:4).

The Psalmist speaks of their enjoying "plenty" (Psa. 37:18,19) and makes the carefully considered observation: "I was young and now am old, yet I have never seen the righteous forsaken or their children begging bread" (Psa. 37:25). David prays, "You still the hunger of those you cherish; their sons have plenty, and they store up wealth for their children" (Psa. 17:14). In the worst of times, the covenant people rest on the truth that "the eyes of the Lord are on those who fear him . . . to . . . keep them alive in famine" (Psa. 33:18). Of course many spiritual blessings will excel the material ones, such as when God fills the "heart with greater joy than when their grain and new wine abound" (Psa. 4:7), or when God's ordinances prove to be "more precious than gold, than much pure gold" (Psa. 19:9,10).

The God of Abraham, Isaac and Jacob knows that "the wicked man , , , who blesses the greedy" seems often to be "always prosperous" (Psa. 10:2,3,5). Such "sinners" follow "wicked schemes" and have "right hands . . . full of bribes" (Psa. 26:9,10). But let the righteous remain only in the way of righteousness and he will not go hungry. Should there be a slack time, remember that "better the little that the righteous have than the wealth of many wicked" (Psa. 32:16). Let him know that the person, "who lends his money without usury and does not accept a bribe against the innocent" may dwell in God's sanctuary (Psa. 15:1,5). The foolish "men of this world" have a reward that only "is in this life" (Psa. 17:14). A vain man "heaps up wealth, not knowing who will get it" (Psa. 39:6).

It is the trait of heaven to "give generously" (Psa. 37:21) for "the Lord is a refuge for the oppressed" (Psa. 9:9,18; 14:6). A protector and "deliverer" of the "needy" (Psa. 12:5; 40:17), a "helper of the fatherless" (Psa. 10:12,14,15). Such a self-description of duty is not to be taken frivilously for "the words of the Lord are flawless, like silver refined in a furnace of clay, purified seven times" (Psa. 12:6). Concerning our God, it can be asked, "Who is like you, O Lord? You rescue the poor from those too strong for them, the poor and needy from those who rob them" (Psa. 35:10). Regarding our Creator it can be stated, "This poor man called, and the Lord heard him; he saved him out of all his troubles" (Psa. 34:6). As to our Provider, it ought to be remembered that while he looks after those in poverty, it is also he who has "placed a crown of pure gold" on the king's head (Psa. 21:1,3). The basis of human stewardship is the foundational truth that "the earth is the Lord's, and everything in it, the world and all who live in it" (Psa. 24:1).

Book Two of the Psalms reveals money to be an inadequate god. How unthinking "is the man who did not make God his stronghold but trusted in his great wealth" (Psa. 52:6,7).

"Rich and poor alike" need to beware of "those who trust in their wealth and boast of their great riches" (Psa. 49:6). Only the true God can pay sufficient "ransom for a life," for it is "costly, no payment is ever enough" (Psa. 49:7,8).

Observe the plight of mortal men who live only for the present world. "All can see that wise men die; the foolish and the senseless alike perish and leave their wealth to others" (Psa. 49:10). "Man, despite his riches, does not endure" (Psa. 49:12). That being beyond debate, follow this wise advice; "Do not be overawed when a man grows rich, when the splendor of his house increases; for he will take nothing with him when he dies, his splendor will not descend with him. Though while he lived he counted himself blessed — and men praise you when you prosper — he will join the generation of his fathers, who will never see the light of life. A man who has riches without understanding is like the beasts that perish" (Psa. 49:16-20).

There is but one God to meet our needs both in this world and in that to come. He is the adequacy for our inadequacy. "Every animal of the forest . . . the cattle on a thousand hills," plus "the world . . . and all that is in it," belongs to him (Psa. 50:10,12). From his "bounty" he provides "for the poor" (Psa. 68:10). He is "a father to the fatherless, a defender of widows" (Psa. 68:5; 59:32,33; 70:5). He endows Israel's kings with sufficient prosperity to "deliver the needy who cry out, the afflicted who have no one to help" (Psa. 72:3,4,7,10,12-16).

Such a compassionate Lord is worthy of the "freewill offering" (Psa. 54:6), the "thank offerings" (Psa. 56:12) and all "gifts from men" including "kings" (Psa. 68:18,29,30). Kings may abide in "palaces adorned with ivory" and princesses may wear gowns "interwoven with gold" (Psa. 45:8,13), but all this can all be "plundered" (Psa. 44:10,12). Royalty ought to share in righteousness and neither act like thieves (Psa. 50:18) nor practice "extortion" (Psa. 62:10). Let all believers be "refined . . . as silver" and "comes to [God's] temple with burnt offerings and fulfil [their] vows" (Psa. 66:10,13,14).

In Books Three and Four of Psalms, prayers go up to God that he care for the underdog: "Do not let the oppressed retreat in disgrace; may the poor and needy praise your name" (Psa. 74:21). "Defend the cause of the weak and fatherless; maintain the rights of the poor and oppressed. Rescue the weak and needy; deliver them from the hand of the wicked. . . . Rise up, O God, judge the earth, for all nations are your inheritance" (Psa. 82:3,4,8). "Hear, O Lord, and answer me, for I am poor and needy" (Psa. 86:1). Those in need are to remember that God "will respond to the prayer of the destitute; he will not despise their plea" (Psa. 102:17). Let the needy be warned that desiring riches can entrap a soul. Affluent people may appear "always carefree" and increasing "in wealth." But, hear the testimony from the Psalmist's experience, "as for me, my feet had almost slipped; I had nearly lost my foothold. For I envied the arrogant when I saw the prosperity of the wicked" (Psa. 73:2,3,12). Much of the evil men's wealth is tainted, because "they slay the widow and the alien; they murder the fatherless" (Psa. 94:6). They "take possession of the pastureland of God" (Psa. 83:12) and share the loot of plunder (Psa. 89:41).

Every human should avoid greed and look to God. It is good to "bring gifts to the One to be feared" (Psa. 76:11), to "bring an offering and come into his courts" (Psa. 96:8). After all, it is "the LORD" who has given the "land" and "its harvest" (Psa. 85:12; 105:44). It was the God of Jacob, who in "famine" days when "supplies of food" were destroyed, "sent a man before them — Joseph, sold as a slave" (Psa. 105:16,17). When gratitude to the Creator is combined with human effort, needs can be met. So if the "man goes out to his work, to his labor until evening," such divine-human cooperation will produce a people "satisfied with good things" (Psa. 104:23,28).

Book Five of the Psalter continues to stress the Almighty's compassion for the down-trodden. He is stated to have "lifted the needy out of their affliction" (Psa. 107:41). He is said to "uphold the cause of the oppressed" and give "food to the hungry," while sustaining "the fatherless and the widow" (Psa. 146:7,9). Imprecatory Psalms scathe the inhumane person who has forced fellow humans into penury. The understandable but unforgiving petition is, "May his children be wandering beggars . . . may a creditor seize all he has; may strangers plunder the fruits of his labor" (Psa. 109:10,11). The "wounded" person sees justice in such a prayer that the table is turned, because the avaricious person "never thought of doing a kindness, but hounded to death the poor and the needy and the brokenhearted" (Psa.

109:16,22).

How different in character are God and those that follow his law, which is "more precious . . . than thousands of pieces of silver and gold" (Psa. 119:72,127). The Lord of heaven "raises the poor from the dust and lifts the needy from the ash heap; he seats them with princes, with the princes of their people" (Psa. 113:7,8). The God of the universe promises, "Good will come to him who is generous and lends freely, who conducts his affairs with justice" (Psa. 112:5). It is suggested that the person who "has scattered abroad his gifts to the poor" shall himself enjoy "wealth and riches . . . in his house" (Psa. 112:3,9).

The Psalmist assures all those "who fear the LORD," "You will eat the fruit of your labor; blessings and prosperity will be yours" (Psa. 128:1,2,5). It is true of God to declare, "He satisfies the thirsty and fills the hungry with good things" (Psa. 107:9,36-38). Because "the LORD is gracious and compassionate, he provides food for those who fear him" (Psa. 111:4,5). He offers "abundant provisions" (Psa. 132:15), and "inheritance" (Psa. 145:15,16). David himself lived in the confidence, "Our barns will be filled with every kind of provision. Our sheep will increase by thousands, by tens of thousands . . . there will be . . . no cry of distress in our streets" (Psa. 144:13,14).

No idols of "silver and gold, made by the hands of men" (Psa. 115:3,4; 135:15), can hear a prayer or provide for a need. No human toil without God's blessing will meet human wants, for "in vain" do men "rise early and stay up late, toiling for food to eat" without reliance on the Lord (Psa. 127:2). Since the Creator and Sustainer has covenanted to bless the nation of Israel if it is faithful to the covenant of Sinai, the Psalmist gratefully sings, "I will sacrifice a thank offering to you and call on the name of the LORD. I will fulfill my vows to the LORD in the presence of all his people." (Psa. 116:17,18).

JOB

The book of Job, by all counts, is one of the world's greatest poems and deals with one of the world's keenest problems. The book of Proverbs had generalized that those who do evil suffer for it. The book of Job reminds us that these apparent rules have exceptions. How is a man to act in those times, when for unknown reasons the rule does not hold? This undated work will never be outdated, for it deals with the insoluble problem of the righteous facing human suffering.

For our limited purpose of finding the teaching on money in its chapters, we first note in its prose prologue that Job is living in patriarchal times and that he is a man of both piety and wealth. He "owned seven thousand sheep, three thousand camels, five hundred yoke of oxen and five hundred donkeys, and had a large number of servants" (Job 1:3). Satan charges that these material blessings are the reason for Job's allegiance to God. Would a human "fear God for nothing?" If the rule was reversed and there was no protective "hedge" for the righteous nor blessing in "flocks and herds," would the Lord have followers? (Job 1:9-12). The rest of the story contains the answer in the face of Satan's accusation, "A man will give all he has for his life" (Job 2:4).

"Sabeans" carried off Job's oxen and donkeys, "fire burned up sheep and the servants" and Chaldean riding parties carried off his "camels" (Job 1:15-17). Clinging to his faith amid financial loss, the sufferer worshipped his God, saying, "Naked I came from my mother's womb, and naked I will depart. The LORD gave and the LORD has taken away; may the name of the LORD be praised" (Job 1:21). At the end of the testing time, once again the rule replaces the exception and "the LORD [has] made him prosperous again," so that he has "twice as much as he had before" (Job 42:10). His relatives and associates "each . . . gave him a piece of silver and a gold ring." As the curtain drops at the end of the drama, Job owns "fourteen thousand sheep, six thousand camels, a thousand yoke of oxen and a thousand donkeys" (Job 42:10-12) exactly twice what he had prior to the calamities that befell him.

Job's poetic speeches throughout show his business acumen. He knows the meaning of "ransom payments" (Job 6:22), "barter" (Job 6:27), "hired" men and "wages" (Job 7:1-2). He is cognizant of mining for "silver," refining "gold" and digging for "sapphires" (Job 28:1,5,6,10). He is observant that rulers have "had gold" and "filled their houses with silver" (Job 3:15), yet many of them have been wicked in the attainment of that wealth. Describing their evil means of gaining riches, he expounds, "Men move boundary stones; they pasture flocks they have stolen. They drive away the orphan's donkey and take the widow's ox in pledge. They thrust the needy from the path and force all the poor of the land into hiding . . . they [the poor] are drenched by mountain rains and hug the rocks for lack of shelter" etc. (Job 24:2-12,14,16,21). Concerning these wicked men Job is aware that they appear to "spend their years in prosperity and go down to their grave in peace," while asking "Who is the Almighty. . . . What would we gain by praying to him?" (Job 21:13,15). Yet he is certain that "their prosperity is not in their own hands" (Job 21:16) and that in the end though a rich man "lies down wealthy . . . when he opens his eyes, all is gone" (Job 27:16,17,19).

Job's speeches reveal the past use of his riches for the needy. They tell of the community speaking well of him because he "rescued the poor who cried for help, and the fatherless who had none to assist him." He was "father to the needy" (Job 29:11,12,16). He can ask, "Has not my soul grieved for the poor?" (Job 30:25). He can cry unto God to be weighed "in honest scales" (Job 31:6) arguing, "if I have denied the desires of the poor . . . kept my bread to myself, not sharing it with the father . . . seen anyone perish for lack of clothing, or a needy man without a garment, and his heart did not bless me for warming him with the fleece from my sheep . . . then let my arm fall from my shoulder" (Job 31:16,17,19-22). He can claim, "no stranger had to spend the night in the street, for my door was always open to the traveler" (Job 31:32).

From Job's own lips we learn that he denies either having put his "trust in gold," called it "his security" or "rejoiced over" it (Job 31:24,25). From Job's own mouth we are pointed to God's wisdom as the object of his search. He considered wisdom a value that "cannot be bought with the finest gold . . . weighed in silver . . . bought with . . . precious onyx or sapphires." He adds, "Neither gold nor crystal can compare with it. . . . Coral and jasper are not worthy of mention; the price of wisdom is beyond rubies. The topaz of Cush cannot compare with it" (Job 28:12,15-19). It is through that wisdom that he can say while in the fire of adversity, "when he [God] has tested me, I will come forth as gold" (Job 23:10).

The three speeches of Eliphaz reason that God cares for the poor (Job 5:5,15,16,20,24), withholds possessions from the corrupt (Job 15:29; 22:20), grants good things to the righteous (Job 22:17,18) and doubts that Job has been as concerned for the poor as he should have been (Job 22:6-10). His advice to Job is "assign your nuggets to the dust, your gold of Ophir to the rocks in the ravines, then the Almighty will be your gold, the choicest silver for you" (Job 22:24,25). Bildad calls also for Job's repentance, promising a "prosperous . . . future" upon admission of guilt (Job 8:7). He warns that what the "godless . . . trusts in is fragile; what he relies on is a spider's web. He leans on his web, but it gives way; he clings to it, but it does not hold" (Job 8:13-15). Zophar, too, finds history teaching that the wicked "must give back his wealth" for "he will spit out the riches he swallowed; God will make his stomach vomit them up" (Job 20:10,15). The verdict against a man like Job is, "What he toiled for he must give back uneaten; he will not enjoy the profit from his trading . . . he cannot save himself by his treasure . . . in the midst of his plenty, distress will overtake him" (Job 20:18-22).

Before God speaks, reminding everyone of the conversants that "everything under heaven belongs to him," Elihu joins in the debate. He agrees that God hears "the cry of the needy" (Job 34:28) and gives "prosperity and . . . years in contentment" to the obedient (Job 36:11,31). He sees that riches can be an enticement and that even large bribes will not sustain a man in distress (Job 36:18,19). The only dependable help is God who "comes in golden splendor . . . in awesome majesty" (Job 37:22).

29

WHAT JESUS' BIBLE SAID ABOUT MONEY IN THE WRITINGS (PROVERBS)

PROVERBS

The one hundred fifty Psalms find special meaning on holy days and at devotional times, but the wisdom of the many Proverbs uniquely applies to the modern world from Monday through Friday between the daylight hours of nine to five. The book of Proverbs deals with ethical conduct in the pragmatic considerations of everyday life. To live under God and in accordance with his law, how are young or old to discpline their actions? Solomon and other wise men give pithy generalizations to which they know there can be occasional exceptions. Yet what may not prove out in every single situation is usually true, so that no known exception should change the rule by which the people of God live. He who follows the ten commandments delivered by Moses is wise to follow the ten commitments regarding money made by Solomon and other men of wisdom.

BE MONOTHEISTS

(1) Commitment one is to recognize that material wealth is not the highest good. God should come before gold in life as well as in the dictionary. A person that "gains respect" has more than the individuals that "gain only wealth" (Prov. 11:16), for "whoever trusts in his riches will fall" (Prov. 11:28). "A good name is more desirable than great riches; to be esteemed is better than silver or gold" (Prov. 22:1). Poverty is no dishonor to the person that is "blameless" (Prov. 28:6; 19:1), lives in "righteousness" (Prov. 16:8) and is no "liar" (Prov. 19:22). To be without great wealth does not signify lack of "discernment" (Prov. 28:11), although it may contribute to lack of both pride (Prov. 16:19) and threats against one's person (Prov. 13:7,8). Do not men, who with one mind strive for wealth, often agree in heart to the wisdom of Solomon in Proverbs 15,16 and 17? He stated, "Better a little with fear of the LORD than great wealth with turmoil. Better a meal of vegetables where there is love than a fattened calf with hatred." Elsewhere he wrote, "Better a dry crust with peace and quiet than a house full of feasting, with strife" (Prov. 17:1).

Cognizant that wealth is not the highest good, the wisdom writers still viewed riches as a potential good rather than an evil. They found cities to rejoice "when the righteous prosper" (Prov. 11:10; 29:2). To them "prosperity is the reward of the righteous" (Prov. 13:21; 11:18; 14:11; 15:6; 21:21). To Solomon "the blessing of the LORD brings wealth" (Prov. 10:22). He knows that all his palaces and storehouses will mean nothing when he stands before his God, because "wealth is worthless in the day of wrath" (Prov. 11:4). He is further convinced that "he who conceals his sin does not prosper" (Prov. 28:13), but if you "commit to the LORD whatever you do . . . your plans will succeed" (Prov. 16:3).

BE HONEST

(2) A second commitment for people in covenant with God is

to be thoroughly honest in everything. "Ill-gotten gain . . . takes away the lives of those who get it" (Prov. 1:18,19). "Ill-gotten treasures are of no value" (Prov. 10:2,20) and they bring "punishment" (Prov. 10:16; 6:30,31) because "the LORD abhors dishonest scales, but accurate weights are his delight" (Prov. 11:1; 16:11; 20:10,23). Learn from the experience of others that "dishonest money dwindles away" (Prov. 13:11). Bribery is taboo (Prov. 17:8) as is robbery (Prov. 19:26; 29:24), fraud (Prov. 20:17) and the moving of boundary lines (Prov. 23:10,11) or the raiding of a residence (Prov. 24:15,16). It is right to "detest the dishonest" (Prov. 29:27) and to "hate ill-gotten gain" (Prov. 28:16). It is the essence of wisdom to learn that "a fortune made by a lying tongue is a fleeting vapor and a deadly snare" (Prov. 21:6). On the slate of dishonest acts, forbidden in improving one's bank total, is usury. "He who increases his wealth by exorbitant interest amasses it for another, who will be kind to the poor" (Prov. 28:8).

BE DILIGENT

(3) Commitment three calls for diligence and hard effort. It is a business axiom, "Lazy hands make a man poor, but diligent hands bring wealth" (Prov. 10:4; 12:14). It is a political observation, "Diligent hands will rule, but laziness ends in slave labor" (Prov. 12:24). It is a workman's truism, "All hard work brings a profit, but mere talk leads only to poverty" (Prov. 14:23). It is the considered opinion of the sages that a lazy man will go "hungry" (Prov. 19:15), "get nothing" (Prov. 13:4; 20:4), "grow poor" (Prov. 20:13) and go soon to his "death" (Prov. 21:25).

The writers of the Proverbs look with disdain at laziness. In an Old Testament setting the phrase "Protestant work ethic" seems inappropriate, but it is a Biblical work ethic indeed. A sluggard is looked down upon as one who "does not roast his game" (Prov. 12:27) and as "one who chases fantasies (Prov. 28:19). His "way . . . is blocked with thorns" (Prov. 15:19). He is viewed as one so lazy that when he "buries his hand in the dish; he will not even bring it back to his mouth" (Prov. 19:24; 26:15). He is pictured as one making ingenious excuses for his inaction by saying, "There is a lion outside" (Prov. 22:13; 26:13). Descriptively Solomon writes, "As vinegar to the teeth and smoke to the eyes, so is the sluggard to those who send him" (Prov. 10:26). He is "brother to one who destroys" (Prov. 18:9).

The model to follow is the hard-to-find virtuous wife of chapter 31. She is comparable to "the merchant ships bringing . . . food from afar" (verse 14). She considerately "buys" fields, "plants" vineyards and trades profitably (verses 16-18). She "makes" and "sells" "linen garments" and saves her gain, so that "she can laugh at the days to come" (verses 24 and 25). At the time she accumulates profit, she also "opens her arms to the poor and extends her hands to the needy" (verse 20). No wonder her husband considers her "worth far more than rubies" and of incomparable "value" (verses 10 and 11).

Another example of industry to ponder and follow is the lowly ant. While "ants are creatures of little strength, yet they store up their food in the summer" (Prov. 30:25). The sluggard is admonished to "go to the ant . . . consider its ways and be wise!" (Prov. 6:6,8). To not buy up the opportunity of the day is the path to want. "A little sleep, a little slumber, a little folding of the hands to rest — and poverty will come on you like a bandit and scarcity like an armed man" (Prov. 6:10,11; 24:30-34). In words pathetic but descriptive, Solomon declares, "as a door turns on its hinges, so a sluggard turns on his bed" (Prov. 26:14).

The call to rise from apathy is accompanied with a motivating promise, "He who tends a fig tree will eat its fruit" (Prov. 27:18; 12:11). In establishing priorities, "finish your outdoor work and get your fields ready; after that, build your house" (Prov. 24:27). Early in life learn at the school of hard knocks that going hungry can be a good teacher. "The laborer's appetite works for him; his

BE INTELLIGENT

(4) Another commitment of God's person is to act wisely. If God is wise, shall his people be otherwise? They ought rather demonstrate that they are made in the image of the Intelligence behind the universe. Wisdom literature advises that we "call out for insight and . . . understanding," searching for it "as for silver and . . . hidden treasure" (Prov. 2:3,4). Though it cost all we have, "we are to gain it" (Prov. 4:7). Wisdom is worth far more than "silver . . . choice gold" and "rubies" (Prov. 8:10,11,19; 3:14,15; 14:24; 16:16). It is not only of higher value, it leads to the attaining of the values lower down on the scale. Wisdom personified speaks into all opened ears, "With me are honor, enduring wealth and prosperity. My fruit is better than gold; what I yield surpasses choice silver . . . bestowing wealth on those who love me and making their treasuries full" (Prov. 6:18-21; 3:16; 20:15). After all, it is "by wisdom a house is built . . . through knowledge its rooms are filled with rare and beautiful treasures (Prov. 24:3,4).

"It is not fitting for a fool to live in luxury" (Prov. 19:10). "Of what use is money in the hand of a fool, since he has no desire to get wisdom" (Prov. 17:16)? It is never appropriate to lack judgment and "chase fantasies" (Prov. 12:11). But it is never improper to lay wise "plans" that "lead to profit" (Prov. 21:5) nor is it wrong to become "skilled" in a work so that we may "serve before kings" (Prov. 22:29).

BE OPEN TO ADVICE

(5) Commitment to a chain of command makes financial sense. Following orders from higher authority leads to business success. In the words of Solomon, "whoever gives heed to instruction prospers" (Prov. 16:20). Constructive criticism "aptly spoken is like apples of gold in settings of silver." That "rebuke to a listening ear" is "like an earring of gold or an ornament of fine

gold" (Prov. 25:11,12).

To learn from wiser heads "will prolong your life many years [to say nothing of your job] and bring you prosperity" (Prov. 3:1,2). Such openness to suggestions wins both "favor," "a good name," "riches . . . honor" and "peace" (Prov. 3:4,16,17).

BE CONSIDERATE

(6) Consideration of co-workers and equipment is commitment six. It is a foregone conclusion that those whom we have chosen as associates and partners hold to the basic moral standards of Israel's Deity. Never would consideration be given to "go along with," or "throw in [one's] lot with," any whose goal is "valuable things" and "plunder" unjustly taken (Prov. 1:11,13-15).

In Solomon's time caring for the equipment used in making a living would include a man taking thought "for the needs of his animals" (Prov. 12:10). Therefore the instruction is given, "Be sure to know the condition of your flocks, give careful attention to your herds; for riches do not endure forever" (Prov. 27:23,24). When such sage advice is followed, "the lambs will provide . . . with clothing and the goats with the price of a field," resulting in "plenty of goats' milk to feed you and your family and to nourish your servant girls" (Prov. 27:26,27). Should the call for consideration of flock or work animals be ignored, the proverb will come to pass, "Where there are no oxen, the manger is empty, but from the strength of an ox comes an abundant harvest" (Prov. 14:4).

Consideration for animals carries with it the higher consideration for people. The book of Proverbs overflows with brotherly concern. We read, "Do not withhold good from those who deserve it, when it is in your power to act. Do not say to your neighbor, 'Come back later; I'll give it tomorrow' — when you now have it with you" (Prov. 3:27,28). We discover, "He who is kind to the poor lends to the LORD, and he will reward him for what he has done" (Prov. 19:17) and "He who gives to the poor will lack nothing, but he who closes his eyes to them receives many curses" (Prov. 28:27).

Godliness demands being like God, who "does not let the righteous go hungry" (Prov. 10:3). Hence, "he who oppresses the poor shows contempt for their Maker, but whoever is kind to the needy honors God" (Prov. 14:31; 17:5). No man living in the BC era, or in the twentieth century AD, can let his eyes be blinded by silver and forget the needy who sleep on the streets or the unemployed who hunger for justice. It is not acceptable to God that "a poor man's field . . . produce abundant food, but injustice sweeps it away" (Prov. 13:23). It is not right that "the poor are shunned even by their neighbors," when heaven blesses the man "kind to the needy" (Prov. 14:20,21; 19:4,7). Harsh "answers" are not what the poor man needs when he "pleads for mercy" (Prov. 18:23). Poor people need "justice" (Prov. 29:7) and defense of "rights" (Prov. 31:9), rather than "beer" or "wine" to "drink and forget their poverty" (Prov. 31:6,7).

If God "keeps the widow's boundaries intact" (Prov. 15:25) and plunders "those who plunder" the needy (Prov. 22:23), will he not bless those who "speak up and judge fairly," defending the rights of the poor and needy (Prov. 31:9). The sure answer is, "Blessed is he who is kind to the needy" (Prov. 14:21) and "shares his food with the poor" (Prov. 22:9). The certain warning is, "If a man shuts his ears to the cry of the poor, he too will cry out and not be answered" (Prov. 21:13). He too will "come to poverty" (Prov. 22:16). No conclusion can be reached by labor or management that will "exploit" or "crush" the other (Prov. 22:22). It is inhumane to take "away a garment on a cold day" or cause "a heavy heart" (Prov. 25:20). The persons who are warm and well fed dare not forget what it means to be cold or hungry. "He who is full loaths honey, but to the hungry even what is bitter tastes sweet" (Prov. 27:7). To be "secure" in your present position (Prov. 29:14) or "blessed" in your future days, be "kind to the needy" (Prov. 14:21). To give the "hungry . . . food to eat" and the "thirsty . . . water to drink," is to find "the LORD will reward you" (Prov. 25:21,22). To be one who "oppresses the poor is [to be] like a driving rain that leaves no crops" (Prov. 28:3).

BE FRUGAL

(7) Commitment to prudence in spending, borrowing and saving is worthy of the young business man envisioned by Solomon. Borrowing is to be carefully done in that "the borrower is servant to the lender" (Prov. 22:7). But one thing never to be done — as if it were the unpardonable sin in business — is to co-sign for another's debt. "He who puts up security for another will surely suffer, but whoever refuses to strike hands in pledge is safe" (Prov. 11:15). Such foolishness indicates one is "lacking in judgment" (Prov. 17:18), especially if he "puts up security for a stranger" or "a wayward woman" (Prov. 20;16; 27:13). The end result is apt to be the experience of "your very bed" being "snatched from under you" (Prov. 22:26,27).

Early in the book, Solomon speaks at length to this folly. "My son, if you have put up security for your neighbor, if you have struck hands in pledge for another . . . free yourself. . . . Allow no sleep to your eyes, no slumber to your eyelids. Free yourself, like a gazelle from the hand of the hunter, like a bird from the snare of the fowler" (Prov. 6:1-5).

In contrast to being in the red-ink or debt side of the ledger, it is comforting to find yourself listed with modest assets on the credit side. A maxim to be learned is, "In the house of the wise are stores of choice food and oil, but a foolish man devours all he has" (Prov. 21:20). Wealth is a "fortified city," but only the blind "imagine it an unscalable wall" (Prov. 18:11; 10:15). Total security rests in the unchanging God, for the value of gold varies in the market day by day.

Frugality in saving will never be a trait of the person imprudent in spending. As it is written, "He who loves pleasure will become poor; whoever loves wine and oil will never be rich" (Prov. 21:17). To form association with "those who drink too much wine or gorge themselves on meat" is to learn too late that "drunkards and gluttons become poor, and drowsiness clothes them in rags" (Prov. 23:20-21). Any hasty purchase "leads to poverty," as does always craving "for more" (Prov. 21:5,26).

The most idiotic of all long-range, poor investments is that in momentary sensual pleasure. The "prostitute is a deep pit . . . a bandit [who] lies in wait" (Prov. 23:27,28). Solomon warns his sons, "Keep to a path far from her . . . lest strangers feast on your wealth and your toil enrich another man's house" (Prov. 5:8,10). Such sons will be reduced "to a loaf of bread" (Prov. 6:26). The whore's empty assurance may be, "My husband is not home; he has gone on a long journey. He took his purse filled with money and will not be home till full moon" (Prov. 7:19,20). The trap may go off in the scam, leaving the poor dupe with the woman's furious husband, who "will not accept any compensation" and will "refuse the bribe, however great it is" (Prov. 6:34,35).

BE GREEDLESS

(8) Commitment number eight is that the Christian creed does not allow for greed. It is the wicked humans who inordinately "desire the plunder of evil men" (Prov. 12:12). Each "greedy man brings trouble to his family" (Prov. 15:27), "stirs up dissension" (Prov. 28:25) and "will not go unpunished" (Prov. 28:20). Covetous men are a curse to their parents. They have "teeth [that] are swords and . . . jaws [that] are knives to devour the poor from the earth, and the needy from among mankind. The leech has two daughters. 'Give! Give!' they cry" (Prov. 30:14,15).

Moderation in all things goes for amassing wealth as well as other actions. The men of wisdom call out, "Do not wear yourself out to get rich; have the wisdom to show restraint. Cast but a glance at riches, and they are gone, for they will sprout wings and fly off to the sky like an eagle" (Prov. 23:4,5). Agur the son of Jakeh prayed, "Two things I ask you, O LORD; do not refuse me before I die: Keep falsehood and lies far from me; give me neither poverty nor riches, but give me only my daily bread. Otherwise, I may have too much and disown you . . . Or I may become poor and steal and so dishonor the name of my God" (Prov. 30:7-9).

BE TESTATE

(9) Commitment to the future of your family and your assets is an evidence of good planning. Why should persons of lesser standards determine how your goods will be distributed after your death? Why should people with less concern for your loved ones be charged at your demise with providing for their needs? Proverbs states that "a good man leaves an inheritance for his children's children" (Prov. 13:22). This book of wisdom suggests that "houses and wealth are inherited from parents" (Prov. 19:14). It also observes, as in the case of the younger son in Jesus' story of the prodigal, "an inheritance quickly gained at the beginning will not be blessed at the end" (Proverbs 20:21).

BE GENEROUS

(10) Last but not least of the monetary commitments advocated in the Proverbs is the dedication to sharing the wealth one has amassed. Keeping one's riches for the means of serving others, rather than letting money become the end of all existence, calls for the discipline of giving. On the crucial point "the LORD tests the heart" as silver and gold are tried in the "cruci-

ble . . . and . . . furnace" (Prov. 17:3; 25:4).

Generosity toward God comes first. Solomon taught, "Honor the Lord with your wealth, with the firstfruits of all your crops; then your barns will be filled to overflowing, and your vats will brim over with new wine" (Prov. 3:9,10).

Giving to other men holds a high, although secondary place. The "righteous" are those "who give without sparing" (Prov. 21:26). The "stingy" are those "who . . .always [are] thinking about the cost" (Prov. 23:6-8) and pursuing "selfish ends" (Prov. 18:1). Such are "unaware that poverty awaits" them (Prov. 28:22). Real largess in giving does not lead to personal loss but to personal gain. The Bible says, "One man gives freely, yet gains even more; another withholds unduly, but comes to poverty. A generous man will prosper; he who refreshes others will himself be refreshed" (Prov. 11:24,25). Experience proves that "a gift opens the way for the giver" (Prov. 18:16) "soothes anger, and . . . pacifies great wrath" (Prov. 21:14). "Everyone is the friend of a man who gives gifts" (Prov. 19:6).

30

WHAT JESUS' BIBLE SAID ABOUT MONEY IN THE WRITINGS (SCROLLS, HISTORY)

SONG OF SOLOMON

In the Hebrew Bible the third section, called the Sacred Writings, has following the Poetical books (Psalms, Proverbs and Job), the Five Scrolls that were read at various Jewish feasts. The first is the Song of Solomon read privately (or in some areas publicly) during Passover week.

In romantic language the object of the lover's affection is said to have "cheeks . . . beautiful with earrings" and a "neck with strings of jewels." He promises to make for her "earrings of gold, studded with silver" (Song of Solomon 1:9-11). Her legs are said to be graceful "like jewels" (Song of Solomon 7:1). Her friends promise to "build towers of silver on her," the day she is spoken for (Song of Solomon 8:9). In turn she considers him to have a "head" of "purest gold," "arms" like "rods of gold set with chrysolite." His body is comparable to "polished ivory decorated with sapphires." His legs are likened to "pillars of marble set on bases of pure gold" (Song of Solomon 5:11,14,15). His aroma is that of "myrrh and incense made from all the spices of the merchant" (Song of Solomon 3:6). His carriage has "posts . . . made of silver, its base of gold" (Song of Solomon 3:9,10). Solomon may have such wealth that a single vineyard would bring "a thousand shekels of silver" (Song of Solomon 8:11,12), but the stewardship lesson of his love song is that it is impossible to do too much toward the object of one's love.

RUTH

The second scroll, the delightful book of Ruth, was for reading during the harvest festival of Pentecost. Hidden in this love story with a "famine" setting (Ruth 1:1) is the account of a business transaction where Naomi sells a "piece of land" to Boaz. Ruth, as "the dead man's widow," is included in the property exchange. The explanation is given, "Now in earlier time in Israel, for the redemption and transfer of property to become final, one party took off his sandal and gave it to the other," as the "method of legalizing transactions in Israel." Boaz announces to the elders of the community, "Today you are witnesses that I have bought from Naomi all the property of Elimelech, Kihon and Mahlon. I have also acquired Ruth the Moabitess, Mahlon's widow, as my wife, in order to maintain the name of the dead with his property" (Ruth 4:3-10).

LAMENTATIONS

The five chapters of Lamentations, containing five separate poems (four of which are acrostics), is read in the Synagogues on the ninth day of Ab, a fast day commemorating Jerusalem's destruction back in the days of Nebuchadnezzer. It is lamentable to remember "all the treasures that were hers [Jerusalem's] in days of old" (Lam. 1:7). Now the city's people "groan as they search for bread" and they find themselves having to "barter their treasures for food to keep themselves alive" (Lam. 1:10,11). They have to plead with God for the lives of their "children, who faint from hunger" (Lam. 2:19). The cry goes on as the nation remembers its former glory, "How the gold has lost its luster, the fine gold become dull! The sacred gems are scattered at the head of every street. How the precious sons of Zion, once worth their weight in gold, are now considered as pots of clay, the work of a potter's hands! Even jackals offer their breasts to nurse their young, but my people have become heartless like ostriches in the desert. Because of thirst the infant's tongue sticks to the roof of its mouth, the children beg for bread, but no one gives it to them. Those who once ate delicacies are destitute in the streets. Those nurtured in purple now lie on ash heaps" (Lam. 4:1-5). The writer considers the slain better off than the living "racked with hunger" (Lam. 4:9). Heirs have become orphans. Every drop of "water" and stick of "wood" has to be purchased at a price. Every bite of bread is gained at the risk of life itself (Lam. 5:2-4,6,9).

ECCLESIASTES

The fourth of the Scrolls is Ecclesiastes, a book to be read in the Synagogues on the third day of the Feast of Tabernacles. Such a festive, cheerful day was to be qualified by reading Ecclesiastes and being reminded of life's transiency lived "under the sun." At the fall celebration people lived in booths, recalling how they as nomads had wandered for forty years until they were given their permanent abode in Palestine. It is good to be reminded that even life in the promised land would not be worth the living, were it not for the heaven-sent commandments and the plans for the man's future known to the Creator above the sun. Ancient Israel and present day residents of earth are to reject confident humanism that leaves God out. Without him life is meaningless.

The opening question of the book has a monetary ring, "What does man gain from all his labor at which he toils under the sun?" (Eccl. 1:3). The closing chapter considers death the severing of "the silver cord" or the breaking of "the golden bowl" (Eccl. 12:6). In between the first and last chapters runs the argument that living exclusively for wealth is to be choosing a road that leads to disappointment. "The Teacher, son of David, king of Jerusalem," tells from experience of building "houses" for himself and planting "vineyards" until he "owned more herds and flocks than anyone in Jerusalem." He "amassed silver and gold . . . and the treasure of kings and provinces." The achievement of his life's purpose proved to be shallow and he laments, "Yet when I surveyed all that my hands had done and what I had toiled to achieve, everything was meaningless, a chasing after the wind; nothing was gained under the sun" (Eccl. 2:4,7,8,11).

The disappointment came because the toil was "grievous" and the wealth he attained he had to "leave" to those coming after him (Eccl. 2:17,18,21: 6:2,3). Surely all "this toil and anxious striving," "the pain and grief" with nights when the "mind does not rest," ought to result in more than "storing up wealth to hand . . . over" to others (Eccl. 2:21-23,26). But, like it or not, the man wedded to this work entered it "naked" and departs taking "nothing from his labor that he can carry in his hand" (Eccl. 5:15,16). "A stillborn child is better off" (Eccl. 6:3).

Life with God and the eternal world as the "duty of man" (Eccl. 12:13), however, put perspective on possessions. Finding "satisfaction in . . . toil — this is the gift of God" (Eccl. 3:13; 5:18,19). Avoid greed and the "envy of . . . neighbor" (Eccl. 4:4), for "whoever loves money never has money enough; whoever loves wealth is never satisfied with his income" (Eccl. 5:10). In a world of both poor (Eccl. 4:1,13,14; 5:8,9; 6:8; 9:15,16) and rich (Eccl. 4:8,9; 9:11; 10:20) wise men live modestly, aware that the adage is true, "Better one handful with tranquility than two handfuls with toil and chasing after wind" (Eccl. 4:6). True also are the sayings, "As goods increase . . . what benefit are they to the owner except to feast his eyes on them" and "the abundance of a rich man permits him no sleep" (Eccl. 5:11,12). The facts are that "wealth hoarded" can "harm . . . its owner" (Eccl. 5:13), "extortion turns a wise man into a fool and a bribe corrupts the heart" (Eccl. 7:7).

Solomonic wisdom calls for learning to recognize when it is "time to keep and . . . time to throw away" (Eccl. 3:6). There is a time to save, for "money is a shelter" (Eccl. 7:12). There is a time to "give portions to seven, yes to eight, for you do not know what disaster may come." A good promise to rely on is the teaching, "Cast your bread upon the waters, for after many days you will find it again" (Eccl. 11:1,2).

ESTHER

In the order of reading by calendar, the scroll of Esther is last of the five. But, in the affections of the Jewish people, it ranks first and is of all five scrolls known often as *the* Scroll. The Feast of Purim, instituted to memorialize this history recorded in the book of Esther, falls on the forteenth and fifteenth of Adar. The thirteenth day of Adar is termed the Fast of Esther. Neither the name of God nor ethical religion is found in the ten chapters of the book, but there is enough Jewish patriotism to make up for the lack.

Moneywise, the scroll begins by describing the empire of Xerxes who "ruled over 127 provinces stretching from India to Cush," (Esther 1:1) "displayed . . . vast wealth" (Esther 1:4) and built the renowned gardens with "hangings of white and blue linen, fastened with cords of white linen and purple material to silver rings on marble pillars." In the gardens "were couches of gold and silver on a mosaic pavement of porphry, marble, mother-of-pearl and other costly stones." In that beauty spot was

277

served "wine . . . in goblets of gold" (Esther 1:6,7).

Haman, plotting to destroy God's people offers to "put ten thousand talents of silver into the royal treasury" to pay any men who will destroy the Jews. Xerxes rejected the money but gave his "signet ring" to Haman authorizing the death and plundering of Jews (Esther 3:9-11,13,14; 4:7). Events are reversed as "the gold scepter" of the king is offered to Esther (Esther 4:11; 5:2; 8:4). This spares her life. The "signet ring" retrieved from Haman is presented to Mordecai (Esther 8:2). Now it is the Jews who are granted authority to "plunder the property of their enemies" (Esther 8:11), but while defeating them they refuse the plunder (Esther 9:10,16). The story ends with Mordecai "wearing royal garments of blue and white, a large crown of gold and a purple robe of fine linen" (Esther 8:15). He writes to the Jews, ordering "them to observe the days [in Adar] as days of feasting and joy and giving presents of food to one another and gifts to the poor" (Esther 9:22).

DANIEL

When the Jews of Jesus' day and our day look at the book of Daniel, they classify it with the Writings rather than the Prophets. We might use the catagories of Major and Minor Prophets and put Daniel with the Major Prophets. In the words of Christ regarding "the Law of Moses, the Prophets and the Psalms" (Luke 24:44), Daniel with other historical works is in the third portion of this third section. The "Psalms," or the Sacred Writings, referred to the poetry (Psalms, Proverbs, Job), the scrolls (Song of Solomon, Ruth, Lamentations, Ecclesiastes, Esther) and history (Daniel, Ezra-Nehemiah, Chronicles).

Since the rest of Jesus' Bible revealed information on money, we expect our search to be rewarded in this final section of the Old Testament as well as the former. Daniel contains dependable history and optimistic visions. These visions in apocalyptic style show the triumph of God's kingdom.

Nebuchadnezzar has a disturbing dream that his astrologers cannot interpret, even though offered "gifts and rewards and great honor" (Dan. 2:5). The king, with money on his mind, sees in his sleep a "dazzling statue" with "head . . . of pure gold . . . chest and arms of silver . . . belly and thighs of bronze, . . . legs of iron, etc." (Dan. 2:31,32). The statue and its bronze, silver and gold parts are broken to pieces. Daniel informs the king that the metals stand for world empires that will follow in succession until God sets up his reign that shall never end. He calls Nebuchadnezzar the "head of gold" (Dan. 2:35,38,39,45). In appreciation for the meaning of his dream the king of Babylon "ordered that an offering . . . be presented" to Daniel and he "lavished many gifts on him" (Dan. 2:46,48).

The good news of chapter two is followed by the bad news of the next chapter, where the king "made an image of gold, ninety feet high and nine feet wide, and set it up on the plain of Dura," ordering that when instruments of music sounded the people "must fall down and worship the image of gold" (Dan. 3:1,5,7,10,11). This order some Jews refused to obey (Dan. 3:12,14,18), making names like Shadrach, Meshach and Abednego heroic names for Jewish children to remember.

In the first half of the book are six stories about Daniel (chapter 1-6). One of these events has to do with a "great banquet for a thousand of his [Belshazzar's] nobles." At this feast the king ordered "the gold and silver goblets," stolen from the Jerusalem temple by his father, be used in drinking wine as "they praised the gods of gold and silver, of bronze, iron, wood and stone" (Dan. 5:1-4,23). Writing on the wall by the fingers of a human hand caused the frightened king to collapse. He sought from his "enchanters, astrologers and diviners" the meaning of the words written, offering that the successful interpreter "be clothed in purple and have a gold chain placed around his neck" (Dan. 5:7,16). They fail and Daniel succeeds, at first protesting all "gifts . . . and . . . rewards," but, nevertheless, finally accepting them (Dan. 4:17,29).

The second half of Daniel contains not stories about Daniel but visions that he received. One of these had to do with a "man dressed in linen with a belt of the finest gold around his waist" (Dan. 10:5). His interpretation foretells "three more kings in Persia, and then a fourth, who will be far richer than all the others." This ruler will gain "power by his wealth" (Dan. 11:2). Daniel further sees "valuable articles of silver and gold" being carried off to Egypt" (Dan. 11:8) and tax collectors contributing to a successor's "royal splendor" with "plunder, loot and wealth" (Dan. 11:20,24). He sadly looks ahead to a king who will honor "a god unknown to his fathers . . . with gold and silver, with precious stones and costly gifts" (Dan. 11:38). This future leader "will distribute the land at a price (Dan. 11:39) and "gain control of the treasures of gold and silver and all the riches of Egypt" (Dan. 11:43). Antiochus Epiphanes, thou art the man!

EZRA-NEHEMIAH

Ezra-Nehemiah describes the three-stage return of the Jews from their Babylonian captivity. The returning people under Cyrus, king of Persia, are to build God a temple with the "silver and gold, with . . . freewill offerings" that they as survivors provide. The inventory lists "gold dishes 30, silver dishes 1,000, silver pans 29, gold bowls 30, matching silver bowls 410, other articles 1,000. In all there were 5,400 articles of gold and of silver" (Ezra 1:6-11; Neh. 7:70-72). The temple was built with "free-will offerings" given "according to their [the donors'] ability" and placed "in the treasury" (Ezra 2:68,69; 7:15 18; 8:24 30,33). "Masons and carpenters," with transporters of supplies received "money" in pay for their work (Ezra 3:7; 6:8; Neh. 3:31,32).

Objections were made by the Jews' enemies to Artaxerxes that royal "revenues" would suffer, if the Jews were allowed to continue returning to and building up Jerusalem (Ezra 4:13,20).

Defenses on the other side were given that "the gold and silver" taken from "the temple of Babylon" was simply returning what had previously been stolen from "the house of God" in Jerusalem (Ezra 5:14; 6:4,5). Artaxerxes himself ordered that "all the treasurers of Trans-Euphrates . . . provide with diligence whatever Ezra . . . may ask . . . up to a hundred talents of silver, a hundred cors of wheat, a hundred baths of olive oil, and salt without limit" (Ezra 7:20-22). The king also instructed that no temple worker was to be taxed or told to pay tribute (Ezra 7:24,26). Ezra gave orders to the returning people to avoid inter-marriage with pagans that might "further their welfare or prosperi-ty" (Ezra 9:12). When a person of Judah and Jerusalem failed to respond within three days to Ezra's call to assemble, he "would forfeit all his property" (Ezra 10:8).

Under Nehemiah, the poor are helped. The cry had been heard that the people were having to mortgage "fields" and "homes" to "get grain during . . . famine" and were having to "borrow money for taxes" (Neh. 5:3,4). Also under Nehemiah the practices of "usury" and "selling . . . brothers" into slavery are condemned (Neh. 5:7,8,10-12). Taxes are lowered (Neh. 5:15,18). The people vow not to "buy" or "work" on the Sabbath and to "give a third of a shekel each year for the service of the house of . . .God" (Neh. 10:31,32; 13:15,16,20). They pro-mise to tithe (Neh. 10:36-38; 12:44; 13:5,12,13). Nehemiah makes "provision for contributions . . . at designated times" (Neh. 13:31). This final verse of the final chapter describes Nehemiah's effort to purify "everything foreign" from Jewish life and faith.

CHRONICLES

Reading over the years our Old Testaments from Genesis to Malachi, we easily forget that our familiar ordering of the books was not the way it was in Jesus' day. Then Chronicles (both 1 and

2) fell in the final slot of the third section called the *Hagiographa*.

To some readers of 1 and 2 Chronicles the chapters are considered quite dull, moralistic and repetitive. Much of the historic information of 1 Chronicles was given earlier in 2 Samuel and that of 2 Chronicles in 1 and 2 Kings. But wait! Repetition means importance! The Chronicler is selecting events from the past that illustrate a vital philosophy of history. Emphasizing the Southern Kingdom, the author would have his readers meditate on how God's divine purpose shines forth in the nation's past. Recalling their sacred history, the remnant nation can better reestablish true worship and valid kingship under the God of Abraham, Isaac and Jacob.

1 Chronicles begins with genealogies from the time of Adam through Saul (chapters 1-9) and then deals with the reign of David (chapters 10-29). 2 Chronicles follows with the reign of Solomon (chapters 1-9) and concludes with the kings of Judah up to the days of Ezra (chapters 10-36).

Moneywise the genealogical portion of 1 Chronicles lists the infamous "Achar, who brought disaster on Israel by violating the ban on taking devoted things" (1 Chron. 2:7) and the ambitious Jabez who prayed "to the God of Israel, 'Oh that you would . . . enlarge my territory' " (1 Chron. 4:10). We read in this section of God enriching "the Reubenites, the Gadites and the half-tribe of Manasseh," as he enabled them to seize "the livestock of the Hagrites — fifty thousand camels, two hundred fifty thousand sheep and two thousand donkeys" (1 Chron. 5:18,20,21). We also are informed of four gatekeepers being "entrusted with the responsibility for . . . the treasuries in the house of God" (1 Chron. 9:26 cp. 26:20,22,26,27; 27:31).

Under David, his subjects brought him "tribute." The officers of Hadadezer provided "gold shields" and the towns of Hadadezer furnished great quantities "of bronze, which Solomon used to make the bronze Sea, the pillars and various bronze articles." Hadoram, king of Zobah, also brought "gold and silver and bronze," which David "dedicated . . . to the LORD" (1

Chron. 18:6-8,10,11). Similar accounts tell of great funds coming to David from Ammorites (1 Chron. 19:6,7) and from Rabbah (1 Chron. 20:2).

We learn from King David the way to associate money and worship. Purchasing the threshing floor from Araunah, as the place for an altar to God, David insisted on paying "full price" rather than accept it as a gift. He argued with Araunah, "I will not take for the LORD what is yours, or sacrifice a burnt offering that costs me nothing." The full price was "six hundred shekels of gold" (1 Chron. 21:22-25). In preparing for the temple's construction under Solomon, King David took "great pains to provide for the temple of the LORD a hundred thousand talents of gold, a million talents of silver, etc." (1 Chron. 22:14,16). David's plans for the temple, given to Solomon in elaborate detail, itemize the costly furnishings (1 Chron. 28:12, 14-18). His speech before the public assembly tells of him giving "all" his "resources" in "large quantities," which include his "personal treasures of gold and silver" itemized to the penny (1 Chron. 29:2-5). His example led the rest to give "willingly . . . freely and whole-heartedly to the LORD" (1 Chorn. 29:6-9). His concluding prayer acknowledges that all "wealth and honor" come from God and "belong" to him in the first place. Hence, David prays, "we have given you only what comes from your hand" (1 Chron. 29:12,14,16).

2 Chronicles recalls Solomon's prayer for wisdom rather than for wealth that resulted in him receiving both from God (2 Chron. 1:11,12,14-17). It reiterates the amassing of workers and materials for the temple (2 Chron. 2:7,13,14; 13:11). It describes the profuse use of gold and other rich adornments (2 Chron. 3:4-10; 4:7-10,19-22; 5:1). It details the elaborate dedication of the temple (2 Chron. 7:7) and the wealth of the king which caused the queen of Sheba amazement (2 Chron. 8:18; 9:9,10). His splendor shines from the pages of Chronicles, as the author revels in the size of his annual revenues, his furnishings, his navy, etc. He writes, "King Solomon was greater in

riches . . . than all other kings of the earth . . . the king made silver as common in Jerusalem as stones, and cedar as plentiful as sycamore-fig trees in the foothills" (2 Chron. 9:13-18,20-24,27).

The kings of Judah included good men like Asa, who brought "silver and gold" into God's temple (2 Chron. 15:17,18) and used his wealth to buy peace for his people (2 Chron. 16:2,3). His son Jehoshaphat begins with "great wealth" (2 Chron. 17:5) and acquires even greater riches before his twenty-five year reign ends (2 Chron. 17:11; 18:1; 19:7; 20:25; 21:2,3).

Of special interest is the chest King Josiah had placed outside the temple gate, as a receptional or offering box for the funds needed for temple worship and repair. The money was given "gladly" and came in until the chest "was full" (2 Chron. 25:6,8-14. A later king Hezekiah encouraged "a tithe of everything" from the people and was amazed that with this practice "the priests and Levites . . . had enough to eat and plenty to spare." The only problem then was one of distribution (2 Chron. 31:3-6,9-12,14-17,19,21). Hezekiah was blessed by God resulting in "very great riches" (2 Chron. 32:22,24,27-29).

Under Judah's kings money also is used for hiring "fighting men" (2 Chron. 25:6,9,13), paying tribute (2 Chron. 26:8; 27:5; 36:3), feeding the poor (2 Chron. 28:14,15), building buildings (2 Chron. 32:27-29), remunerating workers (2 Chron. 34:10,11,16,17) and profiting looting armies (2 Chron. 36:10,18; 25:24).

There is little question that the Old Testament teaching on money was the crucible out of which came the New Testament concepts of Jesus and his followers. God is the owner of everything. It is under his blessing that man receives what he has. It is before the Lord's eyes that man lives his life with its reponsibilities toward both God and man. In covenanted, resonsible stewardship the believer so lives that at the end of life he shall stand with head unbowed before the moral scrutiny of his Creator-Judge. Money and possessions have their dangers when allowed to move from the category of servant to that of master.

Prophetic admonitions, priestly obligations and the record of past national heroes should help Scripture readers keep their priorities in proper order. If it is the nature of God to give, it is the essence of God-like living to love at any cost. As Jesus concluded, "A man's life does not consist in the abundance of his possessions" (Luke 12:15), all materialists to the contrary.

CONCLUSION

Reader, you are important to God. As you ask questions (Part One), ponder doctrines (Part Two) or study texts (Parts Three and Four), each Biblical path leads to knowledge of your personal value. God's love for you led him to give his only Son to make possible your redemption (John 3:16). His love for you led him to reveal the way of living that would bring you happiness. In that revelation — the Scripture of Old and New Testaments — are vital secrets that make sense out of life in this world.

What the Bible Says About Money is a call for you to choose making life's goal your becoming Christ-like, rather than your becoming rich. It is an effort not only to remind you that "the earth is the Lord's" (Psa. 24:1), but so are you. If you are a child of God, don't forget to whom you belong and do not fail to remember the special relationship you have with Him. Master your possessions and do not let them master you.

From the creation of all to the consummation of all, the

destroyer of souls would make your life unfruitful through "the worries of this life and the deceitfulness of wealth" (Matt. 13:22). Christian stewardship is the prescription of the Great Physician that removes the poison from things and turns earthly wealth into assets for the kingdom of heaven.

"God loves a cheerful giver" (2 Cor. 9:7). God is a cheerful giver (Rom. 8:32)! You be a cheerful giver and all the way to heaven will be heaven. As Solomon wrote long ago, "All has been heard; here is the conclusion of the matter: Fear God and keep his commandments, for this is the whole duty of man" (Eccl. 12:13). In your fear, awe and reverence of God include this commandment: "Ascribe to the LORD the glory due his name; bring an offering and come into his courts" (Psa. 96:8).

Index of Topics

Index of Scriptures